Famine in Cambodia

GEOGRAPHIES OF JUSTICE AND SOCIAL TRANSFORMATION

SERIES EDITORS

Mathew Coleman, *Ohio State University*
Sapana Doshi, *University of California, Merced*

FOUNDING EDITOR

Nik Heynen, *University of Georgia*

ADVISORY BOARD

Deborah Cowen, *University of Toronto*
Zeynep Gambetti, *Boğaziçi University*
Geoff Mann, *Simon Fraser University*
James McCarthy, *Clark University*
Beverley Mullings, *Queen's University*
Harvey Neo, *Singapore University of Technology and Design*
Geraldine Pratt, *University of British Columbia*
Ananya Roy, *University of California, Los Angeles*
Michael Watts, *University of California, Berkeley*
Ruth Wilson Gilmore, *CUNY Graduate Center*
Jamie Winders, *Syracuse University*
Melissa W. Wright, *Pennsylvania State University*
Brenda S. A. Yeoh, *National University of Singapore*

Famine in Cambodia

GEOPOLITICS, BIOPOLITICS, NECROPOLITICS

JAMES A. TYNER

THE UNIVERSITY OF GEORGIA PRESS
Athens

© 2023 by the University of Georgia Press
Athens, Georgia 30602
www.ugapress.org
All rights reserved

Set in 10.25/13.5 Minion 3 Regular

Most University of Georgia Press titles are
available from popular e-book vendors.

Printed digitally

Library of Congress Cataloging-in-Publication Data

Names: Tyner, James A., 1966– author.
Title: Famine in Cambodia : geopolitics, biopolitics, necropolitics /
  James A. Tyner.
Description: Athens [Georgia] : The University of Georgia Press, 2023.
  | Series: Geographies of justice and social transformation | Includes
  bibliographical references and index.
Identifiers: LCCN 2022037193 | ISBN 9780820363738 (hardback) |
  ISBN 9780820363721 (paperback) | ISBN 9780820363745 (epub) |
  ISBN 9780820363752 (pdf)
Subjects: LCSH: Famines—Cambodia. | Cambodia—History—1953-1975.
  | Cambodia—History—1975-1979. | Cambodia—History—1979-1993. |
  Cambodia—Social conditions—20th century. | Cambodia—Politics and
  government—20th century.
Classification: LCC HC79.F3 T96 2023 | DDC 363.809596—dc23/eng/20221104
LC record available at https://lccn.loc.gov/2022037193

To the memory of Curt Roseman

CONTENTS

List of Figures ix
Acknowledgments xi

Introduction 1
CHAPTER 1 No One Starves in Cambodia 16
CHAPTER 2 With Fatal Prognosis 46
CHAPTER 3 Work More, Gain More, but Spend Less Capital 75
CHAPTER 4 Another Cambodian War 100

Epilogue 127

Notes 155
Index 197

FIGURES

1. Cambodia 19
2. North Vietnam, South Vietnam, Laos, and Cambodia during the Second Indochina War 40
3. The Ho Chi Minh and Sihanouk Trails during the Second Indochina War 50
4. U.S. bombing of Cambodia 53
5. Areas of Khmer Rouge control during the Cambodian Civil War 63
6. Administrative boundaries of Democratic Kampuchea 79
7. Actual and proposed dams along the Mekong River and tributaries 148

ACKNOWLEDGMENTS

Throughout the course of my studies on the Cambodian genocide, it became all too evident that famine factored prominently in the premature death of hundreds of thousands of men, women, and children. However, there was no sustained engagement with famine *in its totality*. That is, famine appeared during the Cambodian civil war, and famine reappeared both during the genocide and postgenocide periods. So began my effort to understand Cambodia's famines as a series of interconnected historical-geographical processes—in short, to understand famine more widely as mediated by state actors, both foreign and domestic.

It is not hyperbole to say that this project would not have materialized without the support, encouragement, and guidance of Mick Gusinde-Duffy. As always, Mick's editorial insight has greatly enriched the quality of this book. I extend thanks to Bethany Snead, Jon Davies, and the entire staff at the University of Georgia Press, who shepherded the manuscript from initial proposal submission through final production; and to Elizabeth Crowder, who copyedited the manuscript. In addition, I thank the editorial board and the anonymous reviewers who provided critical feedback and constructive criticism on the various drafts of the proposal and the completed manuscript. I extend also my heartfelt thanks to Mandy Munro-Stasiuk, Scott Sheridan, and Marcello Fantoni of Kent State University, for their long-standing support of my research.

Several individuals, through in-person or electronic conversations, have contributed to the broader shaping of this book, notably Randle DeFalco, Craig Etcheson, Helen Jarvis, Ben Kiernan, and Stian Rice. Over the years, their knowledge and understanding of Cambodian history and geography, from both a conceptual and empirical standpoint, has greatly shaped my perception of events and has helped frame my arguments. Special thanks also to Sokvisal Kimsroy, Chhunly Chhay, Kok-Chhay Ly, and Savina Sirik for their knowledge, their assistance, and the translation of documents relating to the Cambodian genocide, all of which provided a critical foundation for this study. In addition, I have benefitted from both the writings of, and conversations with, several people who have challenged and expanded my thinking over the years: Stuart Aitken, Derek Alderman, Katherine Brickell, Thom Davies, Colin Flint, Charles Fogelman, Jim Glassman, Don Mitchell, Heidi Nast, Richard Peet, Simon Springer, and Melissa Wright.

During my twenty-five years at Kent State I have had the privilege to serve as advisor to a constellation of truly remarkable students: Gabriela Brindis Alvarez, Steve Butcher, Sutapa Chattopadhyay, Chhunly Chhay, Jaerin Chung, Alex Colucci, Gordon Cromley, Sam Henkin, Donna Houston, Josh Inwood, Sokvisal Kimsroy, Robert Kruse, Olaf Kuhlke, Kok-Chhay Ly, Gabe Popescue, Stian Rice, Savina Sirik, Andy Shears, Dave Stasiuk, Rachel Will, and Manoka Y. In retrospect, I have probably learned more from them than the other way around.

I thank my family for their unwavering support and encouragement: first and foremost, my parents, Dr. Gerald and Dr. Judith Tyner, for the sacrifices they made when I was a student; and to my brother, David, my aunt, Karen, and my uncle, Bill, for their encouragement over the years. I extend my thanks also to my daughters, Jessica and Anica Lyn, who have both grown into strong young women. My deepest gratitude goes to my wife and life partner, Belinda. I am truly blessed to have traveled through the years with Belinda; she has been and remains my North Star, the guiding light of our family. And of course, this project would not be possible without the loving company of Carter and Bubba, our six-year-old and three-year-old rescue dog and cat, respectively.

Finally, to Curt Roseman. Curt was my PhD advisor, but more important, he was my friend and my greatest supporter. For over three decades, Curt has been a part of my life, and his imprint extends far beyond the walls of academia. Years ago, he surprised me with a signed copy of a book he wrote. The inscription reads: "Jimmie—You seem like a lad who might make a fine geographer some day. Good luck." During the writing of this project, Curt passed away. It is difficult to put into words what Curt meant to me; his kindness, his generosity, his humor. His death has left a hollow in my soul that can never be healed. I will miss him.

Famine in Cambodia

INTRODUCTION

> Sovereignty means the capacity to define who matters and
> who does not, who is disposable and who is not.
> —Achille Mbembe

On May 28, 1977, a local cadre from Region 4 sent a telegram to senior members of the Central Committee of the Communist Party of Kampuchea (CPK). The telegram provides an update on the conditions experienced and activities pursued in the region. For example, 71 hectares of dry-season rice seedlings were transplanted, 920 hectares of short-term rice seedlings were transplanted, and 447 hectares of maize were planted. In addition, the telegram indicates the availability of 7,721 pairs of cattle capable of labor and the presence of 2,744 pigs and 12,703 chickens. The report continues by noting that while "people's health improved" in some areas, in other parts of the country, living conditions were "insufficient." Notably, the telegram continues, "All collectives have run out of food and people's strength is getting weaker." Local officials recommended that food rations be further reduced, as "people [were] running out of rice to eat." Perhaps indicative of the dire conditions that prevailed throughout rural Cambodia, the report acknowledges that on May 26, "two people committed suicide by hanging themselves."[1]

Read in isolation, the telegram offers a grim analysis of an emergent famine. It hints of ongoing efforts to transform existing food provisioning systems and suggests that such efforts were contributing to widespread inequalities among the population. However, the telegram is also a tangible document that provides a glimpse into the inner workings of famine conditions and the political economy of famine. For the telegram is but one document among thousands that, in their totality, reveal the unfolding of a crisis of monumental proportions. Between 1975 and 1979 senior officials of the CPK initiated a series of economic and political programs that resulted in the death of approximately 1.7 million men, women, and children. Many deaths were direct, the result of torture and execution; other deaths resulted from structural conditions imposed by the Khmer Rouge. Indeed, during the Cambodian genocide, starvation-related conditions claimed hundreds of thousands of lives and traumatized a generation.[2]

It is common to attribute Cambodia's famine to the machinations of the Khmer Rouge, and certainly, there is considerable truth to this assertion. Programmatically, CPK officials introduced a wholesale transformation of Khmer society in an effort to accumulate capital rapidly to develop a modern industry. Identifying rice as their competitive advantage, the CPK leadership embarked on a massive infrastructure project to manage effectively and efficiently the country's water resources to expand agricultural production. Conventional accounts accordingly focus on the destructive practices initiated by the Khmer Rouge: the brutal evacuation of towns and cities; the forced relocation of people into communes and work camps; the suspension of currency and the elimination of private property; and the targeted execution of doctors, teachers, engineers, and other "classes" of people who did not conform to the planned utopia envisioned by the Khmer Rouge.

The broader conditions contributing to famine in Cambodia between 1975 and 1979 thus appear all too obvious. A tragic conjunction of political instability, armed conflict, and genocide coalesced in such a way that agricultural systems collapsed, distribution systems failed, and mass starvation followed. Indeed, the famine that occurred during the Khmer Rouge regime appears as an inflection point, a tragic bend of Cambodia's historical arc from "primitive" farming to "modern" systems of agriculture.

Such an account is erroneous, however, for famine was recurrent throughout Cambodia during the 1970s, a period marked by military interventions and occupations, armed conflict, political coups and regime change, economic collapse, and failures of humanitarian relief efforts. On this point, the proximate cause of famine during the long decade of the 1970s was located thirty-four thousand feet above the bloodred sandy soils and waterlogged rice fields; the trigger mechanism was neither drought nor flood but the MSQ-77 computer-based command guidance system of a B-52 bomber. It was neither accidental nor unintentional for famine to sweep over Cambodia like fighter jets; rather, the continuation of mass starvation, disease, and death was the acknowledged and accepted end result of numerous actions and inactions perpetrated by a constellation of sovereign powers indifferent to the welfare of Cambodia's people.

Cambodia experienced three consecutive famines throughout the 1970s set against the backdrop of four distinct governments: the Kingdom of Cambodia (1953–1970), the U.S.-supported Khmer Republic (1970–1975), the Communist Democratic Kampuchea (1975–1979), and the Vietnamese-controlled People's Republic of Kampuchea (1979–1989). Indeed, it is significant that from the time of independence in 1953 until the early 1990s, there was no peaceful transfer of power in Cambodia.[3] Whether originating in political coups or armed conflict, violence has marked Cambodia's recent political past. It has done so not because of some Orientalist imaginary of a Khmer "culture of violence," but because of the country's geopolitics.[4] On this point, for competing sovereign powers—France, the United States, China, Vietnam, Thailand—Cambodia's territory has factored in broader biopolitical and necropolitical calculations that effectively marginalized and traumatized the people of Cambodia. In the end, famine and the threat of famines in Cambodia were always and necessarily geopolitical.

Yet most scholarly accounts of famine in Cambodia limit discussions exclusively to the brutal policies and practices of the Khmer Rouge, failing to consider the equally brutal humanitarian crises in Cambodia both prior to and following the period of 1975–1979.[5] Indeed, there remains an implicit assumption that Cambodia—despite having endured five years of civil war—retained a functioning economy and viable health sector prior to the Khmer Rouge coming to power, and that it was solely disastrous actions taken by the Khmer Rouge that resulted in widespread famine. Similarly, the famine that followed the collapse of Democratic Kampuchea is understood as a continuation of Khmer Rouge failures.

Without doubt, the shadow of the Khmer Rouge darkens the history of Cambodia in the years leading up to and following the genocide. Yet the black-clad figures of the Khmer Rouge too often appear as silhouettes projected against the backdrop of Plato's cave. Famine in Cambodia was, to a degree, the proximate result of Khmer Rouge activities. This should not imply, however, that other shadowy figures played no role. The central plot of *Famine in Cambodia* is straightforward: to chronicle what actually happened in Cambodia during the famine years of the 1970s, and to assess what lessons this traumatic period holds for the future. Unlike conventional approaches to Cambodia's famines, however, this work eschews an overdetermined role of the Khmer Rouge. This is not an attempt to minimize the brutality or culpability of the group. Instead, I underscore the responsibility of other states that, through their biopolitical and necropolitical interventions, contributed to and sustained famine in Cambodia. When the story is told, ample blame is to be found among others without detracting from the moral or criminal liability of the Khmer Rouge.

Famines do not simply happen; rather, they mark the conjuncture of myriad socionatural processes. I situate Cambodia's serial famines of the 1970s within the longer arc of Cambodian history—notably, the prolonged and uneven integration of traditional Khmer farming practices into the capitalist world economy. From this vantage point, it becomes possible to underscore the varied dynamics in operation both within and between the three famines. That is, each famine—if viewed in isolation—highlights particular social and structural transformations of Cambodian agriculture; concurrently, however, the famines appear also as a single, decade-long event, presided over by three different regimes and continuing across them. In demonstrating these facts, I think through how the conditions of famine "accumulate" from one to the next and what this implies for how we think about famine dynamics.

More broadly, my work extends beyond the particular temporal and spatial coordinates of Cambodia, not in an effort to articulate a "Grand Theory" or "metatheory" of famine, but instead to speak conceptually to the growing body of work on state-induced famines.[6] For state-induced famine constitutes a peculiar form of sovereign violence, a geopolitical violence whereby famine conditions are created and maintained in the course of political struggle.[7] *Famine in Cambodia* contributes to those studies concerned with the sovereign management of life (biopolitics) and death (necropolitics), for an interrogation of state-induced famines ultimately provides a critical lens through which to question how scarcity and abundance, privilege and suffering, and life and death are mutually constituted.[8]

Famine Crimes and State-Induced Famines

In my pursuit of a geopolitically informed framework of state-induced famines, I begin with Alex de Waal's provocative statement that starvation isn't something that just happens; it is something people do to one another.[9] Indeed, from his early work on famine in Darfur, de Waal has over the years forwarded an explicit (state-centered) political theory of famine, demonstrating how famines are anthropogenic rather than an inevitable outcome of an imbalance between population and food resources. He begins, as do I, with a critique of the Malthusian specter of famine.

Thomas Malthus, writing in the late eighteenth and early nineteenth centuries, explained famine as a condition of too many mouths and too little food. For Malthus, societies have a tendency to multiply beyond the conditions of subsistence—that is, while human populations increase exponentially, food production increases arithmetically. History revealed, for Malthus, a constant oscillation of the pendulum between population and food.[10] Periodically, the number of mouths that required food exceeded the capacity to feed them, leading to misery, poverty, deprivation, and mass starvation, a reduction in population, and a return to sufficient food provisioning.[11] Reflecting his class position, Malthus attributed blame largely to the lack of "moral restraint" among the impoverished classes who, through their unrestrained propagation, burdened society with hungry mouths. However, poverty was not simply a "natural" calamity, according to Malthus, but instead an admission on the part of the poor for breaking natural and divine law. In other words, through their selfish behavior, the multiplying poor were acting contrary to God and thus brought on themselves the scourges of disease and starvation.

The postulate of famine as caused by a shortage of food is challenged by Amartya Sen.[12] He argues that famines have little to do with how much food is available and almost everything to do with the politics and economics of food distribution. On this point, Sen contends that a decline in "food availability" is not necessary for famine to occur; rather, the key consideration is whether people have access to sufficient food. Indeed, according to Devereux, the most valuable contribution of Sen's approach to famine theorizing is that it shifts the analytical focus away from a fixation on food supplies—the Malthusian logic of "too many people, too little food"—and directs it on the inability of groups to acquire food.[13]

Sen's work has been influential, but it is not without limitations.[14] To begin, while Sen moves away from the notion of famine as a failure of food production, he retains the idea of breakdown or collapse. Therefore, his approach avoids engaging with the highly politicized context within which famines invariably occur.[15] Effectively, Sen does not consider the possibility that famines can be a *product* of the social or economy system rather than its failure.[16] And yet, as Devereux identifies, most of the major famines of the twentieth century were triggered either by political instability or by civil war. In addition, many other famines that had "natural" or economic triggers such as drought, flood, or food hoarding became politicized by failures of government or international response—sometimes involving the deliberate withholding of food aid for political reasons.[17] Indeed, behind the structural causes of hunger lie the machinations of politicians, legislators, creditors, landowners, and myriad other actors that contribute through their actions and inactions to famine conditions.[18] Thus, a growing number of scholars have refocused attention toward the perpetration of state-induced famine crimes.[19]

Scholars such as de Waal, Michael Watts, David Keen, and Jenny Edkins understand famine not only as being socially produced but also as being a political *choice*. That is, famines can, through government action and inaction, be engineered, fabricated to achieve some strategic objective. Scholars have documented numerous such instances in the historical record, exposing the role colonial institutions, development programs, unfettered markets, and war played not just in the deepening and prolonging of mass starvation but in its very creation.[20] Accordingly, David Marcus has coined the term "faminogenesis" to describe state actions that create famine; he offers a fourfold classification of "faminogenic acts" or "famine crimes."[21]

Marcus's typology is useful in that it calls attention to the political intent and responsibility of identifiable government authorities for specific famines.[22] Category one famine crimes are those in which governments knowingly and deliberately create, inflict, or prolong conditions that result in, or contribute to, the starvation of a significant number of persons.[23] Forced mass starvation is the archetypical case of first-degree famine crimes.[24] Notable examples include Joseph Stalin's starvation of Ukrainians (the Holodomor) in the early 1930s, and the Nazis' "Hunger Plan" during the Second World War. Category two famine crimes are those that result from government recklessness. Here, governments implement policies that unintentionally produce famine conditions but, despite having awareness and the capacity to respond to problems, continue to pursue these policies regardless of the suffering that follows. According to de Waal, these constitute the largest number of famine crimes identified in the twentieth century, with Mao Zedong's "Great Leap Forward" of 1958–1960 as the paradigmatic case.[25]

Category three famine crimes are those in which public authorities are indifferent—that is, they are impervious to the fate of their populations even though they possess the means to respond to unfolding crises. Last, category four famine crimes result from the inability or incapacity of "incompetent or hopelessly corrupt governments."[26] For example, when faced with food crises created by drought or price shocks, ineffectual government agencies are unable to respond to their citizens' needs and starvation may follow.

Marcus's forwarding of famine crimes and the subsequent interest in state-induced famines has been highly influential, particularly among legal scholars. Central to the legal and moral evaluation of state-induced famine crimes is the concept of mens rea, or intentionality. Thus, when interrogating the responsibility or accountability of governing authorities, it is necessary to evaluate the intent of the authorities and the link between their actions (or inactions) and outcomes.[27] Devereux, for example, draws a distinction between acts of commission, such as the deliberate attempt to create famine conditions, and acts of omission, or the failure to intervene to prevent or remedy famine.[28]

Related to the distinction between crimes of omission and crimes of commission, we may consider state obligations as taking two forms. On the one hand, there are negative duties in which states refrain from committing harm toward others. On the other hand, there are positive duties, or requirements, that must be performed. Expressed differently, a distinction appears between negative rights that supposedly require no action other than forbearance by the state, and positive rights that require actions and resources. These may be codified, for example, in a nation's constitution and legal system. A country's obligation to not withhold food from its citizens can be understood as a negative right—that is, a requirement that the country not prevent its citizens from accessing food that is otherwise available to them. Conversely, the provision of food by a state constitutes a positive right and requires necessary material resources and different types of policy interventions.[29]

Duties and responsibilities of states have received considerable attention in recent years, both in theory and in practice.[30] Notably, much of this focus centers on the obligations of states *beyond* their territorial limits, as seen, for example, in the "responsibility to protect" doctrine. Here, the operative questions are, first, whether states have duties beyond their domestic borders and, second, what kind of duties states actually have toward others.[31] For instance, in the aftermath of the Second World War and the Holocaust, the intonation "never again" entered our collective lexicon, and with it came the ideal that sovereign states have an obligation to prevent genocide.[32] In subsequent decades, this commitment has extended to other forms of mass atrocities, including famine crimes. The aforementioned "responsibility to protect," by way of illustration, advocates the following: (1) states are responsible for the functions of protecting the safety and lives of citizens and promoting their welfare; (2) states are responsible to citizens internally and to the international community through the United Nations; and (3) states are responsible for their actions—that is, they are accountable for their acts of commission and omission.[33] Consequently, if a state is unable or unwilling to fulfill these charges, perhaps under the rubric of third- or fourth-degree famine crimes, other states have a responsibility to intervene.

The limitations, however, are all too apparent, for appeals to prevent or to stop wrongdoings operate on the assumption that states are committed to the amelioration of violent conditions. The fact remains, throughout the twentieth and now twenty-first centuries, states can and do benefit from the perpetuation of sovereign violence, both within and beyond their borders. For this reason, the concept of state-induced famine necessarily requires a more nuanced geopolitical engagement with that of sovereign violence. The former is unavoidably located within the domain of the latter.

Following Michel Foucault, in the classic conception of sovereignty, the right of life and death was one of the sovereign's basic attributes. Notably, sovereignty here was embodied in the figure of the king or queen, the emperor or empress, whose rule extended over his or her subjects. To say that "the sovereign has a right of life and death means that he [sic] can ... either have people put to death or let them live."[34] Life and death, to a great degree, were removed from the realm of the natural and assumed by the sovereign. However, Foucault cautions that the sovereign cannot grant life in the same way that he or she can inflict death. The right of life and death is "always exercised in an unbalanced way: the balance is always tipped in favor of death." Consequently, the "very essence of the right of life and death is actually the right to kill: it is at the moment when the sovereign can kill that he [sic] exercises his right over life."[35]

With the transformation of sovereignty from embodiment in the form of a person to embodiment in the impersonal collective of the modern state, the ancient right to take life or to let live was similarly transformed into a twofold power to foster life or to disallow life to the point of death. In other words, there was a profound alteration in sovereigns' relation to their subjects, where the crucial pivot was that of "making life" or "letting die." This is not to say, however, that the modern state's right to make or to disallow life completely revoked the classical right to kill. This privilege is seen, for example, when states wage war, execute convicted felons, and engage in political assassinations and targeted killings. The operative calculation was to interrogate the "value" of the individual or population at hand. Thus, what the modern state reveals is a decidedly more nuanced and complex management of life and death, a form of sovereign violence composed of two broad "biopowers."

Subsequently, there emerged an anatomo-politics of the human body: a micropolitics that sought to maximize the forces of the body and to integrate it into efficient, productive systems. Here, Foucault explains that "it is largely as a force of production that the body is invested with relations of power and domination; but, on the other hand, its constitution as labor power is possible only if it is caught up in the system of subjection.... The body becomes a useful force only if it is both a productive body and a subjected body."[36] There also emerged a suite of regulatory practices that Foucault terms "biopolitics." This latter development was imbued with the mechanisms, the calculations, of life in its totality: birth, morbidity, mortality, longevity.[37] From this point onward, it became possible to talk of a state's population as if it had a transcendental existence and experience above and beyond the government—facets that were intensely managed and analyzed by new and specialized academic disciplines and institutions, such as demography, sociology, and epidemiology. In other words, the birth and death of individual subjects was no longer the limit point of sovereignty but rather its site of mediation and operation.[38]

It is at this point, Foucault argues, that we "see the appearance of a State racism: a racism that society will direct against itself, against its own elements and its own products."[39] In other words, this state racism is co-constitutive of sovereign power that mediates the calculation of deciding who may live and who must die. However, as Gavin Rae explains, Foucault's notion of "racism" is of a specific variety—that is, it simply entails an inner division within society.[40] Racism, in this usage, "distinguishes between those who, we might say, are 'pure' and so entitled and welcome to belong to the society and those who are considered 'impure' and so not welcome. This initial bifurcation permits a justification for killing the latter and for the degraded ways in which they will be treated."[41]

Racism, for Foucault, is foundational to sovereign violence, for the first function of racism is to fragment, to create caesuras, within the population.[42] State racism, consequently, is "the indispensable precondition that allows someone to be killed, that allows others to be killed." Foucault is quick to point out, however, that by "killing" he does not simply mean "murder as such, but also every form of indirect murder: the fact of exposing someone to death, increasing the risk of death for some people, or, quite simply, political death, expulsion, rejection, and so on."[43] On this point, therefore, state racism enables the exercise of sovereign violence through both acts of commission (killing) and acts of omission (the disallowing of life).

The distinction between acts of commission and acts of omission aligns with the sovereign distinction between "killing" and "letting die." On this point, we may readily understand acts of commission—first-degree famine crimes—as the active taking of life, or killing. Second-degree famine crimes, where famine is the unintentional result of specific policies, are generally held to be acts of omission, in that the responsible authorities refuse to mitigate the harmful policies. In this case, governments through inaction "let die" people from starvation-related conditions. Likewise, both third-degree and fourth-degree famine crimes can be considered acts of omission, the difference being that governments in these situations are not considered culpable through their inactions, although substantial numbers of people may still be left to die.

Here, the work of Achille Mbembe becomes relevant for our conceptualization of state-induced famine as a form of sovereign violence. Expanding the insights of Foucault, Mbembe forwards the proposition that "to exercise sovereignty is to exercise control over mortality and to define life as the deployment and manifestation of power."[44] In other words, we begin to see how the intentional infliction of mass starvation is a necropolitical means to achieve particular ends. Mbembe, for example, understands necropolitics as the "synthesis between massacre and bureaucracy."[45] In this usage of the word, "massacres" can refer to the whole slaughter of soldiers and civilians in war but can also refer to the intentional mass starvation of a people. The denial of food can kill just as certainly as the dropping of bombs. Indeed, the necropolitical use of famine is to a degree more effective than other more conventional forms of violence. Unlike the indiscriminate mortality that often accompanies warfare, famine can be highly selective, with targeted populations denied food. As Jamie Allinson explains, "It is the old sovereign power of death, operative in a biopolitical setting, implying therefore a division between populations, the making of a 'caesura' between the population worthy of being made to live, and that subject to the right to command death."[46] This is point well emphasized by de Waal, who notes that such an approach "obliges us to consider starvation as a *method* of mass killing."[47] From the vantage point of the state, the operative calculation is straightforward: Who lives and who dies?

The caesura between life and death that appeared with the modern state followed a changed ethic of the sovereign subject—that is, those subjected to the biopolitical and necropolitical calculations that determined the making, taking, or disallowing of life. According to Giorgio Agamben, the first move of classical Western politics was the separation of the biological and the political.[48] Under Greek law, the natural life of *zoe*, "the simple fact of living common to all living things," was excluded from the polis (political space) and confined to the *oikos*, or "domestic sphere." The life of the polis was *bios*, a qualified life particular to an individual or group.[49] Agamben argues that the separation of *zoe* and *bios* is a practice of inclusion by exclusion that is constitutive of sovereignty in the modern Western sense from the beginning.[50] As Edkins highlights, feminist political theorists have long argued the political has operated through the inclusion by exclusion of the female, and of the inclusion by exclusion of the domestic to the public (political) sphere.[51] This distinction is made possible predominantly because of a key paradox Agamben places at the center of sovereign power: "[The] sovereign is, at the same time, outside and inside the juridical order."[52]

Building on the work of Carl Schmitt, Agamben argues that "the sovereign, having the legal power to suspend the validity of the law, legally places himself outside the law."[53] That said, the sovereign belongs to the legal order because the decisions of authority are themselves an aspect of law.[54] The state is both included and excluded from the law, suspended, as it were, in a state of exception. Following Rae, this conceptual legal space—the state of exception—located between the inside and outside of law reveals much about sovereignty-law relations and, by extension, sovereignty-violence relations. Thus, this postulate has also a tremendous bearing on our understanding of state-induced famines. As Edkins explains, "The exception that defines the structure of sovereignty is more complex than the inclusion of what is outside by the very fact that it is placed outside or forbidden. It is not just a question of creating a distinction between inside and outside."[55] In other words, it is more than a matter of determining, for example, who might be considered eligible for legal representation or citizenship; rather, it is a matter of existence or extinction. As Agamben concludes, "If the law employs the exception ... as its original means of referring to and encompassing life, then a theory of the state of exception is the preliminary condition for any definition of the relation that binds and, at the same time, abandons the living being to law."[56]

Thus, in an extension of Foucault's work, Agamben forwards the argument that sovereign power (and its corollary, sovereign violence) is amplified because the sovereign has the force of law without being constrained by law per se.[57] Agamben reveals how sovereignty operates on bare life—that is, those political lives rendered disposable through state racism. Between *zoe* and *bios* exists a liminal figure, *homo sacer*, that could be killed (or let die) with impunity. Accordingly, this figure is subject to two exceptions: exclusion from human life (killing it does not count as homicide) and exclusion from divine law (killing it is not a ritual killing and does not count as sacrilege).[58]

Homo sacer, as one who is positioned outside both human and divine law, is included in the political domain only through its exclusion. On this point, Agamben explains, the fundamental subject of Western politics—and of sovereign violence—is not the distinction of friend or enemy, civilian or soldier, citizen or alien. Instead, it is the distinction between bare life and political existence. Bare life, or *homo sacer*, as Edkins writes, "becomes both the subject and the object of the political order: it is both the place for the organization of state power, in the forms of discipline and objectification described by Foucault, and the place for emancipation from it, through the birth of modern democracy and the demand for human rights."[59] Accordingly, sovereign violence continuously navigates a grievous paradox whereby, in order to secure life, it may be necessary to destroy life. For instance, the sovereign project of "making life" for one's citizens frequently comes at the expense of subjects, whether through their exclusion—by such means as bans on immigration—or elimination—by the killing or letting die of subjects deemed unworthy for inclusion.

State-induced famine constitutes a form of sovereign violence. It operates within a state of exception whereby sovereign authorities subject political life to judgments of worth, of inclusion or exclusion, of participation or abandonment. One the one hand, there are subjects who are allowed a biopolitical existence, and through administrative measures their lives are subjugated and managed with a view to the betterment and greater security of humankind.[60] On the other hand, there are subjects rendered as bare life, subjugated to a necropolitical existence. For the former, sovereign power extends to make life through, for example, food provisioning systems, relief agencies, and healthcare facilities. For the latter, sovereign power is withheld or, rather, transferred toward the administrative making of life *elsewhere*. Necropolitical power, according to Mbembe, proceeds by a sort of inversion between life and death, as if life was merely death's medium. Indeed, for those killed or disallowed life, their "death is something to which nobody feels any obligation to respond. Nobody even bears the slightest feelings of responsibility or justice."[61] Sovereign geopolitical violence, including state-induced famine, is constitutive of and indifferent to bare life. Mass starvation is manifest not as calamity but as objective; the distinction between means and ends, challenges and opportunities, peril and purpose is blurred, intentionally so. By extension, the faminogenesis of state-induced famines is blurred as well.

Outline of the Book

When Michael Watts powerfully describes famine as the "terror of the possible," he highlights that famines are effectively about the exercise of power and rights—specifically the power to command premature dying through the command of food access and availability.[62] In other words, there is an irreducible violence associated with the condition of famine that is rooted in the everyday geographies of life itself.[63] To paraphrase Jamey Essex, famine is not conditioned or experienced the same way in every place or time, nor is it always the result of economic and political processes unbounded from time and space.[64] Therefore, I provide a critical interrogation of the violent geopolitical conditions of state-induced famine in Cambodia and, in doing so, call attention to those governments responsible for the premature dying and death that followed. I demonstrate how Cambodia's serial famines were mediated by particular configurations of geopolitics, biopolitics, and necropolitics. My story begins, however, not in the 1970s but several centuries earlier. As David Nally explains, famines do not necessarily start with crop failures, droughts, or equivalent climatic hazards; rather, conditions of possibility are formed much earlier, when, for example, a population is made progressively vulnerable or slowly brought to the point of collapse.[65]

Building on Nally's insight, I premise that the etiology of state-induced famines is also found in the transformation of key social and structural relations that make life possible. Chapter 1 provides a chronology of Cambodia's political economy from precolonial times to the 1960s. Here, I focus explicitly on the social and structural relations of traditional Khmer farming practices, and how these were transformed during the French colonial period and the subsequent postindependent Sihanouk regime. This is not to argue that the mass starvation experienced by Cambodia's people constitutes an "imperial" famine. That said, the famine dynamics of the 1970s are manifestly conditioned by Cambodia's colonial past.

Cambodia's three consecutive famines of the 1970s are the subject of chapters 2 through 4. And while these are presented as distinct "moments," it is important to recognize the continuities of famine's violent conditions and the subsequent responses of successive governments. Chapter 2 begins with an account of the interlocking geopolitical events of the late 1960s, as the war in neighboring Vietnam expanded. Under Sihanouk, Cambodia's food provisioning system was worsening, and the spread of war undermined efforts to sustain the country's rice-based economy. Continued aerial bombing and ground operations combined to render much of eastern Cambodia's rice fields uncultivable, and to force peasants off their lands and concentrate them in the cities. Insufficient relief efforts on behalf of the international community—and notably by the United States—contributed to the precarity of Cambodia's peoples.

However, the geopolitical machinations of the United States were the most proximate cause of Cambodians' dire situation. America's military intervention in Cambodia is inseparable from the former's intervention in South Vietnam. That is, the principle objective of the United States was to protect and defend South Vietnam, hailed as both a sovereign state and a key ally in the region, against the foreign aggression of North Vietnam. From the vantage point of U.S. officials, this goal seemingly justified the subsequent military intervention in Cambodia, itself a neutral, sovereign state. The ensuing mass starvation in Cambodia, therefore, is most appropriately viewed as a form of state-induced famine initiated by the United States. In turn, once the violent conditions of famine became apparent, U.S. officials were unwilling, both for military and economic reasons, to mitigate them. Meanwhile, Cambodia's people were reduced to the status of bare life.

With the fall of the Lon Nol government, many people cheered, hoping that the arrival of the Khmer Rouge would bring an end to the violence and famine. Hopes were soon dashed, as CPK officials forcibly evacuated the cities and compelled everyone—farmers, civil servants, merchants—into the fields to grow rice. As detailed in chapter 3, the famine during Democratic Kampuchea was not, strictly speaking, a "war famine"; rather, it was a transformation of the war famine induced by U.S. military intervention. This is a point that cannot be overemphasized. By the time the Khmer Rouge assumed power in 1975, hundreds of thousands of Cambodians had endured years of hardship and deprivation. Hunger, malnutrition, and disease were chronic; and the country lacked a viable infrastructure. Under these circumstances, the Khmer Rouge introduced a number of draconian policies designed to ease famine conditions, but in doing so, the group actually augmented the problem. And like their political predecessors, when incontrovertible evidence demonstrated the continuation of famine, senior leaders of the CPK refused to intervene directly to alleviate those conditions.

In other words, at least in late 1975, the ideal of the Khmer Rouge was to transform rapidly traditional Khmer farming with mechanized, modern agricultural practices in an effort to accumulate capital to further develop industry. To this point, the *structural* changes initiated by the Khmer Rouge differed little from those of their predecessors, including both the French and Sihanouk regimes, although the intended *social* transformations were radically different. Senior leaders of the Khmer Rouge did not *withhold* food as a political weapon; rather, they provided food, but only that of insufficient quantity and nutritional value. To that end, the famine of 1975–1979 was necropolitical in orientation, as the Khmer Rouge was indifferent to the premature death of its people in the quest to accumulate capital rapidly to sustain their revolution.

For nearly four years, hunger, sickness, and death remained constant. When the Vietnamese military overthrew the Khmer Rouge in 1979, the people of Cambodia yet again turned hopeful. Newly liberated from the brutality of the Khmer Rouge, people tried to reclaim their lives, only to find their expectations wanting. According to Meng-Try Ea, 1979 saw the most catastrophic famine in the history of the Khmer people; and yet this "third" famine of the 1970s has received comparatively little attention from either famine scholars or scholars of Cambodia.[66] In part, this lacuna exists because the famine in 1979 is frequently (and erroneously) considered an extension of the Khmer Rouge–induced famine. However, the geopolitical context of this last famine—the subject of chapter 4—is considerably different. Indeed, two competing governments vied for sovereignty, a struggle replicated within the international community. To this end, efforts to provide relief were often thwarted in their attempts to address the human suffering that came about following the collapse of Democratic Kampuchea's food provisioning system.

Initially, relief agencies were denied permission to provide much-needed food supplies *not* principally to deny a particular group of people—although that certainly factored into the decisions—but because such aid was perceived as providing international legitimacy to an illegitimate government. On the one hand, the Vietnamese-installed government of the People's Republic of Kampuchea had ousted the Khmer Rouge and brought an end to Democratic Kampuchea. On the other hand, the remnants of the Khmer Rouge re-formed along the Thai-Cambodian border. In a strange twist of geopolitics, most members of the international community, including China and the United States, supported the continuation of the Communist Party of Kampuchea as the rightful sovereign of Cambodia, as opposed to the PRK government, supported primarily by Vietnam and the Soviet Union. Consequently, those states in support of the exiled Khmer Rouge worked to prevent the distribution of famine relief *within* Cambodia, favoring only the provision of assistance to the refugees along the border—many of whom were Khmer Rouge cadres and their supporters. Those states that recognized the newly installed PRK government, conversely, wanted to deny aid from reaching the border regions and to only allow aid to be distributed to those under their authority.

In the final chapter I revisit the main arguments forwarded in the book and cast a speculative look to the possibility of famine in Cambodia's future. In so doing, I argue that the state-induced famines of the 1970s should not be seen as aberrational but instead as harbingers of complex geopolitical conjunctures. In other words, to restrict our interpretation of Cambodia's famines of the 1970s to the actions and inactions of the Khmer Rouge is to fail to see how competing biopolitical and necropolitical practices can coalesce in violent ways. Food insecurities remain in Cambodia not because of the immediacy of armed conflict but because of the vulnerabilities of the country's farmers and fishers to social and structural transformations that remain very much in place.

CHAPTER 1

No One Starves in Cambodia

> You have created property [in Cambodia]; and thus you have created the poor.
> —Prince Yukanthor

Throughout the centuries, hunger was not unknown among the people of Cambodia. A poor harvest resultant from flood or drought, for example, could contribute to localized and even more widespread hunger. However, until the 1970s, there was no documented famine that ravaged Cambodian society. As Michael Watts explains, "The anticipation of food shortage gives rise to practices and behaviors that attempt to preserve a margin of economic security and the demand for subsistence security emerges from the concrete conditions of peasant life."[1] And to this point, Cambodia's farmers historically displayed a resiliency that mitigated their vulnerability to famine. In response to the impulses of the nation's monsoonal climate, they modified their farming practices, adapting to fluctuations in the timing and duration of precipitation. Seeds were selected based on localized knowledges of a complex assemblage of geomorphological and hydrological conditions. The resiliency of Cambodia's farmers throughout the twentieth century was pervasive—there remained a widespread belief among government officials and development experts that "no one starves in Cambodia" because "rice and fish are always available."[2]

But on the eve of the 1970s, Cambodia's farmers were vulnerable. On the surface, Cambodia's rural communities appeared unchanged, with their wood-and-thatch homes on stilts situated in clusters near fields and forests from which residents derived their spiritual and material sustenance.[3] And yet behind the facade of fixity was a land in flux. Misguided development projects mixed with malign neglect contributed to a growing precarity within the rural economy. Changes in landownership and the introduction of a market economy introduced under French colonial rule irrevocably unsettled the seeming tranquility of a landscape laden with fecund fields, bountiful forests, and steadfast water buffalo. War would soon scar the land and lay waste to hamlets that had stood for centuries; and war would maim and wound and kill Cambodia's people. The pagodas that nourished the soul like water from a well would be emptied, leaving the communal fabric frayed, and the deep, gentle tones of morning bells calling for monks to pray replaced by mourning.

Any understanding of famine, as Watts explains, presupposes a grasp of the form and functioning of the food system in question.[4] This holds even for state-induced famines resultant from sovereign geopolitical violence. In this chapter I provide a sweeping overview of Cambodia's changing political economy up to the 1960s. My purpose is to identify key geopolitical transformations that conditioned the production, distribution, and consumption of food. In so doing, I highlight the material conditions on which war—and famine—came to Cambodia.

Precolonial Cambodia

Cambodia has a tropical climate dominated by two monsoons, a summer monsoon that starts in late May and brings heavy rains, and a winter monsoon that begins in November and brings dry, cooler air. However, the timing of these winds is irregular, and farmers must make adjustments to their planting schedule accordingly. Precipitation amounts also vary widely. Whereas most of the prime rice-growing regions of Cambodia receive between 1,250 and 1,750 millimeters annually, other areas experience more or less. The coastal areas surrounding the Cardamom Mountains, for example, receive upward of 4,000 millimeters per year.

The physical geography of Cambodia consists of a large central plain, dominated by the Mekong River and the Tonle Sap Lake, surrounded by a series of mountain ranges. The lake is fed by several small streams as well as the Tonle Sap River, a tributary of the Mekong. Heavy precipitation and thunderstorms throughout Southeast Asia during the summer monsoon cause the Mekong River to swell. This in turn causes the Tonle Sap River to reverse its course and flow into the central basin, expanding the already vast Tonle Sap up to five times its areal extent.

Over the millennia, local climatic, hydrologic, and geomorphic conditions have influenced farming practices, especially the cultivation of rice. Rice has long been a staple in Khmer society. Khmer farmers have been growing rainfed lowland rice for at least 2,000 years, and irrigated rice has been cultivated for at least 1,500 years.[5] And over the millennia farmers have developed and refined farming strategies based on a combination of seed selection, planting techniques (e.g., broadcast or transplanting), and water management. Given the complexities of rice production, indigenous local knowledge is of great importance. Cultivation techniques, for example, need to be adapted to local conditions, including topography, precipitation, and soil.[6] It is hardly surprising that over two thousand traditional varieties of rice have been identified as being unique to Cambodia.[7]

Throughout precolonial Cambodia, four main rice cultivation "ecosystems" predominated: rain-fed lowland rice, dry-season rice, deep-water rice, and rain-fed upland rice.[8] The most prevalent form is rain-fed lowland rice farming (*srov tumneap*). Geographically, this crop is widely distributed, although it is predominant around the Tonle Sap Lake, Tonle-Bassac River system, and Mekong River (figure 1). Rain-fed lowland rice is almost completely dependent on local rainfall for its growth. Small-scale irrigation methods may be used, however, to either increase water availability in times of drought or promote drainage in times of excess rainfall.

The typical landscape associated with rain-fed lowland rice appears as a patchwork of irregular fields separated by small earthen bunds (*phleu sre*) used to retain water for weed control and for crop growth. Field size is usually a function of soil fertility, labor availability, and topological gradient: in a place where the land is flat and labor is abundant, larger fields are preferred. However, higher fertility encourages denser planting but requires more labor during planting and harvesting.[9] Morphological variation, even on the order of a few meters, has a deciding influence on growing cycles. In part, this is related to the amount and duration of water availability, in that the yields of rain-fed lowland rice production are a function of a plant maturation–water depth relationship.[10] For example, since lower fields remain flooded longer, a correspondingly longer growth period is permitted. This inverse relationship between slope height and standing water enables farmers to determine which variety to plant in order to "match" the maximum experienced water.

Rain-fed lowland rice is classified according to the elevation of the fields. High fields (*srai leu*) are those located relatively higher in elevation; lower down the slope are middle fields (*srai kandal*) and low fields (*srai kraom*). In upper fields, where the deepest standing water is usually in the range of twenty to thirty centimeters, early maturing varieties (*srau sral*) are planted. Harvested in late November or early December, these are typically drought tolerant. In terms of quality, these types are considered good "subsistence" rice. In medium fields, where the average water depth ranges between twenty and forty centimeters, medium to medium-late maturation varieties (*srau kandal*)

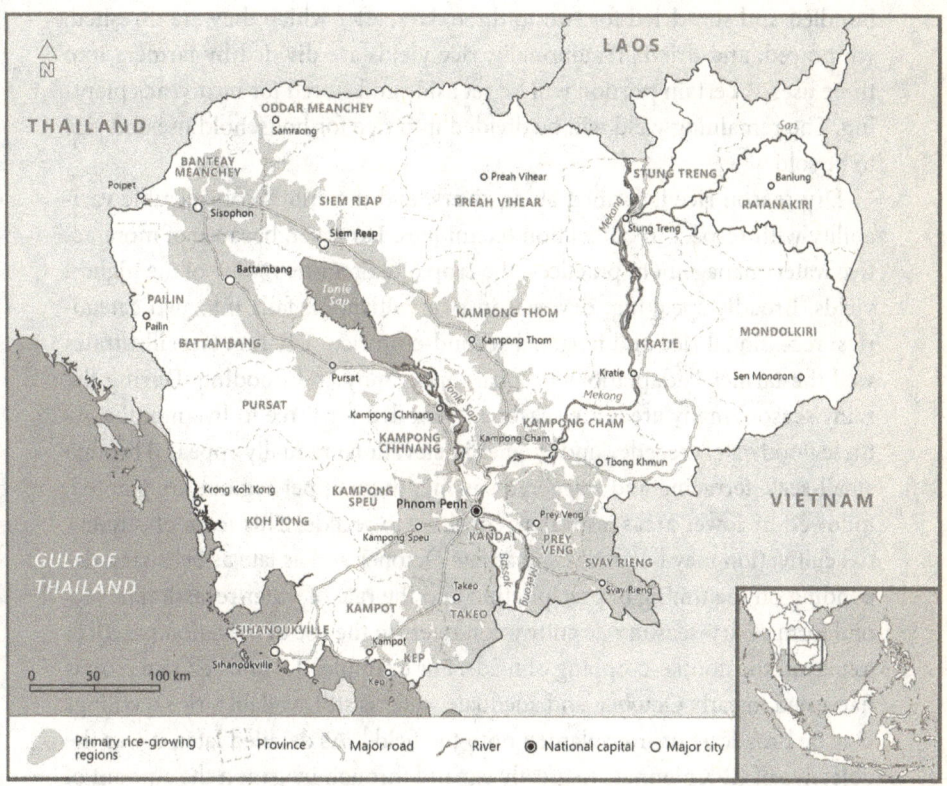

FIGURE 1. Cambodia. Courtesy of Stian Rice.

are planted. These are harvested later in the year, usually around mid- to late December, and are generally thought to be the best cooking rice. These varieties also normally enjoy the highest market price. Last, in those fields where the deepest standing water ranges from forty centimeters to upward of fifty centimeters, late-maturing rice (*srau thungu*) is planted. These type of rice is considerably more flood tolerant and is known for having a good cooking quality. Harvesting of these fields usually occurs in January or February.[11]

The actual planting of rice seedlings takes one of two forms. Transplanting rice is a process whereby pre-germinated seedlings are sowed first in small, carefully tended nurseries (*santoung*). After twenty to thirty days, the "baby rice" (*samnap*) is bundled and transplanted into the primary rice fields in a series of carefully aligned rows. The second form of planting consists of broadcast sowing. Here, the pre-germinated rice seedlings are sowed directly onto the primary rice fields. This technique is common where labor shortages exist.[12] Upon the crop's maturation, harvesting is done by hand. Rice plants are bundled and sun-dried for two to three days, after which they are threshed, winnowed, and dried. Traditionally, rice yields are divided by farmers into three uses. A certain portion will be set aside and stored for next year's planting. The remaining yield will be divided into rice for household use and rice to be sold.

Dry-season rice is farmed along rivers, and it exhibits considerable variability with respect to cultivation techniques. However, because of more active water-management practices, the crop often registers some of the highest yields. Broadly speaking, dry-season rice cultivation falls into two categories: recessional rice and irrigated second-crop rice. The first type illustrates well the farmers' adaptations to local topography and flooding. During the rainy season, many areas are seasonally flooded for three to five months. As these floodwaters recede, lands higher in elevation gradually appear. Through small-scale terracing and staggered sowing, these upper regions are planted, followed by lower areas, as waters continue to recede. This form of sequential cultivation may begin as early as late October and as late as February, depending on the timing of precipitation and the rate of water recession. A second form of dry-season rice cultivation refers to the use of irrigation practices to permit the double-cropping of fields. For example, if a rain-fed rice crop is harvested in early October, and adequate water is still available, rice seedlings may be broadcast or transplanted onto the field.[13] As detailed later, it was the objective of CPK planners to greatly expand through irrigation the amount of dry-season rice.

Two other forms of rice cultivation have traditionally been practiced throughout Cambodia: deep-water rice farming and rain-fed upland rice farming. The former entails the cultivation of rice in low-lying areas and depressions and in some respects mirrors recessional forms of dry-season rice. Following the onset of the summer monsoon, water levels in low-lying areas rise between July and August, with maximum depths registered between September and November. Rice is planted as the water recedes, usually between November and early January, and is adjusted to the rate of recession, which may be either gradual or rapid, depending on soil type. Rain-fed upland rice farming is practiced in hilly or mountainous areas, usually in unbounded, nonterraced fields, with water provided entirely by local rainfall. During the dry season (February to April), trees are cleared and underlying brush is burned. This provides both clearance for planting and natural fertilizers. Seeding follows sometime between April and June, with harvesting taking place in August. Most upland farmers diversify their crops, also growing maize, sesame, cucumber, sweet potato, pumpkin, cassava, papaya, and banana.[14]

Although rice production was the core activity in Cambodian peasant production systems, it was frequently integrated into a larger portfolio of livelihood strategies, such as *chamcar*-based (nonrice) agricultural systems, swidden agriculture, and the collection and management of natural resources on "commons," which individual farmers co-manage with others.[15] These include fisheries, grasslands used for grazing cattle, and both shrublands and forests where nontimber products are gathered or harvested.[16] The different forms of land-use activities ensured a flexible and diverse supply of natural products for local livelihoods and, in turn, minimized the risk of mass starvation.[17]

For centuries, very low population pressures throughout the Tonle Sap Basin precluded the need for strong regulation with respect to land use. In Khmer rural communities, the central decision-making institution for both land and natural-resource use was that of the household. Traditionally, it was not dictated to by a superior community-based organization.[18] Decisions related to land and resource management in Cambodian peasant societies were socially negotiated between households and influenced by two important institutions, or norms, that evolved over many generations. On the one hand, social relations were traditionally based on a form of trust linked to the moral obligations between a patron and a client. Indeed, patron-client relationships have been a continuous and central element of the Khmer social fabric throughout history, and they still influence contemporary society.[19] The myriad associations and committees created and structured around the pagoda formed a second core institution mediating communal activities. These associations were usually transitory and meant only to address a specific need or problem in the community.[20]

Beginning in the ninth century A.D., the Kingdom of Angkor was founded on the productive plains north of the Tonle Sap Lake. At its zenith, Angkor was a densely populated center of religious importance, political power, regional economic trade, and commercial activity.[21] Indeed, from its central core, the functional reach of Angkor encompassed more than 3,000 square kilometers and was home to over 750,000 people. Notably, the rise of the Angkorian kingdom integrated a rural hinterland composed of myriad hamlets and farms, and it marked the onset of large-scale surplus production and the emergence of an agrarian-class society. Angkor's political economy depended on a bureaucratic system centered around the universal authority of the Khmer king and a nonmonetized economy based on rice production, land acquisition, and taxation.[22] That said, Angkor's agricultural successes were almost entirely dependent on the construction of an elaborate water-management system that harnessed Cambodia's natural hydrology to intensify and expand rice production. In other words, while rice formed the agricultural and political backbone of the Angkor Kingdom, the administration of water made this possible. Indeed, the stability of the food supply and necessary surpluses depended on the modification and management of the area's hydrology.[23]

Every monsoon season, tremendous amounts of water flow down from the Kulen Hills, drain across the floodplain of the Siem Reap River and its tributaries, and empty into the Great Lake, itself pulsating with the seasonal ebb and flow of water that comes with the annual reversal of the Tonle Sap River. And for centuries prior to the emergence of Angkor, these ecosystems provided an abundance of rice, fish, and other aquatic resources for the Khmer for their subsistence. For the rulers of Angkor, the modification of these agro-ecosystems enabled the Khmer empire to prosper as the commercial center of the region.[24]

From an engineering standpoint, the water-management system of Angkor was composed of three main sectors: a northern zone, where water was spread across the landscape and its flow rate could be reduced; a central zone around the main temples, where water was held in massive reservoirs; and a southern zone between the center of Angkor and the lake, where water was either rapidly dispersed to the lake in the wet season or slowly distributed from west to east across the slope of the landscape, providing much-needed irrigation during the dry season.[25] This latter component was critical for Angkor, in that dry-season flow in the rivers was always insufficient to meet potential demand for water. Consequently, modification and canalization of the rivers ensured that the countless hamlets and rice fields of the empire received adequate year-round supplies.[26] In this way, Angkor's hydraulic system enabled farmers throughout the capital's hinterland to control the watering of their fields at the critical beginning and end point of the rice-growing season. Indeed, it was this temporal element that effectively transformed farming from a basic subsistence-level practice and created the kinds of surpluses needed to support a vast agrarian urban complex.[27]

To encourage the expansion of wet rice cultivation surrounding Angkor's capital, royal assignments of landed estates were extended to Khmer elite; in addition, agricultural workforces were also provided to the Khmer king as necessary to facilitate rice production and to construct and maintain the ever-expanding hydraulic system.[28] Frequently, these labor pools were composed of indentured servants and war captives. Khmer peasants were subject also to corvée—that is, compulsory labor for the ruling classes by private and public workers. Effectively, peasants worked as part-time laborers on whom the Khmer economy depended, for Angkor's rulers could effectively relocate their workforce into new lands to be cultivated.[29] Apart from expanding Angkor's agricultural productivity, the allocation of farmlands to a growing elite class more tightly integrated the hamlets scattered throughout the empire. For example, to acquire and maintain their legitimacy, local temples, founded on the new landed estates by the Khmer elite, were required to relinquish a certain percentage of their annual harvest in order to support the state's central temples.[30] Rice surpluses thus fed into Angkor's territorial expansion and flourishing regional trade networks. While agricultural expansion financed the political expansion of Angkor, merchants active throughout the empire shared in the prosperity generated by the agrarian base.[31]

By the late thirteenth and early fourteenth centuries the pinnacle of Angkor had passed. By the sixteenth century the political, economic, and cultural center of Khmer civilization shifted irrevocably from the long-standing agricultural heartland surrounding Angkor to the area around the confluence of the Mekong, Tonle Sap, and Bassac Rivers.[32] From here, the Khmer merchants had better access to the profitable maritime trade networks, notably around the South China Sea, and they were able to capitalize on new opportunities for trade with China.[33] Indeed, Phnom Penh would emerge as the primary urban center, due in part to its Mekong River commercial connections, as well as to its status as the sometimes residency of the Cambodian court, and the base of the most prominent Cambodian Theravada Buddhist clerical order.[34] European merchants and traders, a growing presence in the country, likewise perceived Phnom Penh to be the strategic market clearinghouse for Cambodian goods arriving from upstream and downstream, transported by various local and international Khmer, Lao, Thai, and Vietnamese diaspora communities.[35]

Between the Angkorian period and the arrival of the French in Cambodia, traditional Khmer society was broadly organized into three classes: peasants, government officials, and royalty.[36] At the apex stood the king, symbolizing the cosmic order and embodying the kingdom in the name of *deva-raja* (god-king).[37] As Chandler explains, people's ideas about the king tended to be grounded in mythology rather than their own experience; and because the king was rarely seen by ordinary peasants, his power and divinity was limited only by one's imagination. This was important, for the king, as ultimate arbiter of truth and justice, was often "the only political source of hope among peasants."[38]

In theory, the king held absolute political and administrative power; in practice, the actual exercise of power was closely linked to high-ranking officials, or *okya*. Personally assigned by the king—a key instrument for shaping the broader political landscape—these functionaries conducted the quotidian tasks of governance but did so within intricate networks of alliances, including those between patrons and clients. On this point, however, the functions of these officials were anything but codified, for the king could adjust their titles and tasks on a moment's notice. Chandler clarifies that sometimes a title carried a rank, and at other times it was associated with a job, such as maintaining the king's elephants, guarding his regalia, or collecting taxes.[39] Regardless of the specific task at hand, the *okya* were responsible for the day-to-day activities of the kingdom. They also provided the only real tangible connection the peasantry had with the ruling class.

The most influential among the *okya* were the five king ministers and myriad *chovay srok*—provincial governors—who attended to the political, social, and economic functions unique to their district.[40] For example, a royal tax of 10 percent was levied on rice production and labor to keep those activities under the effective control of the kingdom. The *chovay srok* were authorized to collect these taxes in their jurisdiction, from which they could also mobilize labor for public works. As Diepart and Sem conclude, access to labor and rice meant that in practice the *chovay srok* controlled the balance of power in the kingdom.[41]

Cambodia's population was overwhelmingly rural. Phnom Penh, the largest settlement and preeminent market town, was home to only about twenty-five thousand people; and the royal capital at Udong, only ten thousand. Battambang, another important market town 180 miles (296 kilometers) northwest of Phnom Penh, had only three thousand inhabitants.[42] Beyond these few commercial centers, the vast majority of Cambodians lived in villages widely scattered across the fertile central plain, a settlement pattern reflecting the physical conditions of subsistence agriculture that formed the bedrock of daily life. First, there were *kompongs*, larger villages of several hundred people that served as political and economic centers and were administered by the influential *chovay srok*. Located especially along the Mekong and Tonle Sap Rivers and their attendant tributaries, *kompongs* were key nodes through which goods and people circulated.[43]

In the hinterlands of the *kompong* were numerous rice-growing villages known as *srae*. Geographically disbursed and clustered irregularly around ponds or streams, these often housed Buddhist monasteries, or wats, that served as focal point for the Khmer.[44] Here, traditional Khmer society centered on the nuclear family, as families worked together as a unit, responsible for both household production and consumption.⁴⁵ Women and men contributed to farming and other income-generating activities, although gendered divisions of labor existed. Men would typically plow the fields, transport goods, and maintain localized irrigation schemes, while women would prepare seed rice, sow and transplant the seedlings, and harvest the crops.⁴⁶ Typically, families cultivated vegetables and herbs in small gardens around their homes; families also tended fruit trees and palms. Most households raised livestock, such as chickens, ducks, and pigs, while families that were more prosperous might maintain a stable of draft animals, including oxen and water buffalo. Women were mostly responsible for the cultivation of vegetable gardens and the raising of livestock. Depending on their home environment, families could supplement their resources through fishing and hunting (both normally male activities) and the manufacture (often by the elderly) of small household items, such as baskets, for immediate use.

Last, there were smaller, more isolated villages (*prei*) located in the forested mountain regions to the northeast and in the Cardamom and Elephant ranges southwest of Phnom Penh. Predominantly non-Khmer, the people who lived in the forests were neither Buddhists nor rice farmers and thus stood apart from the majority of the population. That said, *prei* played an essential role in the kingdom's political economy, for these villages provided essential forest resources that were valued in the market towns and beyond.⁴⁷

On the eve of colonialism, life continued much as before for most Cambodian peasants. Farmers kept cultivating rice, and fisherfolk went on catching fish. Water was still stored, diverted, and used to irrigate rice paddies, albeit on a limited, localized scale. And for most Khmer, spiritual life continued to revolve around the myriad Buddhist temples found in most villages and hamlets. Social positions were mostly fixed, the possibilities of accumulating wealth were limited, and the prospects to rise above the class into which one was born were almost nonexistent.⁴⁸

The French Protectorate Era (1863–1953)

Of all the political creations that the age of imperialism brought to Southeast Asia, arguably none was more artificial than French Indochina.⁴⁹ Composed of present-day Cambodia, Laos, and Vietnam, French Indochina was an amalgam of five separate administrative regions. Southern Vietnam (Cochinchina), under the ultimate authority of the colonial and naval ministries in Paris, was the only colony in the narrow constitutional sense. Politically, central Vietnam (Annam), northern Vietnam (Tonkin), Cambodia, and Laos were administered as distinct and autonomous protectorates under the auspices of the French Foreign Ministry. From 1887, however, all five political entities were brought under the authority of a single governor-general headquartered in Hanoi. Five regional heads served under the governor-general: the governor of Cochinchina and the *résidents supérieurs* of Annam, Tonkin, Cambodia, and Laos.[50]

Under French rule, the colonial economy of Indochina *as a whole* centered on land transactions, taxation, and the export of agricultural products. Consequently, public investment in land development and the transportation of agricultural commodities became government priorities throughout all of French Indochina, including Cambodia.[51] These investments, however, were exceptionally uneven—a factor that would mediate anti-colonial resistance in the twentieth century. From the outset, French authorities sought to capitalize on the productive potential of the Mekong Delta, and Cochinchina therefore received the lion's share of investment moneys. This is seen especially in the engineering efforts directed toward rice cultivation in the Mekong Delta. From 1890 to 1930, for example, new transportation and irrigation canals were dredged exceeding 165 million cubic meters in volume; the outcome was that almost 1.5 million hectares of land were cleared and put under cultivation. Another area of public investment was in railways throughout Indochina, but particularly in Tonkin. As Montserrat López Jerez explains, the objectives of moving what the government considered the excess population of the North to the South, and of moving rice from the surplus areas in the South to the deficit districts in the North, remained an important policy priority during the colonial period.[52] In Cambodia, French investment was substantially less, both in scale and scope.

The Cambodian Protectorate was, from the French vantage point, largely secondary to the economic possibilities in Vietnam—notably the rice fields of Cochinchina, but also the mines and rubber plantations of Tonkin. Accordingly, French authorities financed almost all their activities in Cambodia, including constructing public works and paying the salaries of French officials, through a complex and onerous system of taxes on salt, alcohol, opium, rice, and other crops, and by levying extensive fees for all government services.[53] In addition, throughout most of the colonial reign, French administrators delegated many of the day-to-day functions to intermediaries, whether Khmer, Chinese, or Vietnamese. Taxes, for example, were routinely collected by Khmer officials. However, French officials sought to more actively exploit the potential resource wealth of their protectorate through the export of agricultural products such as rice, rubber, and livestock. These exports were to augment the French agro-processing facilities and international export trade system centered in Cochinchina. Effectively, Cambodia's position within the larger regional economy of French Indochina was to supply low-cost raw materials.[54] Even this, however, required sweeping changes both economic and legal—indeed, a dialectic of productive and ideological structures and social relations that would have a lasting impact on the geography of Cambodia.

To boost rice yields, French administrators implemented a dual economic strategy composed of two subsectors. The first consisted of large-scale rice plantations established on land concessions and concentrated in Battambang Province. Owned and operated by French settlers, these plantations mainly hired migrant workers, many of them displaced Vietnamese peasants from neighboring Cochinchina. Operationally, rice plantations were heavily subsidized by the French government and organized around "modern" agricultural technologies geared toward the intensification of crop yields. For example, the colonial administration helped fund the necessary agricultural infrastructure, including the construction of irrigation systems, research stations for fertilizers and plant breeding, and a research farm involved in testing rice-mechanization technologies. To facilitate the distribution of rice, a rail line was constructed from Battambang City to Phnom Penh; from the latter city, barges would carry rice to Saigon via the Mekong River.[55]

The second subsector of colonial rice production comprised almost the entirety of the Khmer peasantry. Local smallholders of family-oriented plots grew rice for subsistence and commercial exchange using traditional methods. French officials, in turn, acquired rice through a direct tax on farmers, and this became the largest source of governmental revenue.[56] Notably, little technical innovation was achieved in rice production within the peasant subsector. Indeed, throughout the colonial period, French authorities provided only minimal investments for traditional farming methods, believing that the Khmer peasants "were incapable of developing or mastering innovations."[57] Consequently, for the vast majority of peasant farmers, the day-to-day activities of rice *production* changed very little during the period of French administration. Cambodian growers continued to cultivate rice using traditional techniques on small landholdings. Indeed, as Slocomb details, typical rice farmers still tended only those areas of land that their family units could till, and that produced sufficient rice for their families' immediate needs.[58] That said, the turn toward a market economy greatly increased the vulnerability of the peasantry.

French plans to boost agricultural exports and to generate revenues from taxes necessarily entailed substantial social and structural transformations of Cambodia's rural economy. Foremost among these changes was the conception of landownership. As Slocomb explains, in terms of meeting French needs, Cambodia's most valuable natural resource was what the administration regarded as vacant lands; the promise of economic growth and development in the protectorate lay in increasing land values—that is, capitalized rents.[59] Consequently, France's policies of land reform initiated a process of so-called primitive accumulation. These policies also created the conditions mediating the transformation of Khmer farming practices toward a path of agrarian capitalism.

The modern conception of private ownership did not exist in traditional Cambodian landholdings.[60] Prior to colonialism, all lands throughout Cambodia were held by the king, with substantial territories apportioned to princes and other members of the ruling class. However, ordinary farmers could claim the right to land access and use by clearing and cultivating vacant lands, a practice commonly known as appropriation "by the plough." Through this process, farmers traditionally retained possession rights (*paukeas*) of land.[61] In return, a royal tax of 10 percent was levied on all rice yields in order to place rice production and labor under the effective control of the sovereign king. The *chovay srok* were authorized to collect taxes in their jurisdiction, from which they could also mobilize labor for public works or military necessity.[62] If farmers produced more, they paid more in taxes; if they produced less, they still paid only 10 percent. In practice, the system discouraged the production of large surpluses as farmers were often reluctant to produce above and beyond their immediate needs.[63] For profit-seeking French administrators, this traditional landownership system was an enormous barrier that catalyzed a broad array of legal practices designed to more fully integrate Khmer farming into the embryonic colonial economy. Most notably, these practices coalesced around the commodification of land.

Land registration and titling procedures introduced during the French colonial era consisted of two consecutive steps that followed distinct procedures and involved different categories of actors. The registration of land as fixed asset was based on the productive occupation of a plot of land for five years. This restriction, in turn, required technical measures and registration in a landbook, and the procedure was supervised by the commune chief. Subsequently, the land title and transfer of the ownership right could be delivered. This step, however, required a written property-transfer document and registration from the French-administered cadastral office.[64] For many Cambodian peasants, the system was both confusing and cumbersome. On the one hand, the legal difference between "possession" and "ownership" rights was unclear because farmers assumed they retained full land tenure security on account of local recognition of the possession certificate. The added step of acquiring ownership rights appeared excessive and unnecessary. On the other hand, many peasants balked at obtaining land titles because they did not trust the French authorities. Consequently, whereas the delivery of possession certification was fairly widespread, few landholdings were effectively titled—a pattern that continued long after the French departed. Effectively, and with few local exceptions, the claim of land right through occupation—the traditional "acquisition by the plough"—remained the norm throughout much of the country.[65]

In liberalizing land markets and favoring access to land for French and other foreign investors, the administration attempted to increase the exchange value of land in order to transfer it to the most productive farmers. This was to be achieved through the institution of a new tax system, obliging peasants to pay a certain percentage of their crop yield in cash. Consequently, peasants were compelled to engage in the market economy by selling part of their harvest; and if yields were insufficient, farmers were forced to solicit waged employment.[66] Effectively, these administrative policies contributed further to the embryonic proletarianization of the peasantry and hastened the path toward agrarian capitalism. As Diepart and Sem explain, this cash economy deepened usury credit systems and resulted in widespread indebtedness among the peasant class. Combined with the development of land markets, indebtedness led to a growth in land dispossession through mortgage or sale, and to the emergence of a small but no less significant class of landless laborers.[67]

Aside from development projects oriented around rice production, land concessions for rubber plantations and forest reserves were also important instruments of French colonization in Cambodia.[68] The first major rubber plantation in Cambodia, the Chup Plantation, was established by the French in 1921. By the 1930s sizable plantations were operating in the favorable soils of northeastern Cambodia, notably in the provinces of Kompong Cham, Kompong Thom, and Katie.[69] Within a decade, rubber became the third-largest export from the country and would remain a key foreign-exchange earner until independence in 1953.

French authorities also turned to the extraction of profits from Cambodia's forests.[70] On this point, the French administration initiated a system of forest reserves. Starting in 1902, logging activities were regulated within these state enclosures according to licenses signed between French companies and the forest administration. These regulations were introduced to sustain colonial rents and substitute small-scale indigenous forest use with large-scale entrepreneurial exploitation. Indeed, through these concessions, Cambodians were denied access to many forests throughout the protectorate.[71] Consequently, changes in ownership rights and the imposition of land concessions and enclosures contributed to the dissolution of the commons, further reorienting Khmer quotidian life to the market economy. And this, in fact, was by design. The replacement of possession rights by ownership rights enabled and facilitated the expansion of plantation agriculture through the permanent acquisition of land, for the French needed both to commodify land *and* to provide secure title for foreign owners in perpetuity.

On the eve of independence, Cambodia's economy remained rural in its focus, with the majority of the country's population engaged in subsistence agriculture or other small-scale extractive activities. As Slocomb documents, aside from an embryonic plantation agriculture that was foreign owned, served foreign industrial purposes, and earned profits for foreign shareholders, there was little capital investment in Cambodian agriculture. Consequently, there was limited industrialization of the local economy and virtually no industrial proletariat. Indeed, because of the lack of capitalist development in the agrarian section, there were no surplus agricultural workers to supply labor for the few plantations in operation. Foreign owners imported migrant workers displaced from neighboring Vietnam. That said, private wealth certainly existed in Cambodia; high officials serving in collaboration with the French grew rich by taxing the surplus product of the farmers and lending money against future harvests. Overall, though, these individuals acquired riches primarily for prestige and power, not for the creation of capital.[72] In addition, as Vickery explains, potential capitalists were foreign, mostly Chinese, or they came from a small group of Khmer bureaucrats and a limited number of plantations. Members of the nonproducing ruling class extracted wealth from the agricultural sector through usury, taxation, or payment for favors, not by direct intervention to increase production.[73]

The end result of French colonialism was neither a substantial concentration of landholdings among an absentee landlord class, nor a substantial capitalist development of agriculture. By the time of independence, most of the Khmer peasantry did not have a landowning aristocracy pressing down on them. However, unequal distribution of land among the peasantry was a growing problem: 80 percent of Cambodian landowners who each owned less than five hectares of land in 1930 accounted for only 44 percent of the land cultivated. More than half of the land was owned by the wealthiest 20 percent of the farmers.[74]

More pressing was the fact that Cambodia's smallholding farmers were increasingly caught in networks of debt and traditional obligations.[75] On that point, French colonial practices significantly increased Khmer farmers' vulnerability to hunger, starvation, and possible famine. With land commodified and the commons under threat, farmers were placed in ever more precarious positions and subject to indebtedness or landlessness. The nascent market economy created usury credit systems and resulted in widespread liabilities among the peasants. In turn, insurmountable debt led to land dispossession and the emergence of a floating, landless population forced to work as agricultural wage laborers.[76] Vulnerability to hunger or dispossession increased precipitously, for one or two poor crops were often enough to plunge farmers into a cycle of debt or force them to sell their land to creditors. As Slocomb concludes, "If Cambodian farmers were not actually starving, neither were they prosperous."[77]

The Sihanouk Regime (1953–1970)

On November 9, 1953, Cambodia regained the independence it had lost decades earlier when it became part of French Indochina.[78] The struggle for autonomy, notably, was neither a widespread mass movement nor a social revolution. Somewhat disingenuously, King Norodom Sihanouk claimed that it was his "royal crusade" for independence, a series of international diplomatic appeals, that won political and military freedom for Cambodia.[79] In fact, liberation was offered by French officials who, mired by a failing war in neighboring Vietnam, granted independence to their former protectorate.

Cambodia achieved its independence during the maelstrom of the First Indochina War, also known as the Franco–Viet Minh War. The Viet Minh, a Communist-led revolutionary movement in Vietnam, waged an armed struggle against the French starting in 1946. After a brief interlude of Japanese occupation during the Second World War, French authorities sought to regain and retain possession of their former colonies. In turn, numerous nationalist groups throughout Vietnam formed and re-formed in opposition to the French. The most notable of them was the Viet Minh, led by Nguyen Sinh Cung, better known as Ho Chi Minh.

For strategic reasons, the Viet Minh believed that independence from colonial rule could only be ensured if the French were defeated throughout the entirety of Indochina. This led to the establishment in 1951 of a Vietnamese-sponsored Cambodian Communist movement, the Khmer People's Revolutionary Party (KPRP). Prior to this watershed event, no dominant or united opposition group in Cambodia had challenged French authority. Instead, a disparate assemblage of Khmer Issarak ("independence") forces exhibited vastly different outlooks. The short-lived Khmer People's Liberation Committee, for example, was nationalist in orientation, although some members were sympathetic to Communism. Following independence, the vast majority of Cambodians laid down their arms and returned to village life. Their country was free from foreign rule, and both French and Vietnamese forces were departing. As David Chandler writes, most Khmer "were reluctant to become involved in rebellious politics after Cambodia's independence had been won."[80]

For most observers within and beyond Cambodia, the future appeared promising. Nearly everyone had enough to eat, almost all peasants owned the land they tilled, and—importantly—there was an abundance of land to cultivate. For nonfarmers, towns offered employment.[81] A foreign reporter captured some of this optimism, writing in 1955, "Cambodia seems to stand at the extended new road to life among the many nations. She has passed several tollgates and is entering the main highway.... In certain places in the world, there are unspoiled places awaiting training and education for the new era; Cambodia is one of those places."[82] Over time, this optimism dissipated, replaced by unattained aspirations, increased disillusionment, political factions, and war.[83]

Sihanouk attempted to maintain a neutral position, declaring Cambodia a nonaligned country; however, this strategic move effectively ensured that his government was opposed by social revolutionaries, conservative aristocrats, a pro–U.S. military, and an emerging educated class seeking personal advancement and national modernization.[84] In an effort to consolidate his power, Sihanouk abdicated the throne and formed his own political party, the Sangkum Reastr Niyum (People's Socialist Community).[85] Ideologically, the Sangkum was a conservative amalgam with a few left-wing politicians to balance against the Right, and it espoused a conservative version of Buddhism explaining social inequalities through the workings of karma.[86]

In 1956 Sihanouk embarked on a program of Khmer socialism, later modulated into what he called Buddhist socialism. Here, though, the term "socialism" acquired a particular meaning for him, in that it denoted "a society mobilized to perpetuate the status quo."[87] As Michael Vickery explains, "It was not to be Marxist socialism, but rather a 'Royal Buddhist Socialism'—without class conflict, which was declared non-existent in Cambodia—and dependent on the 'ancient' Cambodian practice of the sovereign always providing for the welfare of its people."[88] In other words, far from a radical or revolutionary ideology, socialism for Sihanouk was conservative in orientation. While state intervention was pervasive in many areas of public life, agriculture and commerce were to remain private.[89] Indeed, according to Kenton Clymer, Sihanouk had no sympathy with Communism and no illusions about the results of a Communist victory in neighboring Vietnam. For Sihanouk, an independent Cambodia would not long survive such an outcome; however, he wanted to confront this threat on his own terms, not as a puppet of the United States.[90] This required a delicate balancing act that offered advantageous diplomatic and political relations from across the ideological spectrum.

In practice, Sihanouk's Khmer (or Buddhist) socialism meant remaining neutral between the capitalist and Communist blocs in the political domain. In the economic sphere, his ideology involved seeking a balanced adaptation of the two systems. As Slocomb explains, under these conditions state capital supplemented private investment. The state would control key economic sectors, such as energy, transportation, and extractive industries (mines), while other sectors, notably industry, agriculture, and commerce, were targeted for mixed enterprise.[91]

From 1955 onward, Cambodia's economy seemingly prospered. Exports of primary products such as rice, rubber, and pepper earned foreign exchange sufficient for Cambodia's needs; and foreign aid from France, the United States, and the Sino-Soviet bloc translated into new hospitals and schools. In turn, health care and sanitation improved dramatically, and the incidence of malaria and infant mortality decreased. Literacy also improved as hundreds of thousands of children were able to attend school. The country's long-neglected infrastructure likewise received much-needed upgrades, including the construction of a deep-water port.[92]

Yet the most ambitious plans for development centered on the transformation of Cambodia's rice economy. The government assumed control of the large-scale French rice plantations in Battambang Province and looked also to continue the expansion of irrigation started by the French. With support from the U.S. Agency for International Development (USAID), national water-control infrastructure was improved, as irrigation schemes, barrages, canals, and reservoirs were constructed in Siem Reap, Kompong Cham, Kandal, and Kampot Provinces. In addition, a USAID rice production program was established in 1955, with six rice-research stations developed for yield trials and seed production.[93] To facilitate the expected increases in rice productivity, the United States funded the construction of the Khmer-American Friendship Highway (now National Road No. 4), which connected Phnom Penh with the newly built port of Kompong Som. This road allowed Cambodia to import and export goods without having to rely on the Mekong River route through Vietnam.[94]

Despite massive investment in agricultural infrastructure, results were marginal but not disastrous. Rice production increased to levels of around 2.3 million tons per year during the first decade of independence, but productivity measures barely registered any change. When development programs first started in 1955, average yields were 1 metric ton per hectare; when the projects were canceled ten years later, yields were only up to 1.1 tons per hectare.[95] The discrepancy lies in the limited scale and scope of state-sponsored development programs. For example, large-scale irrigation had not yet reached the vast majority of Cambodia's farmers by 1968. Between 1954 and 1968, irrigated rice cultivation expanded only from 34,762 to 79,926 hectares, approximately 3 percent of the total area under rice. Consequently, dry-season rice production remained on the whole inconsequential.

In addition, chemical fertilizer use nationwide totaled only 32,000 tons; while crop protection using pesticides had begun, it was not yet applied to rice. Agricultural mechanization also had expanded to include the use of 1,500 tractors, but these remained largely confined to the large landholdings in Battambang Province. Finally, a shortage of skilled technical and management staff in agriculture remained.[96] Simply put, as Stian Rice concludes, rice production was growing as it had throughout history: by getting bigger, not more efficient.[97] The area of land under rice cultivation, for example, expanded from 1.7 million to 2.2 million hectares, growth that generally aligned with rural population growth.[98]

More pressing, the government-sponsored agrarian programs failed to address the growing inequalities among the peasant sector. Inherited from the French colonial era, such inequities arguably were a byproduct of Sihanouk's forwarding of Khmer socialism. As Slocomb explains, "The roots of Khmer socialism were in the past, originating with the kings of Angkor and the patterns they established for land use and ownership as well as for social action.... Through Khmer agrarian socialism, each rural family would be assured of full ownership of the land it was capable of developing as well as freedom over disposal of the 'fruits' of its work."[99] However, as Courtney Work and Alice Beban note, Sihanouk's limited efforts to address land reform often led smallholders to contract unpayable debts and to suffer subsequent landlessness.[100] Indeed, through the 1960s landlessness was becoming more widespread. In 1962, for example, 16 percent of agricultural households were landless, and by 1970, the figure rose to 20 percent.

Even more pressing, this period was characterized by the rise of land inequality, as seen in the growing class of peasants who retained very few ties to the land. And of those who retained possession of their holdings, most lacked operating capital and were subject to indebtedness and a dependency on usury.[101] On this point, the underlying financial situation of the peasant class remained quite like it was under the French. Smallholder farmers sold what little surplus they produced to acquire money with which to pay taxes. From this exchange, the government received revenue from rice exported through Phnom Penh and Saigon, and from taxation. However, to increase profits, the domestic price offered to farmers for their harvest was kept artificially low, despite rising global prices. Peasants in need of short-term capital thus sought out private moneylenders or rice brokers and either borrowed rice (if they had a deficit caused by a poor harvest), borrowed money, or sold property. Bank credit was largely unavailable in rural Cambodia, as most short-term credit given by the country's fledgling private banks went to commercial enterprises, as opposed to desperate farmers.

In an effort to confront the growing problem of rural poverty, Sihanouk established the Office of Royal Cooperation (OROC) to expand the role of rural cooperatives, extend credit lines, and assist those farmers in default. From the outset, however, Sihanouk's program faced serious problems. Merchants, for example, resisted the cooperatives' development, and some of these enterprises suffered from unsound management, lax supervision, and official corruption.[102] In the end, Sihanouk's efforts were too little and too late. By 1966 an estimated two-thirds of Cambodia's peasant farmers had problems repaying debts or obtaining credit.[103]

In November 1963 Sihanouk renounced U.S. military and economic assistance, and in 1965 he severed diplomatic relations with America. These were remarkable moves. Between 1955 and 1963, Cambodia received approximately U.S.$400 million from the United States, equaling 30 percent of Sihanouk's defense budget and 14 percent of Cambodia's total budget.[104] In fact, the amount of U.S. aid surpassed the combined amount of aid provided by China and the Soviet Union. However, Sihanouk worried—rightfully so—that aid programs were creating a military class in Cambodia that was dependent on the United States. More broadly, he feared that Cambodia was becoming an American client state. U.S. officials had for years pressured Sihanouk to join the Southeast Asia Treaty Organization (SEATO), an anti-Communist security alliance loosely modeled after the North Atlantic Treaty Organization (NATO), which included the United States, Thailand, the Philippines, Australia, France, and Pakistan.[105] The U.S.-supported coup and murder of South Vietnam's president Ngo Dinh Diem no doubt affected Sihanouk's thinking.[106]

In order to cope with the loss of U.S. assistance, Sihanouk nationalized major sectors of the Cambodian economy.[107] In early 1964, foreign trade, including rice exports, was placed under the control of a new state corporation given monopoly control, the Société nationale d'exportation et d'importation (SONEXIM). In turn, the existing OROC became responsible for the purchase and processing of the rice export crop, which was then sold through SONEXIM. SONEXIM subsequently controlled the import of agricultural inputs, including fertilizers, pesticides, and farm equipment, that were distributed for sale through OROC.[108]

Initially, Sihanouk's strategy appeared to be working. Cambodia exported 500,000 tons in both 1964 and 1965, with total rice production levels exceeding 2.5 million tons. By 1966, however, reality set in. For example, the nationalization of rice maintained *state* profits by suppressing the domestic price of rice. This development came at the expense of smallholder farmers who could no longer pay their debts after selling their crops at the government-fixed rate. Consequently, the fixing of prices discouraged peasants from growing rice for more than minimal needs. In turn, officials expressed concern that the lack of production incentives might reverberate throughout the country. Despite declines in rice exports, Cambodia grew enough rice to obviate any serious danger of mass starvation for the time being. The unanswered question, though, was whether the production system would degenerate further into an "economy of survival" in which peasant farmers planted only enough for their immediate needs.[109]

Compounding the government's problem was the fact that large portions of rice exports were being sold on the black market, depriving the state of tax revenue.[110] Chinese merchants in Phnom Penh and other urban centers were anxious to sell rice and other goods directly to the Vietnamese Communists because the latter paid in American dollars at international rates. According to Kiernan, in 1966 Cambodia exported an estimated 300,000 tons of rice, of which only 170,000 tons were sold legally, and official agencies collected only one-third of the crop. Dependent on its heavy taxation of rice exports, the government was running short of legitimate sources of income.[111] This impelled Sihanouk to launch a campaign, known as *ramassage du paddy*, to force farmers to sell their rice to the government at artificially low prices.[112] Growers caught selling rice illegally were severely punished.

Conflicts over land tenure also contributed to the grievances expressed by both Cambodian farmers and would-be revolutionaries. Following independence, land continued to be claimed in three ways: ownership title, fixed-asset registration, and occupation. While the main growing areas were registered under ownership or through fixed-asset registration, land continued to be cleared, used, and claimed through the customary arrangements of "acquisition by the plough." Indeed, this remained a key legal context for the expansion of rice cultivation throughout the 1950s and 1960s. However, the continuation of customary land clearing and landownership through occupation, coupled with a modern system of property rights, caused conflicts when the government failed to protect vulnerable groups who did not integrate into the modern property system. Thus, by manipulating the legal system, government and military officials frequently invalidated undocumented possession of property that local villagers had cleared and obtained land titles for, *but not ownership titles*.[113]

The struggle over land rights, coupled with government campaigns to forcibly collect rice from recalcitrant peasants, proved volatile. Beginning in March 1967, localized uprisings flared up around Samlaut in western Battambang Province; by the end of the year, these rebellions had developed into armed conflict throughout much of the country.[114] Villagers seized weapons, destroyed government property, and killed government officials, sparking unrest in other provinces among the disaffected rural poor.[115] Sihanouk responded in force, ordering the Cambodian military to wage a bloody counterattack on the "Khmer Rouges," his derogatory term for the protesters. Convinced that the Vietnamese Communists were behind the uprisings—a premise with some validity—Sihanouk offered a bounty for the severed head of any captured insurgent. Retribution became spectacle, with the public execution of suspected leaders and the screening of graphic films of the killings throughout the country. Sihanouk reportedly claimed to have put to death 1,500 Khmer Rouge adherents during the rebellion.[116]

The Samlaut Rebellion, according to Donald Kirk, was "a prelude, in a microcosm, of the conflict that would sweep across the country three years later."[117] And to that point, the unrest that stemmed from deteriorating economic conditions was not limited to the rural area, for Cambodia's faltering economy extended beyond the rice sector. Exports of rubber, the country's most valuable product, fell as a result of declining world prices. The development of other crops for export—for example, pepper, kapok, cotton, and tobacco—was hampered by insufficient foreign investment, lethargic bureaucrats, and state monopolies that stifled initiative.[118] Industrialization was still embryonic in scale and scope: inexperience, mismanagement, poor equipment, isolation from foreign markets, and shortages of raw materials kept the heavy industry from developing.[119] Light industry, however, which had not been nationalized, exhibited modest growth but was insufficient to carry Cambodia's economic burden. As Slocomb details, the pace of economic growth slowed after 1963, with several industrial sectors, including food, textiles, printing, and paper, declining in each successive year.[120]

These economic woes translated into urban discontent. Sihanouk's nationalization policies angered Cambodia's small but vocal commercial class. Likewise, a growing mass of high school and university graduates were unable to find jobs commensurate with their education, and members of the Cambodian armed forces resented budgetary cuts following Sihanouk's decision to sever ties with the United States.[121] Effectively, Sihanouk was accumulating enemies along a broad spectrum of Cambodian society, and he had a diminishing set of options with which to respond: peasants, merchants, and members of the military. The country's future was as clouded and turbulent as the monsoonal rains.

The Origins of the Khmer Rouge

The Khmer Communist movement was born in the struggle for independence from French colonial rule after the Second World War.[122] As mentioned earlier, revolutionary activity in Cambodia was largely insignificant before the 1950s, with two notable exceptions. In 1930 the Buddhist Institute was established in Phnom Penh and became a center of nationalism and anti-colonial activity. Two key members included Son Ngoc Thanh and Achar Sok, later known as Tou Samouth.[123] Also in 1930, the Indochina Communist Party (ICP) was formed in Hong Kong under the leadership of Ho Chi Minh, with an ICP cell subsequently established in Cambodia and composed of ethnic Vietnamese workers recruited from French rubber plantations.[124]

During the Second World War, various armed Khmer Issarak (Khmer Independence) groups were established. Composed mostly of nationalist-oriented revolutionaries, the Khmer Issarak engaged in low-level, primarily rural campaigns against French forces both during and after the war. Notably, Vietnamese Communists attempted to build a united front among the various resistance groups in Cambodia.[125] Still heavily influenced by Soviet advisers, they concluded that only the total defeat of the French in the entirety of the Southeast Asian mainland could ensure their independence. To this end, the Vietnamese provided aid to their Khmer comrades, mostly in support of their own liberation strategies. Operationally, Vietnamese Communists set up guerrilla bases throughout Cambodia, extending mostly over large areas in northwest, southwest, and southern parts of the country. Vietnamese cadres, working with the Khmer, also established people's committees at district and village levels in many provinces in Cambodia, and formed self-defense units to protect villagers from the French army.

During the First Indochina War (1946–1954), Vietnamese Communists expected Cambodian resistance fighters to model their movement on that of the Vietnamese. The Vietnamese cadres told their Khmer counterparts that they could play a small but vital part in liberating Indochina, becoming one part of a greater international movement delivering equity and justice to the downtrodden nations.[126] In the process, Vietnamese Communists gained more influence within the Khmer Communist movement, and they subsequently used Cambodian territory in their own war against the French.[127] More formally, in 1951, the Vietnamese Communists helped found the first Communist organization in Cambodia, the Khmer People's Revolutionary Party (KPRP), even writing the statutes and platform for the KPRP.[128] In doing so, Vietnamese Communists denounced Cambodian ideas of nationalism and local ways of organizing society as "feudal."[129] Indeed, they described the KPRP not as "the vanguard party of the working class[,] but [as] the vanguard party of the nation gathering together all the patriotic and progressive elements of the Khmer population."[130]

When Sihanouk secured independence, the future of the Khmer Communist movement was very much in doubt. In the minds of many Khmer resistance fighters, Sihanouk's crusade for freedom had obviated the need for revolution. During the war against the French, most Khmer—including several members of the KRPR—were not fighting for Communism; rather, the vast majority of Khmer resistance fighters directed their revolutionary activities against French colonialism. For this reason, as Chandler explains, most Khmer "were reluctant to become involved in rebellious politics after Cambodia's independence had been won."[131] Indeed, the removal of the French probably meant little to many Cambodians, who continued to pay taxes to finance an unresponsive government in Phnom Penh. Consequently, because the people in the countryside had never been asked to play a part in any government, they saw few short-term rewards in resisting those in power, who were now at least Cambodians rather than French or Vietnamese.[132] Even had conditions been optimal, the Khmer Communists were in no position to move forward. Numerically, the KPRP had perhaps a thousand members with another five thousand Khmer fighting alongside the Vietnamese.[133]

In 1954, defeat at Dien Bien Phu hastened France's departure from Indochina entirely. The subsequent signing of the Geneva Accords, however, left the future of the region in question. Most pressing was the decision to divide Vietnam into two political entities, the Communist-dominated Democratic Republic of Vietnam (DRV) in the North, and a U.S.-supported Republic of Vietnam in the South (figure 2). In this regard, military victory for the Vietnamese Communists did not bring political victory. Accordingly, in the aftermath of the Geneva Conference, the Vietnamese Communists counseled postponement of the Khmer revolution until conditions in Vietnam, *not Cam-*

FIGURE 2. North Vietnam, South Vietnam, Laos, and Cambodia during the Second Indochina War. Courtesy of Stian Rice.

bodia, warranted armed insurrection. Indeed, in their postwar planning, the leadership in Hanoi anticipated Communist parties in Laos and Cambodia forming the basis of parliamentary governments that would be independent but militarily and politically weak, and thus reliant on the DRV for survival.[134]

Simply put, the Vietnamese Communists considered their revolution a people's democratic revolution, one that would sweep away feudalistic exploitation and build a foundation for socialism throughout Vietnam and beyond. The Cambodian revolution, conversely, was a local revolution, one that was not yet ready to build the foundation for socialism.[135] Practically, this meant that the Khmer Communists must forestall overt revolutionary activities and support Sihanouk. Effectively, it was imperative for the Vietnamese Communists that Cambodia remain neutral—at least in the short term—to prevent the United States from establishing a base of operations on South Vietnam's western border.[136]

From the signing of the Geneva Accords onward, insurgents in the U.S.-supported Republic of Vietnam pressed the DRV for permission to wage armed rebellion. Senior leadership in the North repeatedly refused these requests, worried that a hastily expanded insurgency might draw America into a protracted ground war. The official position of the DRV was to limit revolutionary activities in the South to political agitation; indeed, only in 1956 were armed self-defense units formed.[137] Only in 1959 did the Vietnamese Communists agree to the use of armed struggle with the founding of the National Liberation Front (NLF, colloquially known as the Viet Cong). All the while, Khmer Communists in Cambodia agitated to wage armed revolution.

Conditions of the Geneva Conference decreed that Khmer resistance forces not be given control of any of their national territory in which to regroup. Instead, members of the resistance faced two unpalatable choices—namely, to lay down their arms and participate in national elections organized by the Sihanouk government, or to retreat into exile in North Vietnam.[138] In the end, between one and two thousand Khmer Communists traveled north to receive military and political training; these men and women would not return until the early 1970s. A second group of approximately one thousand Khmer revolutionaries remained in Cambodia. Of this latter group, some participated overtly in political opposition to Sihanouk, while others worked covertly to recruit party members.

The still-embryonic Communist movement in Cambodia was beset by factionalism and ideological differences.[139] Significantly, this enabled the colonization of the KPRP by more radical members such as Pol Pot, Son Sen, Khieu Samphan, Ieng Sary, and Ieng Thirith. Unlike other veteran revolutionaries, these men and women had recently returned from university studies in Paris. Indeed, as May Ebihara explains, the Khmer Rouge did not emerge out of the grass roots—like many revolutionary organizations elsewhere, it was organized by educated leaders from urban or upper-peasant backgrounds—but it obviously required control over much of the rural population.[140] Therefore, the Khmer Rouge constituted a peasant-*composed* movement; it was decidedly not a peasant-*led* revolutionary movement.

Pol Pot and other Khmer students had arrived in Paris when the political climate was vibrant and French intellectuals were shaping the themes that dominated postwar attitudes—a time when the French Communist Party (PCF) was in turmoil following revelations of Stalin's atrocities. However, a growing anti-Americanism replaced much disillusionment with Soviet politics. According to Elizabeth Becker, the Korean War, the American Marshall Plan for the reconstruction of Europe, and the continued American monopoly of the nuclear bomb combined to create an American menace in the eyes of many French Leftists.[141] This attitude permeated the Khmer Marxists, whose conviction only deepened with the United States' overt military intervention in Indochina. Accordingly, these Marxists interpreted contemporary events in Cambodia primarily through the writings of Stalin's "The National Question" and Lenin's *On Imperialism*. The knowledge and experiences Khmer scholars gained from their studies abroad carried over to Cambodia. Pol Pot, for example, held semiclandestine seminars on civic virtue, justice, and corruption. Students attended many of these classes, as did monks, military officials, and bureaucrats disenchanted by the Sihanouk regime. Pol Pot purposely spoke of a new society but rarely mentioned Communism; nor did he actively recruit members to the KPRP. Rather, Pol Pot encouraged participants to question and evaluate the political climate. Absent any direct support from their Vietnamese counterparts, however, the Khmer movement in Cambodia remained weak and vulnerable to intimidation and violence, as Sihanouk's secret police continued suppressing known or suspected Communists.[142] Betrayals and defections further hindered the cause. By the end of the decade, the Khmer Communist movement lost nearly 90 percent of its rural cadres. Some were murdered, many more quit from fear of retribution, and still others simply disappeared.[143]

In 1960, delegates of the moribund KPRP met secretively in a Phnom Penh railway yard to elect new leaders and to draft a political agenda. The meeting marked the first convention of the KPRP in nine years and, significantly, the first concerted effort to step outside the Vietnamese Communists' shadow. Proclaiming themselves to be Marxist-Leninists, the Khmer Communists assumed the title of Workers' Party of Kampuchea (WPK), thus placing themselves on equal footing with the Vietnamese Workers' Party. In addition, attendees agreed on a platform that clearly departed from the Vietnamese one by declaring Sihanouk and the "ruling feudal class" to be "the most important enemy of the Kampuchean revolution."[144] WPK members appointed veteran revolutionary Tou Samouth as party secretary, and elected Nuon Chea and Pol Pot to positions with the second- and third-highest rankings, respectively. However, internal dissent and growing factions hindered the effectiveness of the WPK until the sudden disappearance of Tou Samouth in 1962 opened the door for Pol Pot and his allies to assume greater power. At a meeting convened the following year, delegates formally installed Pol Pot as secretary-general, and he, in turn, initiated a new course of incremental but unwavering steps toward armed revolution.[145] The vanguard, known simply as Angkar, was formed.

During 1965, Pol Pot left Cambodia to spend several months in North Vietnam and China.[146] It was an auspicious time. As Kiernan explains, large numbers of U.S. troops began arriving in South Vietnam, and the benign neutrality of the Sihanouk government was increasingly valued by the Vietnamese Communists. The Vietnamese also valued their ability to use parts of Cambodia's border areas for sanctuary and shipment of supplies.[147] Keenly aware of these developments, Pol Pot pressed his plans to intensify the Khmer Communist movement *against* Sihanouk. In Hanoi, for example, he presented his Vietnamese counterparts drafts of his political platform, which featured a resolution emphasizing self-reliance and endorsing all forms of struggle, including armed violence.[148] It is probable that Pol Pot expected support from his Vietnamese allies to make contingency plans for armed struggle in Cambodia against Sihanouk. At the very least, he probably hoped to acquire weapons needed for revolution.[149]

In the end, Pol Pot's expectations went unfulfilled, as the Vietnamese Communists continued to consider a neutral Cambodia necessary to their immediate and more pressing objective of reunification. Thus, the Vietnamese leadership reprimanded the Khmer Communists for pursuing a nationalist agenda, and for wanting to put the Cambodian revolution ahead of the collective goal of a socialist Indochina. For example, Le Duan, secretary-general of the Vietnamese Communists, stressed the view that the Khmer strategy of "self-reliant struggle" was inappropriate and defeating; moreover, as a revolutionary party the Khmer Rouge was subordinate to the Vietnamese and thus was in no position to make such demands.[150] In view of these facts, Le Duan "recommended that the Cambodians combine building revolutionary bases in the countryside through unarmed mass mobilization with continued infiltration of parliament and government, in order to position the Party to make a bid for power, perhaps through violence, once the Vietnamese had won the war."[151]

Ultimately, Hanoi stressed the need for continued access to sanctuaries within Cambodia, as well as the ability to transport troops and supplies into southern Vietnam along the Ho Chi Minh Trail. In fact, the Vietnamese Communists had recently reached an agreement with Sihanouk that allowed the NLF access to Cambodian territory; in exchange, the Vietnamese pledged to honor all territorial borders at war's end. Given the enfeebled state of the Khmer resistance, the Vietnamese presciently believed that if anything should happen to Sihanouk, he would be replaced not with a socialist government but with a right-wing regime that would ally itself with the United States.[152]

Having failed in his attempt to secure the go-ahead for armed rebellion, Pol Pot and his entourage traveled to China to meet with several high-ranking officials of the Chinese Communist Party (CCP), including Deng Xiaoping and Liu Shaoqi.[153] The Chinese Communists viewed Cambodia as an important piece in the grand scheme of geopolitics. Like the Vietnamese, though, they concluded it was not the decisive piece. Yet Beijing did anticipate a future role for the Khmer Rouge very differently than Hanoi did. Although China and the DRV shared the goal of defeating the United States, they had divergent strategic interests in postwar arrangements. While the Vietnamese saw a united Indochinese Communist front as the best way to guarantee Hanoi's regional influence, a diffused power structure among Vietnam, Laos, and Cambodia best served China's strategic interests.[154] Consequently, the Khmer Rouge was counseled by its Chinese compatriots to suppress its nationalist aspirations for the greater good—that is, the defeat of the Americans. In practice, this meant not only that support for armed revolution was not forthcoming but also that the Khmer Rouge would not strike against Sihanouk.

Although denied immediate support and assistance for armed insurrection, Pol Pot returned to Cambodia with high hopes. Proclaiming his alliance with China as the path to victory, he informed his inner circle, "We need have no more doubts about the correctness of what we are doing."[155] In September 1966 Pol Pot convened a plenum to draft a new party program. The party officially changed its name to the Communist Party of Kampuchea, thereby elevating itself to the level of the CCP and surpassing that of their Vietnamese counterparts.[156] Against this backdrop, the Khmer Rouge interpreted the peasant uprisings in Battambang Province and, according to Steven Heder, decided to abandon cooperation with the Sihanouk regime and form a revolutionary army with which to wage all-out armed struggle against it.[157]

Conclusions

By the end of the 1960s, mass starvation remained off the radar of most Cambodian observers. Despite political turmoil, a stagnating economy, and a looming war, the social fabric of Khmer society remained largely intact. However, decades of social and structural transformations of traditional Cambodian land tenancy and farming practices undermined the adaptive resilience of Khmer farmers. Even without the specter of armed conflict, the vast majority of Cambodia's people faced an uncertain future as they were increasingly dispossessed of their lands and livelihood. Indeed, the heightened vulnerability of the Khmer peasantry spurred demands for reform, if not revolution. The Sihanouk government, the Khmer Rouge, and intelligence experts in the United States all recognized the animosity growing in the countryside. As Kate Frieson explains, all that was necessary for the Khmer Communist movement to make political inroads into the countryside—and for the governments in Phnom Penh and Washington to respond accordingly—was a combination of economic catastrophe and political opportunity. Both conditions would be provided by the coup against Sihanouk in March 1970, after which civil war, foreign invasion, and an unrelenting bombing campaign ultimately obliterated much of Cambodia's social fabric.[158] The violent conditions of an impending famine were fast taking shape.

CHAPTER 2

With Fatal Prognosis

> We'll hope the poor little Cambodians can hang on for a little longer than we think.
> —Richard M. Nixon, August 3, 1973

> I have only committed this mistake of believing in you, the Americans.
> —Sirik Matak, April 12, 1975

On March 17, 1970, Henry Kissinger, the U.S. national security adviser, briefed President Richard Nixon on developments in Cambodia. The country's economy was in trouble, Kissinger informed the president, noting that rice exports had dropped because of Norodom Sihanouk's nationalization of the commercial sector. Sihanouk also appeared politically troubled. According to Kissinger, Sihanouk faced for the first time in years concerted resistance to his domestic policies from conservative right-wing politicians and military officials. In recent days, violent demonstrations had erupted on the streets of Phnom Penh. Motivated by a potent mixture of nationalism and anti-Vietnamese hatred, the protesters called for regime change.[1] The uprisings, however, were far from spontaneous; rather, they were the latest manifestation of a power struggle inside the Cambodian government that had been festering for years.

Throughout the late 1960s the country became more dependent on rice exports to bring in foreign exchange. In addition, more and more rice was diverted from export markets into the Cambodian-Vietnamese black market where payment was mostly in Cambodian riels, not in foreign currency. Consequently, the gravity of Cambodia's faltering economy compelled Sihanouk to negotiate with the World Bank, the International Monetary Fund (IMF), and the Asian Development Bank (ADB) in a desperate attempt to garner funds. These institutions, though, were controlled indirectly by the United States, and U.S. advisers were adamant that Cambodia receive no loans until efforts were made to denationalize the economy. It was thus economic desperation, not military necessity, that forced a rapprochement between Sihanouk and the United States. As William Rosoff concludes, Sihanouk seems to have been forced to turn to the Americans for help, if only because they controlled the capital resources on which he believed economic development depended.[2]

Sihanouk's overtures to the United States went for naught, however. On March 18, 1970, a right-wing coup staged by General Lon Nol, an openly pro-American and anti-Communist figure, and Prince Sirik Matak, a cousin of Sihanouk's, removed Sihanouk from power. In the days following the coup, Sydney Schanberg recalls, "enthusiastic throngs of Cambodians, rallying behind their new anti-Communist, American-backed government, sacked and burned the North Vietnamese and Vietcong embassies—and the smoke and ashes filled the patriotic air."[3] The streets of Phnom Penh echoed with cries of cautious optimism about an uncertain but hopeful future, a future buoyed by the economic and military might of the United States.

Five years later, there would be little joy and little hope, only hunger and hardship. As Schanberg described at the time, "With Phnom Penh largely encircled by the Communist-led insurgents, the United States Embassy is burning some of its files . . . to prepare for the possibility of evacuation—and the ashes drift slowly to the embassy yard." Five years earlier, he explained, "the loudest noise one heard in the soft Cambodian night was the shrieking of the locusts in the tamarind trees. Now mortars and artillery thump away through the hours of darkness." Before the coup, before the war, Phnom Penh was "an uncrowded and untroubled city of flowering trees, temple bells, wide boulevards, floating river restaurants and gentle people who smiled a lot." "Now," Schanberg noted, "rockets fired from insurgent positions a few miles outside the city fall daily, leaving twisted bodies in the streets."[4]

Prior to the coup, Cambodia's economy had been fragile yet unbroken. The structure of rice production was fundamentally the same as it had been on the eve of independence in 1953. Yields remained low compared with those in neighboring Thailand, and yet—buoyed by extensification and infrastructural improvements to plantation agriculture—the national harvest had grown considerably. Indeed, the 1969 growing season produced 3.8 million tons, the largest rice harvest recorded.[5] For most people, food—and especially rice—was both cheap and plentiful. By 1975, the situation was horribly different. Writing that year, Schanberg observed, "Rice is outrageously expensive and five years of thinner and thinner diets have finally bent the population to a point where children by the scores are dying of malnutrition."[6]

Several thousands of miles away, safely ensconced in the White House, U.S. government officials and intelligence experts awaited the fall of Phnom Penh.

They expressed little empathy for the men, women, and children of Cambodia; and while U.S. policy makers were aware of the deplorable conditions—the hunger and disease and mental trauma—they remained largely indifferent to the plight of Cambodia's people. Rather, Cambodia appeared in the abstract, a chess piece no longer useful. Just days after the five-year anniversary of the coup, on March 24, 1975, Kissinger concluded that the time to solicit additional funds and aid for the war-stricken country had come to an end. He explained, "I think we probably ought to just give up on the Cambodia supplemental. Cambodia's finished."[7]

The coup d'état proved decisive in the destabilization of Cambodia and contributed to the famine conditions that would engulf much of the country from 1973 onward. This is not to lay blame solely or even exclusively on regime change, for the significance of Sihanouk's removal is found in the resultant necropolitics of America's expansion of war into Cambodia. On this point, the "first" of Cambodia's famines is rooted foremost in the United States' sacrifice of the Lon Nol regime to achieve the largely chimerical goal of nation building in neighboring South Vietnam.

The Territorial War

The U.S. military intervention in Cambodia was neither an aberration nor an accident. Instead, it resulted from deliberate political and military decisions emanating from the long-standing war in neighboring Vietnam.[8] When the Vietnamese Communists led by Ho Chi Minh defeated the French colonial forces in 1954, the subsequent Geneva Accords partitioned Vietnam into two military zones administered by two civilian governments. North of the seventeenth parallel—an arbitrary demarcation—was the Communist-controlled Democratic Republic of Vietnam. To the south was the State of Vietnam (later renamed the Republic of Vietnam). According to the conditions of the Geneva Accords, free elections were scheduled for 1956, with the goal of reuniting the "two Vietnams" under one sovereign authority.

To prevent the establishment of a Communist-led unified country, the United States assumed the burden of "state-building" in southern Vietnam starting in 1954, in effect "inventing" a sovereign country out of the ruins of French colonialism.[9] As James Carter describes, "During the period of direct American involvement beginning in 1954, the U.S. mission in Vietnam designed and implemented a range of far-reaching economic, political, and eventually military development projects in one of the most thorough and ambitious state-building efforts in the postwar period. The projects consisted of installing a president; building a civil service and training bureaucrats around him; creating a domestic economy, currency, and an industrial base; building ports and airfields, hospitals, and schools; dredging canals and harbors to create a transportation grid; constructing an elaborate network of modern roadways; establishing a telecommunications system; and training, equipping, and funding a national police force and a military, among others."[10]

Initially, Vietnam hardly registered on America's postwar radar. Indeed, U.S. officials during the early years of the Cold War had little knowledge of the region; nor was there much interest in deepening their understanding at a cultural level. However, caught in the vices of the Cold War, Vietnam soon emerged as a crucial "test case" of America's geopolitical credibility, and of its military capability to combat the numerous "national wars of liberation" associated with anti-colonial movements throughout the Global South.[11] A consensus emerged among U.S. officeholders that the Vietnamese revolution was symptomatic of the broader "peasant wars" of the 1950s. These officials feared such efforts would undermine U.S. economic interests elsewhere in the region. In other words, the "backwardness" of Indochina's economic structure was a breeding ground for Communist infections. However, American functionaries incorrectly deduced that money and munitions could substitute for freedom from colonial and postcolonial rule. On this point, a succession of U.S. presidents, from Dwight Eisenhower to Richard Nixon, tried to convince the American public—and probably themselves—that "there existed an independent, noncommunist state south of the seventeenth parallel that compelled American aid and defense."[12] Upholding the country as the last bulwark against unscrupulous and global Communist domination, U.S. officials deceived their way into war.

The Second Indochina War is often described as a "war without front"—that is, an unconventional conflict composed primarily of insurgent and counterinsurgent combat operations.[13] Confronted with a ubiquitous enemy and no clearly defined front lines, U.S. commanders and Washington-based analysts struggled to devise substitutes for gauging progress and effectiveness throughout the course of the war.[14] The necropolitical concept of "body counts" consequently assumed a vital place in military and political planning for American officials. Simply put, given that the primary geostrategic aim of the United States was to compel North Vietnam to agree to the existence of an independent and sovereign South Vietnam, U.S. military operational and tactical plans coalesced around a central assumption: if the Communist forces sustained sufficient military and civilian casualties, they would relent.[15]

The war was in fact inherently territorial, but at the strategic rather than

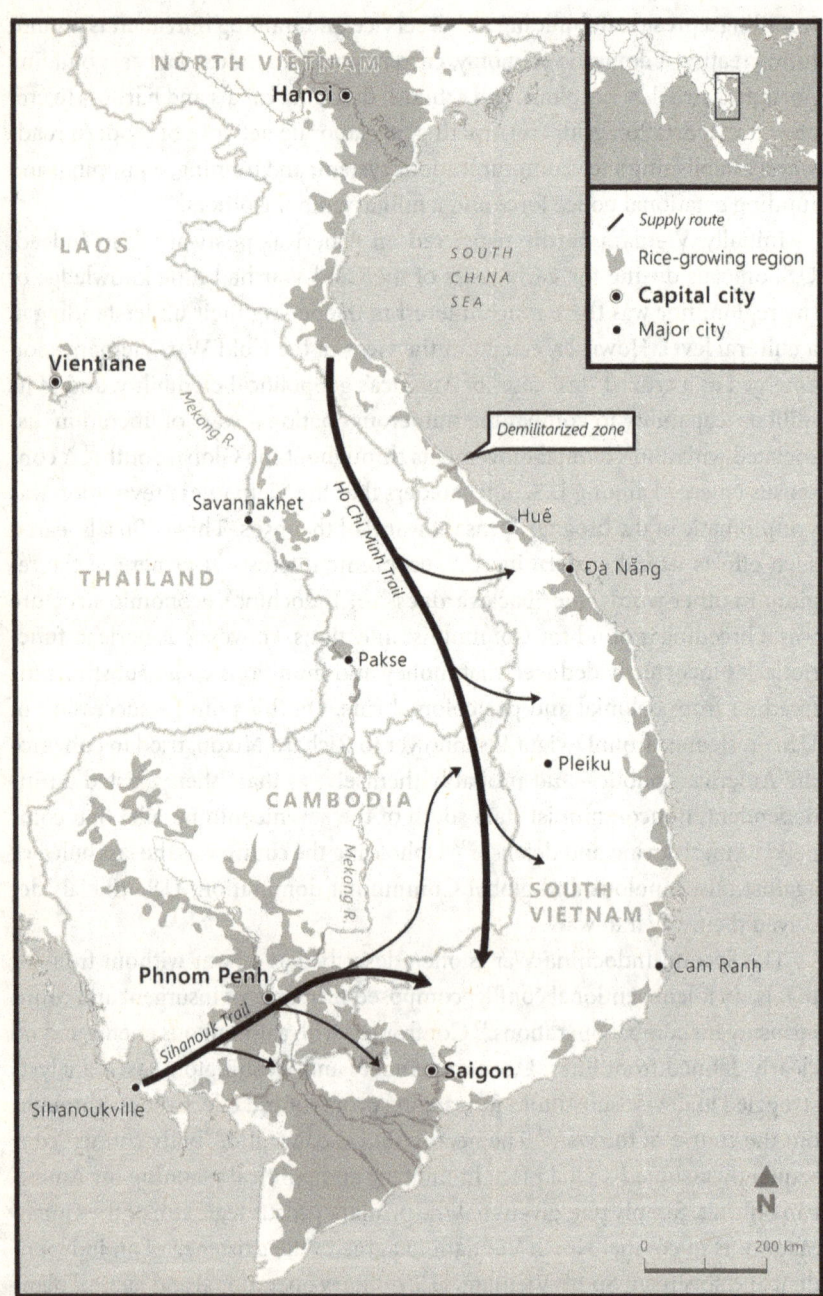

FIGURE 3. The Ho Chi Minh and Sihanouk Trails during the Second Indochina War. Courtesy of Stian Rice.

operational or tactical level. To build up and sustain South Vietnam, it was necessary to maintain the country's territorial integrity—that is, to solidify its borders from external interference and to eliminate domestic insurrection. U.S. objectives accordingly dictated the course of armed conflict to a considerable degree. Indeed, with the survivability of the Republic of Vietnam as the primary aim of U.S. interests, it was almost a certainty that the bulk of military actions would occur both within South Vietnam and in the defense of its borders with Cambodia and Laos. Standing opposite the Army of the Republic of Vietnam (ARVN) and its U.S. allies were the combined forces of the People's Army of Vietnam (PAVN, also referred to as the North Vietnamese Army, or NVA) and the People's Liberation Armed Forces (PLAF), the latter being the military branch of the National Liberation Front (NLF). Derisively known as the Viet Cong, the NLF was a semiautonomous organization operating in southern Vietnam that worked in conjunction with DRV leaders to overthrow the Republic of Vietnam.[16]

For the senior leadership of the Vietnamese Communists, military success required the ability to provision the NLF; this, in turn, required continued access through neighboring Laos and Cambodia. As such, military planners in Hanoi initiated the construction of a series of supply lines through eastern Laos, the Central Highlands of Vietnam, and eastern Cambodia. Known collectively as the Ho Chi Minh Trail, these lines in fact formed three overarching trail "complexes." The most well-known one traversed the length of Laos, permitting egress into central and southern Vietnam. This multicountry supply line consisted of thousands of miles of roads and footpaths carved out of dense forest vegetation; tens of thousands of men and women transported food, weapons, medicines, and other supplies along these routes. Eventually, fully armed North Vietnamese Army (NVA) troops would use the trail to conduct military operations in both South Vietnam and Cambodia (figure 3).

A second trail system originated in Cambodia's port city of Sihanoukville and operated largely on existing roads and rivers until passing through the eastern terminus of Cambodia. Along these routes, Vietnamese and Khmer Communists transported material by sampan or junk on inland waterways, by truck along Cambodia's road network, and by porters on the jungle trails that crossed into South Vietnam. A third system focused on the maritime networks, allowing materials to be shipped by sampan or junk from Cambodia's coastal ports to islands in the Gulf of Siam and subsequently to the east coast of South Vietnam. Collectively, many of these supply routes took advantage of historical commercial patterns; others constituted new pathways engineered specifically to further military objectives.

U.S. military advisers were well aware of the importance of the Ho Chi Minh and Sihanouk Trails to the Vietnamese Communists, for the logistical component of the war was crucial to the objectives and strategies adopted by both the United States and the DRV.[17] Cambodia especially was perceived by U.S. officials as the spatial Achilles' heel of South Vietnam. The porous 675-mile border separating the two countries afforded many crossover points to move weapons, munitions, medical supplies, and foodstuffs into South Vietnam. In addition, the sparsely populated jungles of eastern Cambodia provided ample sanctuary for PLAF and NVA forces. In May 1966, for example, the U.S. Central Intelligence Agency (CIA) prepared an assessment of the use of Cambodian territory by the PAVN/PLAF forces. Noting an overall increase in activities across the countries' border, CIA analysts identified several key routes and means of conveyance for moving resources through Cambodia into South Vietnam.[18] Indeed, estimates at the time suggested that porters along the Sihanouk Trail carried roughly 80 percent of all supplies other than arms and ammunition that were required by Vietnamese Communists in the southern half of South Vietnam. Cambodia itself made a vital contribution to those supplies by putting its rice crop at the disposal of the PLAF and PAVN forces.[19]

North Vietnamese access through Cambodia was conditioned on Sihanouk's assurance of neutrality or, at the minimum, his acceptance of it. This explains in part Hanoi's refusal to abide the demands of the Khmer Rouge. Vietnamese Communists were unwilling to jeopardize their prime objective, a unified Vietnam. Senior leaders of the Vietnamese Communist Party therefore refused Khmer Rouge leaders' requests for support to move against Sihanouk. Essentially, the objectives of the Communist Vietnamese and the neutralist Sihanouk aligned, to the frustration of the Khmer revolutionaries. This meant, in practical terms, that the Khmer Communists were to forestall armed insurrection and support the ostensibly neutralist Sihanouk. For the Vietnamese, the brewing struggle against the United States was all-important, and it was imperative that Cambodia remain neutral—at least in the short term—to prevent America from establishing a base of operations on Vietnam's western border. However, Sihanouk's incessant purge of suspected Communists and apparent deference to his Communist neighbors hindered Pol Pot's efforts to expand their movement. In certain respects, Sihanouk's actions threatened to extinguish the revolution altogether.

Foucault explains that "it is at the moment when the sovereign can kill that he exercises his right over life."[20] And it is from this moment onward that U.S. officials assumed and exercised the sovereign right to grant life or inflict

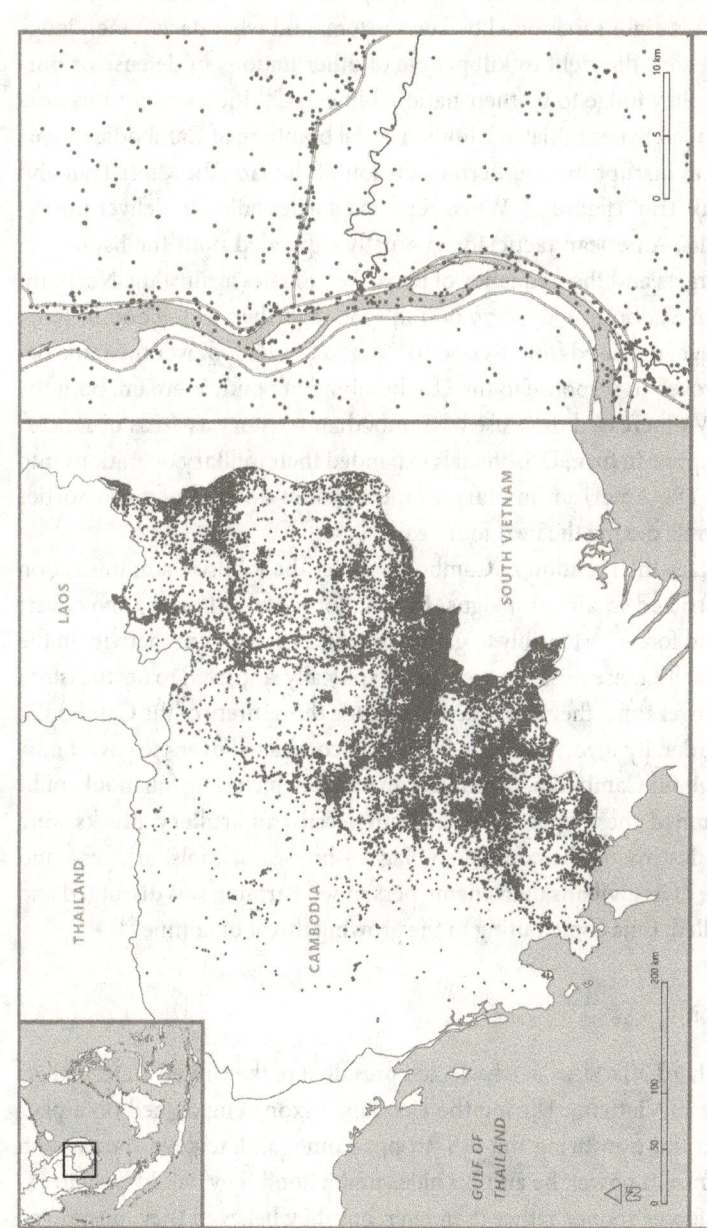

FIGURE 4. U.S. bombing of Cambodia, 1965–1973. Courtesy of Stian Rice.

death in Cambodia. Indeed, as Walt Rostow, a key architect of Johnson's Vietnam policy, explained, "National sovereignty means that nations retain the ultimate right—a right sanctioned by law, custom, and what decent men judge to be legitimate—the right to kill people of other nations in defense or pursuit of what they judge to be their national interest."[21] Indicative of this doctrine, the United States initiated a limited aerial bombing of Cambodia in 1965 in an effort to disrupt the southern extension of the Ho Chi Minh Trail and the Sihanouk Trail (figure 4). When repeated sorties failed to deliver the expected results, American tacticians gradually expanded both the list of "acceptable" targets and the frequency of air strikes. Sorties against the North increased from 25,000 in 1965 to 79,000 in 1966, and then to 108,000 in 1967; bomb tonnage increased from 63,000 to 136,000 to 226,000 over the same period.[22] However, in response to the U.S. bombing of South Vietnam, both the NLF and NVA increased their use of Cambodian territory as areas of sanctuary and resupply. In turn, U.S. officials expanded their military operations into Cambodia. The American military would conduct upward of 2,500 sorties over Cambodia during the next four years.[23]

U.S. military intervention in Cambodia under the Johnson administration was not restricted to air campaigns. In 1967 Johnson authorized the covert use of ground forces, ostensibly to gather intelligence on enemy activity in the country. Initially, these missions were geographically restricted to northeastern Cambodia; over time, they expanded to include the entirety of the Cambodia-Vietnam border. By 1970, American forces had conducted over 550 covert missions throughout Cambodia.[24] Cambodian officials, including Sihanouk, publicly condemned these operations, as both aerial and artillery attacks were more often destroying the country's villages—houses, schools, bridges—and killing more of its civilians than enemy personnel. Farming was disrupted and livestock killed, thus contributing to the growing threat of famine.[25]

Nixon's Gambit

In 1969, Richard Nixon, as newly elected president of the United States, inherited the war in Vietnam. During the election, Nixon campaigned on a platform to end the war, bring the U.S. troops home, and achieve "peace with honor."[26] Once in power, he and his aides understood they would have to extricate U.S. forces sooner rather than later, but they believed they must do so without damaging American credibility on the geopolitical stage. A swift collapse of South Vietnam due to a hasty U.S. withdrawal would imperil America's efforts to shape the international order after the war.[27]

In response to that point, Nixon's advisers premised a strategy based on South Vietnam's military, the Army of the Republic of Vietnam (ARVN), assuming a considerably larger role in the war effort than it previously had.[28] To that end, a center point of Nixon's strategy was the so-called Vietnamization program of training and equipping the Republic of Vietnam to govern and defend itself *without* the presence of U.S. ground forces.[29] The plan was announced publicly on June 8, 1969, with Nixon affirming that a reinvigorated ARVN would steadily replace the withdrawing U.S. personnel. Soon thereafter, his remarks came to be known as the Nixon Doctrine. Far from a coherent set of beliefs, however, Nixon's comments *with respect to Vietnam* reflected two long-standing goals of past U.S. administrations: to win the war in Vietnam—that is, to win a negotiated settlement with the North Vietnamese that allowed the continuation of a sovereign, non-Communist South; and to sustain U.S. global hegemony and credibility.[30] And, as with past presidents, Nixon realized that the neutral territory of Cambodia was vital to American interests.

From the outset, Nixon and his national security adviser Henry Kissinger understood that Vietnamization alone might require years of American patience and congressional largesse—two elements not guaranteed.[31] Indeed, the continued use of Cambodia both as sanctuary and a safe haven to movement troops and matériel remained a viable option for the PAVN and PLAF, and remained a potent threat to the survivability of South Vietnam. Thus far, the limited strikes permitted by the Johnson administration proved woefully inadequate, and Nixon was determined to push the envelope of military operations in Cambodia. Consequently, on March 15, 1969, Nixon authorized the use of B-52s to carpet bomb "Base Area 353" inside Cambodia, a region long suspected of harboring the DRV's and NLF's command-and-control post known as the Central Office for South Vietnam (COSVN).[32] This was the beginning of a fifteen-month bombing campaign known as Operation Menu in which U.S. B-52 pilots flew more than 3,800 sorties and dropped more than 100,000 tons of bombs on the Cambodian countryside.[33]

The overthrow of Sihanouk by Lon Nol and Sirik Matak on March 18, 1970, greatly altered the military and diplomatic terrain.[34] Initially, fighting between all parties paused briefly; the combatants were unsure what the new situation would mean.[35] Two days later, air strikes on Cambodian territory by the South Vietnamese air force commenced, followed a week later by multiple ground probes. The ground operations involved an ARVN infantry battalion with armored vehicles and air and artillery support. In turn, North Vietnamese forces initiated fighting in Cambodia.[36] Notably, the North Vietnamese at this point remained reluctant to expand military activities in Cambodia. In fact, Kissinger's own intelligence groups concluded that the North Vietnamese were not prepared to widen the war. On March 19—*the day after Sihanouk's ouster*—senior advisers informed Kissinger that "the North Vietnamese would not want to get involved in a war on two fronts in the South," and had "no reason to mount an insurgency since they could continue to use Cambodian territory."[37]

Governments elsewhere recalibrated their options in the aftermath of the coup. In Beijing, for example, Chinese leaders made overtures to the embryonic Lon Nol government, apparently with the goal of retaining North Vietnamese access to bases in and supply routes through Cambodia. As Isaacs explains, this was no trivial offer, for it meant that China would not sponsor Sihanouk as head of a rival Khmer government or support a Cambodian liberation war. Certainly, Lon Nol and his associates would have to tolerate a continued illegal Vietnamese occupation of parts of Cambodia. But in return, Lon Nol would remain in power, while Sihanouk—who still commanded strong support in the countryside—would be left with no base, no international backing, and no source of arms.[38] Lon Nol, however, balked at the Chinese offer, deciding instead to side with the Americans. Politically, he hoped to forge a stronger relationship with U.S. forces because he assumed they were all joined in a fight against a common enemy—Communism.[39] In reality, the Nixon administration's war against Communism largely stopped at the borders of South Vietnam. Cambodia was important only insofar as it was used as a base of operations by the Vietnamese Communists.

At this point, Sihanouk made a fateful decision that would have far-reaching consequences. The Chinese Communists, rebuffed in their overture to Lon Nol, encouraged Sihanouk to align with the Khmer insurgency and form a government-in-exile. He was far too astute a politician not to have realized that he was tying himself to interests that could be fatal to Cambodia.[40] Cold War calculus, however, forced the prince into a Faustian bargain. On March 23 Sihanouk announced the formation of the National United Front of Kampuchea (Front Uni National du Kampuchea, or FUNK), a political and military coalition of royalists and Khmer Communist insurgents. Two months later Sihanouk established the Royal Government of National Union of Kampuchea (Gouvernement Royal d'Union Nationale du Kampuchea, or GRUNK) and served as its head of state.[41]

For the Nixon administration, the Lon Nol government constituted little more than a handle with which to wield a blunt instrument. Convinced that military victory was still possible in South Vietnam—and that winning the war was necessary to maintain U.S. credibility, deter further wars of national liberation, and provide leverage over the Soviet Union and China—Nixon concluded that expanding the war into Cambodia would buy him the time needed.[42] As Schmitz explains, Nixon believed he could launch the aggressive Cambodian ground campaign that Johnson had resisted, using it as a decisive military blow to turn the tide of war and force the North Vietnamese to accept a settlement.[43] As a necessary show of force, however, the invasion could not be conducted covertly. As Nixon explained to Kissinger, "I think we need a bold move in Cambodia." Of the Vietnamese Communists in Cambodia, the president grumbled, "They are romping in there and the only government in Cambodia in the last 25 years that had the guts to take a pro-Western and pro-American stand is ready to fall."[44]

Materially, the United States provided Cambodia's armed forces, the Forces Armées Nationales Khmères (FANK), with captured small arms, ammunition, and miscellaneous personal equipment. In May, this aid was followed by Nixon's authorization of military assistance for Cambodia. Significantly, the military and economic support was developed to help the country maintain political stability. In translation, this primarily meant buttressing Lon Nol's military in its attacks against PVAN/PLAF forces operating within Cambodia's territorial limits.[45] However, Nixon was not willing to risk his overall objectives by assuming a secondary role in the developing conflict. On April 30, he informed the American public of a massive offensive into Cambodia against "the headquarters for the entire Communist military operation in South Vietnam."[46] Code-named Operation Shoemaker, the invasion involved more than forty-four thousand ARVN and American troops and was concentrated along the Cambodia-Vietnam border. Nixon remarked shrewdly that the United States undertook the mission not for expanding the war into Cambodia but for ending the fighting in Vietnam and winning the peace.[47] Subsequently, when Kissinger was later asked about the invasion, the national security adviser explained, "We're not interested in Cambodia. We're only interested in it not being used as a base."[48]

Nixon's "bold move" generated substantial political backlash and public opposition throughout the United States. Mass protests boiled over across university campuses, leading to the killing of four students at Kent State University on May 4, 1970. Responding in part to domestic concerns, Nixon subsequently set a June 30 deadline for the use of U.S. ground forces in Cambodia and imposed an arbitrary thirty-kilometer limit on their operations.[49] However, although handcuffed in his ability to deploy boots on the ground, Nixon called for an escalation of the air war. As he explained, "Termination of U.S. ground operations in Cambodia ... underlines the desirability of maintaining maximum pressure on the enemy in Cambodia through U.S. and allied air efforts. For this reason, I want to reaffirm until further notice, all authorities heretofore promulgated for the conduct of U.S. air operations over Cambodia."[50]

As the war in Cambodia stalled, U.S. advisers grew frustrated with the inability of the Lon Nol government to stem the flow of matériel to South Vietnam. The likely collapse of Phnom Penh, intelligence experts warned, foreshadowed the imminent fall of Saigon. A CIA memorandum addresses the situation as follows: "Continuing or increased U.S. assistance to the GKR [Government of the Khmer Republic] might slow the rate of decay, but hardware and material aid do not of themselves affect and cannot offset the major obstacle to improvement: the Phnom Penh government's inability to pull itself together.... This—not hardware or other forms of quantifiable assistance—is the central issue. Unless or until the GKR can start functioning as a government, there is little hope for any significant improvement in its position—no matter what additional assistance the U.S. provides."[51]

With few options available, analysts at the CIA and other government agencies proposed a series of measures to improve the effectiveness of the Lon Nol government. These included the declaration of martial law, a collective defense program that would entail the "arming" of the people, the installation of top-level U.S. advisers to the Lon Nol regime, and additional psychological operations against the Khmer Communists. Yet none of these expedients were considered promising.[52] Ironically, it was the lack of viable options in support of Lon Nol that forced U.S. officials to entertain working with Sihanouk and, indirectly, the Khmer Rouge. Although the Nixon administration had initially welcomed the removal of the mercurial prince, its members grudgingly acknowledged that Sihanouk perhaps offered the best hope for a negotiated settlement in Cambodia.

Despite minor victories, by late 1971 and early 1972 the overall course of the war in Cambodia was clear. For Kissinger and most of his advisers, the Khmer Republic was steadily unraveling, and the best they could do was to "lurch" onward to the inevitable and bitter end.[53] Indeed, by February 1972 CIA analysts premised, "Prospects for driving the communists out of Cambodia by military means must now appear dim in Phnom Penh, and Cambodian leaders probably accept that a negotiated settlement will be necessary at some point in the future."[54] Sihanouk—because of his connections with both the Chinese and the Khmer insurgents, seemingly offered the best hope. As Kissinger explained in January 1973, "We are not in favor of seeing Peking dominate Phnom Penh, because we don't want any great power to dominate Phnom Penh. Therefore, if some accommodations could be reached between

Lon Nol and the Khmer communists... we could get a neutral Cambodia in which no great power exercises a dominant influence."[55]

To achieve a neutral Cambodia, Kissinger warmed to the possibility of a coalition government with Sihanouk as figurehead. On May 30, 1973, for example, Kissinger explained to Ambassador Huang Chen, chief of China's Liaison Office in Washington, D.C., that Nixon was not committed to any one man. Instead, the president wanted to reach a settlement that would "let the warring elements live together."[56] Speaking to this point on June 15, 1973, Kissinger told Tran Kim Phuong, ambassador to the Republic of Vietnam, that the United States didn't "really have a solution" for Cambodia. He explained, "The problem in Phnom Penh is they have never been able to form an adequate government." In turn, Ambassador Phuong questioned whether the United States could deal with the various factions on the other side—that is, the Khmer insurgents. Here, Kissinger equivocated, asking a rhetorical question: "Which is really better, the Khmer Rouge or Sihanouk? Is it better to have the faction controlled by Hanoi or Sihanouk? We simply haven't made up our minds on this matter."[57]

Likewise, when asked in July 1973 whether there was any real interest in getting Sihanouk back into power, Kissinger replied, "There is no interest if he becomes sort of dependent on the Khmer Rouge. We have no interest in getting him back."[58] In other words, Sihanouk was acceptable only to the extent he could wield substantial political power in a neutral government. Kissinger maintained this position as late as November 1974, when he informed Deng Xiaoping, who was then China's vice-premier, that the United States was "not opposed to Sihanouk." Kissinger reaffirmed, "We have no interest in Sihanouk returning to Cambodia as a figurehead for Hanoi. But we have no objection to him if he could head a truly independent government."[59]

Prospects for a negotiated settlement in Cambodia took a turn for the worse in January 1973 with the signing of the Paris Peace Accords. Ostensibly bringing the war in Vietnam to an end, the accords left in doubt both the political future of South Vietnam and the future of Cambodia. Despite the many flaws and limitations of the agreements, Nixon hoped that Saigon and Hanoi would respect them, at least in the short run.[60] As late as May 1973, Nixon said of the state of affairs in Vietnam and Cambodia, "We can hope that this decline [in fighting] will continue until each side accepts the balance of forces as the best of a bad bargain. If events do take this course, there will also be hope that the two sides will commence to negotiate a political settlement in earnest."[61] His hopes were misplaced, as serious fighting between the Vietnamese Communists and the South Vietnamese resumed. With fading prospects for peace, Asselin explains, it was imperative for Nixon that a semblance of peace last long enough to demonstrate the viability of the accords; in other words, a "decent interval" was necessary for the claim of "peace with honor."[62] Cambodia's immediate political future was vital to that outcome. Indeed, in July 1973 George Carver confirmed, "The importance of Cambodia to the U.S. is its impact on South Vietnam." He clarified this contention as follows: "From the point of view of South Vietnam, the longer Hanoi has to wait for unrestricted access in Cambodia, the more difficult it is for them to move in South Vietnam. They longer they have to wait, the less chance they have of improving their political prospects in South Vietnam, which are now fairly bleak. This argues for stretching out the Cambodian unravelling."[63]

Accordingly, in August 1973, Kissinger wanted to know what more could be done to prop up Cambodia. During the course of the conversation, George Aldrich and William Porter in particular discussed bypassing congressional restrictions in order to transfer military equipment in South Vietnam to the Cambodian military. Likewise, talks focused on the possibility of South Vietnamese forces providing additional security along the Mekong to facilitate the distribution of rice and other supplies to a besieged Phnom Penh.[64] These options did not come without a price. As Admiral Moorer explained in an October 1973 meeting, the transfer of South Vietnamese forces *into* Cambodia would be dependent on assurances of U.S. financial support.[65]

In reality, U.S. officials had little hope of a peaceful settlement in Cambodia and became resigned to the possibility of a coalition government.[66] Behind closed doors, members of the Nixon administration conceded that they were willing to work with anyone, even if that meant supporting a coup against Lon Nol. In fact, on March 28, 1973, James Schlesinger, then the director of the CIA, informed Kissinger, "There is some interest in a possible coup." Kissinger did not immediately discount the possibility, instead telling Schlesinger, "You'd better finish your hearings before you start getting into these ideas."[67] Nixon likewise perceived the need to remove Lon Nol but was unsure of any effective strategy for doing so. Indeed, just two days after Schlesinger's comments to Kissinger, Nixon told Alexander Haig, the vice chief of staff of the U.S. Army, "They've got to get Lon Nol the hell out of there, some way or other, but you can't overthrow him."[68] For his part, Lon Nol naively continued to believe—or hope—that the U.S. government remained steadfast in its backing of his regime. In early January 1973, he told reporters, "I can tell you that in the course of that conversation [with Alexander Haig], the assurance of the firm support of the United States for the just struggle of the Khmer Republic against the North Vietnamese aggression was confirmed to me."[69]

For a brief period after the accords, the Nixon administration held one final brutal chip to play in the effort to reach an acceptable settlement in Cambodia—the intensification of the air war. As they did with their strategic approach to the North Vietnamese, Nixon and Kissinger premised that a massive aerial bombardment would force the Khmer insurgents to the negotiating table. Accordingly, eleven days after the Paris agreement, Nixon authorized the bombing of Cambodia, and "for the next six months the air war was waged with unprecedented fury."[70] In March 1973 American B-52s dropped more than 24,000 tons of bombs on Cambodia; by April the tonnage increased to 35,000 tons; and in May the figure surpassed 36,000 tons. According to Shawcross, the bombardment of Cambodia became so intense that the Seventh Air Force faced serious logistical problems. At one point, B-52s sortie rates were has high as eighty-one per day. By the time the bombing campaign ended, American B-52s had dropped more than 260,000 tons of explosives.[71]

In the end, Cambodia was sacrificed for America's geopolitical interests in Southeast Asia. It was necessary to sustain the Khmer Republic only insofar as the Cambodians could prevent the rapid collapse of South Vietnam. Nixon and his advisers were ready and willing to betray Lon Nol in a desperate attempt to keep the Khmer Republic on life support long enough to distance America from the fall of South Vietnam. In the end, the United States had no real plans for Cambodia beyond the immediate destruction of Vietnamese Communist bases; nor was the United States excessively worried about Cambodia's political future, with or without Lon Nol. On this point, the Nixon administration was never committed to "winning" in Cambodia. There was never a question of retaining a non-Communist Khmer Republic. As Kissinger bluntly declared in late 1974, "The United States has nothing to gain in Cambodia."[72]

Famine

The mood of euphoria that swept through Phnom Penh in the weeks following the coup against Sihanouk was short-lived. Any visions of economic improvement were soon shattered, first by the Vietnamese Communists' determination to retain their sanctuaries, bases, and supply routes in eastern Cambodia, and then by the military intervention of South Vietnamese and U.S. troops in Cambodia.[73] By June, just three months into the war, Cambodia's tourism and rubber industries were ruined. Many of the country's small factories and processing plants were already faltering, as the necessary raw materials failed to be delivered or labor forces disappeared. Notably, all development projects had been shut down, including the U.S.$61 million irrigation project at the Prek Thnot Dam. Developers hoped this scheme would bring life to the arid, impoverished rice-growing region southwest of Phnom Penh.[74] The disruption to Cambodia's rice production was most pressing. Indeed, within weeks of the coup, analysts at the CIA cautioned that the rapidly changing political situation posed a significant threat to the economy moving forward.[75] A June 1970 intelligence also warned that Cambodia's rice exports were expected to drop precipitously.[76] Famine loomed on the horizon.[77]

Still, many U.S. and Cambodian officials remained guardedly optimistic. The rice harvest of 1969–1970 was exceptionally good (3.595 million metric tons), and it had been collected and stored before the outbreak of hostilities at the end of April.[78] So confident were these officials that the Ministry of Finance issued a communiqué at the end of May 1970 stating, "The Cambodian economy ... remains relatively healthy and active" despite enemy attacks on road and rail infrastructure.[79] However, the Lon Nol government also recognized that key steps were needed to sustain rice production. In the coming year, sowing and harvesting would be difficult because of insecurity. In addition, the seriously depleted labor force would present difficulties, as many young men joined or were conscripted into the military.[80]

By 1971 the optimism that pervaded Phnom Penh had darkened considerably. As Lon Nol's military suffered a string of defeats, notably along the main transportation arteries north of Phnom Penh, more and more vital rice-producing regions fell under the control of Khmer insurgents (figure 5). By the end of 1973, when the provincial capitals of Kompong Thom and Takeo fell, the government could rely only on harvests from Battambang Province to supply its food needs.[81] As Hildebrand and Porter document, when the war began, the average rice yield in Cambodia was about one metric ton per hectare—one of the lowest in Asia. By 1974, however, yields dropped even further, resultant from the destruction of farm machinery, impressment of farmers into the army, damage to croplands from fighting and the incessant bombing campaign, and shortages of seed and fertilizer.[82] Consequently, because of the combination of loss of control over productive land and declining yields in the remaining areas, paddy production in the Khmer Republic fell from a high of 3.8 million tons in 1969–1970 to 493,000 tons in 1974–1975—a drop of 87 percent.[83]

In June 1971, convoys were hastily organized in an effort to meet the growing need for foodstuffs and other supplies in Phnom Penh. Within a year, shipments from Battambang, Kompong Som, and other market towns delivered over a million sacks of milled rice to the capital, as well as more than half

FIGURE 5. Areas of Khmer Rouge control during the Cambodian Civil War. Courtesy of Stian Rice.

a million sacks of rice derivatives and 75,870 tons of various merchandise. Indeed, all along the Khmer-American Friendship Highway linking Kompong Som and Phnom Penh, trucks carried salt, beer, cement, sawed timber, and tons of other imported goods. In addition, barges came up the Mekong bringing much-needed supplies of petroleum and returned with dwindling amounts of exports destined for Hong Kong and Singapore.[84]

The disruptions of war, Bridget Conley and Alex de Waal write, have the potential to quickly create pockets of profound need. This is not necessarily a matter of food availability; "for populations reliant on purchasing food, such as those people besieged in cities and towns, economic collapse through extended warfare creates conditions in which food is available, but priced out of people's means to access it."[85] The drastic fall in rice production and the increased isolation of Phnom Penh and other towns meant that the free market could no longer function effectively to distribute food.[86] As Hildebrand

and Porter document, market prices for food increased at a staggering rate, rising from 10 riels per kilogram in December 1971 to 125 riels per kilogram in December 1973. By the middle of February 1975, the price skyrocketed to 340 riels. According to a study conducted by the International Monetary Fund (IMF), by September 1974 the average household did not make enough income to feed itself. In desperation, government officials attempted to provide subsidized rice to Phnom Penh residents at the rate of fifteen kilograms per family every ten days, but even this was out of reach for many families. Moreover, since the government bought and sold rice at artificially low prices, much of Cambodia's own production—as well as large quantities of U.S.-imported rice—was resold on the black market, hoarded, or smuggled into Vietnam or Thailand.[87]

As conditions in the countryside worsened, and rural residents sought shelter in Phnom Penh and other government-held urban areas, the plight of the hungry urban poor increased. Throughout much of the country, the unfolding refugee crisis was apparent as early as June 1970. As fighting raged around the provincial capitals of Kompong Speu, Kompong Som, and Kompong Chhnang, the roads leading away from these centers were quickly choked with displaced families moving from hamlet to town, town to city, and city to city as the onslaught of war pursued them with endless determination. For many refugees, Phnom Penh was the main destination. Early on, Schanberg explains, Phnom Penh's evacuees were mostly absorbed into the population. They often found shelter with relatives, and many were able to find work. As the war progressed, however, a "saturation point" was reached: jobs were no longer available, and soaring food prices meant less to eat.[88] By late 1972 insufficient food was becoming a serious problem in the myriad refugee camps constructed in and around Phnom Penh.

During the war, the refugee population was divided administratively into registered and unregistered individuals. Registered refugees included those displaced people who had been forced to flee their homes, and whose experiences had been substantiated by the Cambodian Ministry of Refugee Affairs. They were subsequently issued official identification cards that entitled them to receive rice and other assistance.[89] In September 1971, U.S. government placed the number of registered displaced persons in Phnom Penh and other provincial capitals at 220,000. And by August 1973, there were an estimated 760,992 registered evacuees, including 732,891 in Phnom Penh and 23 government-held provinces, and an additional 30,101 in other countries.[90] There was no systematic accounting of unregistered refugees, although the

U.S. Embassy hazarded a guess of 200,000 in all.[91] Many on-the-ground observers placed the total count significantly higher, most likely well above the number of registered exiles.

Living conditions within Cambodia's refugee camps varied tremendously, although none of them were exceptionally well provisioned. Located in Phnom Penh, for example, the Tuok Kauk Camp (as of September 1971) housed approximately four hundred indigenous people displaced by war and U.S. bombing in Ratanakiri Province. Converted in June 1970 from a former youth camp, the refugee camp consisted of four concrete buildings divided into individual family cubicles. Water was supplied to the encampment, a medical station was available, and a classroom had been established. In addition, small plots of land had been made available to grow vegetables, and a small poultry project had been started. Here, conditions were tolerable, and the majority of families received two hundred kilograms of rice every two weeks. By comparison, on the outskirts of Phnom Penh several ad hoc camps were formed without government assistance or oversight. Here, upward of two hundred thousand men, women, and children crowded into makeshift housing constructed of thatch and other salvaged materials. No sanitary facilities were available, and refugees were forced to purchase drinking water from elsewhere. Nor were medical facilities readily accessible.[92]

In the provinces, conditions within the refugee camps were decidedly worse. In Battambang Province, the Wat Leap Camp housed nearly two thousand ethnic Vietnamese families by September 1971. Surrounded by a barbed-wire fence and military guards, the encampment was densely crowded with few amenities. A common latrine had been constructed, and water was obtained from a city system. Housing was hastily constructed of thatch, tin, wood, burlap, and other scrap materials. Bank Agricole Camp, also located in Battambang Province, housed nearly 1,200 ethnic Vietnamese refugees. Here, no latrine had been constructed, and people defecated in a nearby river.[93]

Overall, insufficient hygiene, unsafe water supplies, and overcrowded conditions in the refugee camps led to frequent epidemics of common diseases.[94] These conditions only worsened as the war continued. By early 1975 health professionals reported that impure water and water supplies throughout the refugee settlements in and around Phnom Penh contributed to localized outbreaks of cholera and typhoid fever, and that incidences of malaria, enteritis, and hookworms were increasing.[95] In addition, food was always in short supply. For the approximately 450,000 *registered* refugees in Phnom Penh, for example, a meager daily allotment of 150 grams of rice per person was available for free from voluntary agencies. For the hundreds of thousands of refugees who were not registered—and were unemployed—there was virtually no assistance from either the United States or the Lon Nol government.[96]

As the war progressed, Kissinger and his advisers identified the urgent need to provide supplies—notably rice—to the beleaguered Cambodians in the capital and other cities and garrisons not yet under control of the Khmer Rouge. However, the immediate need was understood as a military problem and not a humanitarian crisis. Essentially, as military expenditures rose dramatically, the Lon Nol government became intractably dependent on U.S. aid.[97] However, without money from rice or rubber exports, the government could not pay the salaries of its soldiers or afford basic shipments of arms and ammunition. Consequently, for U.S. strategists whose primary interest was delaying Communist victory *in South Vietnam*, financing the Republican military *in Cambodia* became a high priority.[98] That said, aid to Cambodia arrived with significant restrictions imposed by the U.S. Congress. Deeply concerned that a "Vietnam-type" situation might develop, representatives limited U.S. assistance and involvement and sought greater oversight of its disbursement. The chief limitations included prohibition of the deployment of combat troops; restriction of the use of U.S. advisers for the military in Cambodia; limitation of the number of U.S. civilian advisers in Cambodia; and caps on U.S. expenditures on the country.[99]

Moreover, American officials went to great lengths to confirm that foreign backing did not indicate the U.S. commitment to Cambodia's defense but instead underscored that any help provided was to support the Vietnamization program and protect the withdrawal of U.S. troops from South Vietnam. Accordingly, all U.S. aid was for military and economic assistance, not humanitarian needs. By 1973, the United States had disbursed U.S.$516 million in military aid and $216 million in economic aid to Cambodia.[100] The latter provided goods to be sold through the existing official commercial distribution system, and thus also generated Cambodian currency for the Khmer army.[101]

Famine relief, from the vantage point of the U.S. government, was never meant to alleviate the suffering of the Cambodian people, for they existed in a zone of indistinction, a liminal space trapped within the political calculations of the Nixon administration. Directed against Vietnamese enemy combatants, the United States' sovereign violence carried with it the disallowing of life *within Cambodia* of a population reduced to bare life. As *hominis sacer*, the refugees seeking sanctuary in government-held cities and camps registered little in the realpolitik of Kissinger and his aides. Indeed, as George Hildebrand and Gareth Porter contend, during the early 1970s the government of the United States "placed a concern for human suffering so far below a concern for avoiding the failure of its anti-Communist policy in Cambodia that it was prepared to accept mass starvation for an indefinite period in order to postpone the military defeat of its client."[102]

Initially, both U.S. and Cambodian officials downplayed the humanitarian crisis unfolding across the country. On the one hand, many advisers remained wedded to the belief that "no one starves in Cambodia," and that in the Khmer social structure extended families would serve as safety nets. On the other hand, U.S. officials worried that the extension of humanitarian aid would imply a far-greater commitment to the people of Cambodia than the United States was willing to make. In fact, it was U.S. policy not to become involved with civilian war victims in Cambodia. To that end, the U.S. State Department routinely minimized the refugee problem by misrepresenting the size of Phnom Penh's swollen wartime population. Only in late 1972, long after it had become impossible to deny the desperate situation of the exiles, did the U.S. government express a "willingness to help ease the refugees' needs and to assist them in resuming a more productive existence pending their full reintegration into the Cambodian economy and society."[103]

Still determined "to not become involved with the problems of civilian war victims in Cambodia," U.S. officials essentially delegated responsibility to voluntary agencies and third-party countries.[104] USAID contracted with myriad volunteer organizations to assist in the provision of emergency necessities such as food, shelter, and medical care; the improvement of water supplies and sanitary conditions in refugee sites; the construction of clinics, hospitals, and schools; and the returning of displaced persons to a "self-supporting life." Targeted institutions included Catholic Relief Services, the World Vision Relief Organization, the International Committee of the Red Cross, Lutheran World Relief, CARE, and the United Nations Children's Emergency Fund.[105]

The most pressing need of Cambodia's population was food. However, the aid systems put in place by the United States were actually used to generate Cambodian riels for the military budget, not to feed the hungry.[106] Most food assistance to Cambodia from America was "donated" through the so-called Food for Peace program. Established in 1954, the Agricultural Trade Development and Assistance Act (Public Law 480, or simply PL-480) expanded the Mutual Defense Assistance Act of 1949, which stipulated that food aid could be used as a substitute for or supplement to direct military assistance. In other words, PL-480 was a means to directly help foreign military establishments by donating food.

That said, as Israel Yost explains, neither politico-military strategy nor the humanitarian concerns commonly associated with the Food for Peace program were the primary motivation behind the adoption of PL-480. Rather, members of the U.S. Congress worried about the prevailing crisis of American agriculture in the 1950s. In the aftermath of the Second World War, U.S. farmers' massive output resulted in a level of production that exceeded normal domestic consumption and export requirements. The rebuilding of Europe through U.S. aid alleviated some of this surplus, but excess government-procured foodstuffs were soon rotting in warehouses across the country. Not wanting to dump this oversupply on the world market and depress prices, U.S. officials contrived a means to give away or sell it.[107]

Under the PL-480 program, food aid can take several forms, although two assume prominence. One form, called Title I, is designed as a revenue-generating program for foreign governments; it provides food "to a government for sale through commercial or official channels to generate local currencies for military spending."[108] Title II, conversely, is intended to provide food aid for famine-stricken countries, or to offer other urgent relief assistance to any "friendly" government or people deemed to be in need. Also included under Title II are grants of PL-480 commodities to U.S. voluntary agencies to use in their overseas programs; under this component of the plan, the American government not only provides the food but also covers the freight costs involved in its transportation. Throughout the 1960s, Catholic Relief Services and CARE were major distributors of Title II food aid for the United States.[109]

In the Khmer Republic, the vast majority of food aid arrived under Title I. Beginning in July 1974, for example, USAID spent a total of U.S. $72.5 million under PL-480 for Title I food shipments to Cambodia, but only $1 million was used to support free distribution through Title II. In March 1975 USAID announced that it would provide an additional U.S.$15 million to voluntary agencies to buy rice under the Title II program for *registered* refugees, but even this was too little and too late. Hildebrand and Porter estimate that the amount of funds set aside under Title II furnished only fifty tons of rice for free distribution, far short of the estimated six hundred tons necessary to prevent mass starvation.[110] In other words, the vast majority of Food for Peace aid was available only for purchase, with the proceeds used to pay military salaries and procure weapons, munitions, and uniforms. As Rice explains, "Through Title I aid, PL-480 essentially imposed a food market on the city and forced the poor to pay for rice that could have been given away for free. The government was allowed to charge whatever it wanted, so long as the rice was sold. Under PL-480, not only *could* the government run the food program like a for-profit business, it was *obligated to*."[111]

Regardless, the amount of rice and other foodstuffs supplied by the United States was far less than was required to keep consumption in Phnom Penh and the myriad refugee camps at anywhere near normal levels.[112] According to Hildebrand and Porter, by 1974 rice imports provided enough for a daily variable distribution of between 500 and 700 metric tons. This apportionment was far below the estimated 1,000 tons per day necessary to provide adequate nutrition *just* for the population of Phnom Penh. Still, the vast majority of food aid never reached the hungry and sickened people of Cambodia, but instead was diverted by widespread corruption. Indeed, according to some estimates, fully half of the $350 million in U.S. military assistance provided just in fiscal year 1974 was sold by corrupt civilian officials and military officers for private profit.[113] For example, under the Cambodian military pay system, unit commanders were responsible for preparing and paying the unit's payroll. Each unit submitted soldiers' names, serial numbers, and amounts due to a regional military intendant. However, since there was no centralized management of personnel, the regional intendant could not verify that the individual soldiers paid actually existed. The GAO report estimates that Cambodian military officials were padding their troop strength by 10 to 15 percent. An estimated U.S.$750,000 to $1 million went into the pockets of corrupt commanders every month from paychecks of approximately 100,000 nonexistent "phantom soldiers."[114]

Profits diverted from U.S. aid were also made elsewhere. Indeed, the primary source of wealth was derived from the sale of ammunitions, weapons and other military supplies, medicines, and rice to merchants who then resold these items on the free market or to Cambodian and Vietnamese revolutionary forces. Ironically, many of the funds used to buy and resell these goods were probably obtained through payroll padding.[115] Effectively, corrupt officials would fabricate the names of soldiers and receive salaries for these "phantom troops"; they would then use that money to purchase stolen weapons, munitions, uniforms, or other goods to be sold to merchants, North or South Vietnamese soldiers, or even Khmer insurgents through routine commercial channels or the black market.[116]

In turn, parts of Phnom Penh were transformed into a gilded city, as politicians and military officers lived in luxury while the poor went hungry. Schanberg wrote in 1972, "Colonels who never leave the capital, who have never been near a battle, drive around in fancy jeeps with mounted machine guns, flashing red lights and sirens, guarded by soldiers armed with new American M-16 rifles, while some troops in the field are still carrying inferior carbines." These same officials owned "luxury villas . . . in the capital and rent[ed] them to Americans for $700 a month."[117] For these corrupted officers—for the members of the elite in general—starvation was never a consideration. And for those who arrived from rural areas and registered with refugee organizations, food and medical attention was difficult but not impossible to find. The greatest suffering, as Rice concludes, fell to Phnom Penh's urban poor and to the hundreds of thousands of unregistered evacuees who were largely left to fend for themselves.[118]

"Seldom has a people's slide into severe malnourishment been so carefully recorded," Hildebrand and Porter write, "as it was in Cambodia, where both United States and international agencies observed and reported on it regularly."[119] By October 1971, representatives of the World Health Organization, the International Committee of the Red Cross, and the Cambodian Red Cross joined doctors from the Cambodian Ministry of Public Health in stating that the lack of sufficient food was rapidly becoming a serious problem among the population in general, and among the refugees in particular. Signs of malnutrition and vitamin deficiency were noted.[120] On this latter point, health officials noted that an observed higher incidence of vitamin B deficiency was because the urban poor were unable to supplement their meager, rice-dominant diet with fruit or fish.[121] In November 1973, a survey of nine refugee camps in and around Phnom Penh found that 31 percent of the children under age six in the "worst camp" and 16 percent under age six in the "best" camp were "severely malnourished."

The following year, a WHO report found that half the children in Phnom Penh were believed to be moderately malnourished. In February 1975, a U.S. congressional investigation concluded, "The general level of health of almost the entire Cambodian population—the refugees, the poor, families of military servicemen, and particularly the children—has deteriorated rapidly."[122] According to this latter study, both in Phnom Penh and myriad refugee camps, "malnutrition, including the advanced stages of kwashiorkor, marasmus, [had] increased dramatically over the last several months. Measles, malaria, tuberculosis and other respiratory diseases also were increasing in incidence, often with fatal prognosis." The report continued, "Resistance to diseases also is causing the effects of these diseases to be more pronounced and requiring longer recuperating periods in overburdened health facilities."[123] Reporting from a small Catholic Relief Services hospital located outside Phnom Penh, Schanberg wrote, "The children gather by the dozens.... They have swollen bellies. Some are shrunken. A 10-year-old girl has dehydrated to the size of a 4-year-old. Harsh bronchial coughs come from their throats, marking the beginnings of pneumonia and tuberculosis. All have dysentery. Their noses run continuously. Their skin has turned scaly. Every scratch on their legs and arms becomes an ulcer. Without help these children are slipping toward death. Others have already died."[124]

The starving, dying children witnessed by Schanberg personified the violent conditions of famine. The evidence and overall assessment was incontrovertible: incidences of malnutrition and nutrition-related diseases had reached catastrophic levels. According to international standards for weight-for-age relations, a healthy two-year-old child should weigh 12.4 kilograms. However, a sampling of two-year-old children in January 1975 averaged 7.85 kilograms in weight, down nearly 1 kilogram from a survey conducted just four months earlier, and almost 3 kilograms less than children weighed before the war. Most observers concluded that the children of Cambodia were literally "starving to death." Indeed, two doctors affiliated with the International Committee of the Red Cross declared, "There is no hope for the future."[125]

With the deterioration of health services throughout the country, famine conditions worsened. This was particularly true for those rendered as bare life—that is, the unregistered refugees and urban poor of Phnom Penh. Prior to the war, the Sihanouk government had embarked on an ambitious modernization program of the country's medical facilities. The improvements were made possible by substantial foreign aid, notably from the United States, but also with sizable contributions by France, the Soviet Union, and Japan. Indeed, so successful was the effort that by 1969 the number of hospitals and district clinics totaled sixty-nine, and the number of commune dispensaries and infirmaries approached six hundred.[126] With the war, however, shortages in all areas of health services became increasingly severe. By September 1971, ten of the country's forty hospitals were either destroyed or damaged, and a similar number of district health centers likewise destroyed or damaged. In addition, eleven of Cambodia's hospitals and clinics were in areas controlled by the Khmer insurgency. Of the dispensaries and infirmaries, nearly a quarter were either destroyed, damaged, or under insurgent control.[127] As one medical director of a volunteer-operated child nutritional center on the outskirts of Phnom Penh explained in January 1975, there were never enough beds for the thousands of children seeking help. Most were turned away, their fate being almost certain death.[128]

The rapid escalation of war casualties, both civilian and military, placed a tremendous strain on the overcrowded and understaffed health services still available. With the first year of the war, hospital admissions increased from thirty-one thousand to approximately thirty-nine thousand, with the number exceeding fifty thousand by 1971. Medicine was likewise in short supply.

As early as 1972, for example, a hospital director in Phnom Penh reported an alarming rise in child mortality from gastric disorders. These were easily treatable, the doctor explained, but no medicines for treatment were available.[129] By 1975, those dispensaries, clinics, hospitals, and nutrition centers still operating were forced to refuse treatment to gravely ill patients because of the lack of facilities and shortage of doctors. And given the acute shortage of medicines and drugs, those who could be seen often went untreated. Death frequently resulted from infection and lack of adequate care.[130] In the waning days of the war, Schanberg described a six-year-old girl who was brought to a clinic for urgent medical care. She had a gaping shrapnel wound in her chest and was bleeding into her abdomen; her face was already turning white from loss of blood. An attending doctor said, "We could have saved her. All we needed was steady transfusion. But all we had was one pint of blood to give her. She died in an hour."[131]

Throughout Phnom Penh and the remaining government-held centers, schools, athletic stadiums, sporting centers, private houses, and public buildings were hastily converted to ad hoc medical facilities. Invariably, these "hospitals" were operationally inadequate to the burdens placed on them by overcrowding, as well as demands for water, sanitary facilities, electric power, and light. Sporadic and frequent power outages in Phnom Penh and shortages of gasoline in the provinces placed life-threatening limits on the use of critical medical equipment, including sterilizers, operating-room lights, and X-ray machines. Bathroom and sanitary blocks, where available, clogged, overflowed, and were left uncleaned because of understaffing of maintenance personnel.[132]

Conclusions

The "dire plight of the great majority of war victims" in Cambodia, a U.S. congressional investigation concluded in February 1975, "is now being brought into its proper focus and receiving increased attention." The report warned, "Unless humanitarian and relief efforts are expanded to assist those victims who are not presently being helped, health and nutrition of the Cambodians will deteriorate at an ever-increasing rate." This surprisingly frank assessment tragically underscores the disastrous and not unpredictable consequences of the U.S. effort to achieve peace through war. In five years, Cambodia was plunged into an unprecedented humanitarian crisis caused in part by mortal negligence. By war's end in 1975, U.S. officials determined that an estimated three million of the five million Cambodians living under the control of the

Khmer Republic government were "war victims." Yet the small amount of available aid reached "only about one of every three" people in need.[133]

In a moment of frankness, Kissinger ruminated, "For a great nation to have gotten itself into these straits is unbelievable. People just won't believe that we could do this to ourselves."[134] Kissinger's comments, made on November 2, 1973, capture his dawning realization that Nixon's reckless strategy to expand the Vietnam War into Cambodia had backfired. The United States unleashed a maelstrom of violence on a sovereign state with no clear strategy—and no endgame—beyond the furtive use of Cambodia as a sacrificial pawn to delay the inevitable collapse of South Vietnam. Neither Kissinger nor his advisers evinced any great concern for the people of Cambodia; nor did they take responsibility for the death and devastation they wreaked on the country. From the vantage point of the Nixon administration, the people of Cambodia were nothing more than bare life. Excluded from political consideration, their lives were seen only—if at all—in the abstract. As Hildebrand and Porter observe, "Only the United States could make and enforce a decision that Cambodians would not starve to death. But the United States did not have sufficient concern for the problem of starvation to sacrifice interests that loomed larger in U.S. policy."[135]

To justify its fabricated claims of supporting an ally engaged in civil war, the United States launched a monumental project of nation building in South Vietnam from 1954 onward. This itself was window dressing for a larger objective of containing the spread of Communism in Southeast Asia. In the end, however, Cambodia's people were reduced to bare life, killed and disallowed life with impunity, by U.S. actions and inactions. In the end, the state-induced famine of the early 1970s that the United States initiated against Cambodians was predicated on America's claim to defend South Vietnam against North Vietnamese aggression. U.S. officials at the highest level were aware of the onset of famine conditions. But instead of responding to the devolving humanitarian crisis, they continued to interpret events through the lens of geopolitical strategy. In other words, the American government writ large was indifferent to the suffering resultant from Nixon's calculated gambit to expand the war into Cambodia and forestall defeat in South Vietnam.

On July 10, 1973, Kissinger asked his advisory group for "an estimate of the food supplies for Phnom Penh after August 15 and any [foreseeable] problems."[136] His concern, however, was not for the starving people. Kissinger focused on the ability to "delay the North Vietnamese having unrestricted use of Cambodia for as long as possible," and thus to forestall the collapse of South Vietnam.[137] His remarks were echoed in the calculated decisions forwarded by Lieutenant General H. M. Fish, director of the Pentagon's Defense Security Assistance Agency, who testified before Congress on February 3, 1975, "We seek only to keep them [Cambodians] alive and fighting through the remainder of this fiscal year."[138] Together, the statements of Kissinger, Fish, and myriad other U.S. policy makers make clear the necropolitics of American foreign policy, a coalescence of actions and inactions that effectively consigned tens of thousands of Cambodians to premature death. As Hildebrand and Porter conclude, "The temporary survival of an anti-Communist regime in Cambodia was Washington's primary concern, and if tens of thousands of Cambodian children had to starve to keep Phnom Penh in the war for still another dry season, that was apparently an acceptable human cost."[139] The people of Cambodia were in the end considered disposable, collateral damage wrought by American's sovereign power to decide who lives and who will die.

CHAPTER 3

Work More, Gain More, but Spend Less Capital

> Our population need not be anxious about famine.
> —Ieng Sary, October 6, 1976

> Measures have been taken to mix potatoes with the rice in order to conserve rice to prepare for future shortages.
> —Comrade Chhin, September 7, 1976

Prior to the late 1960s, most Cambodians were subsistence cultivators.[1] Women and men contributed to agricultural and other income-generating activities, although gendered divisions of labor were common. Men would typically plow the fields, transport goods, and maintain localized irrigation schemes, while women would prepare seed rice, sow and transplant the seedlings, and harvest the crops.[2] Families commonly owned fruit trees and palms, cultivated vegetables and herbs in kitchen gardens, caught fish in ponds, and raised livestock, such as chickens, ducks, and pigs. More prosperous families maintained a stable of draft animals, including oxen and water buffalo. Households commonly fabricated material necessities, such as baskets and mats. However, most families were not sufficient to satisfy all their material needs; some cash income was required, for example, to purchase foods and goods not produced at home, to pay taxes or debts, or to use for ceremonial purposes, such as giving offerings to the Buddhist wat (pagoda) or sponsoring weddings, funerals, and other domestic rituals.[3]

Daily life centered around one's hamlet, notably the wat, which served as a moral, social, and educational center for villagers. As May Ebihara explains, the Buddhist conception that an individual goes through a cycle of reincarnations exerted a powerful influence on individual behavior, as did the notion that the number of meritorious deeds performed in this lifetime will affect one's position in the next life.[4] To this point, annual festivals were important occasions. They offered meaningful opportunities not only to accumulate merit through prayers and offerings but also to socialize with kin, friends, and acquaintances from other communities.[5] Indeed, social interactions beyond the confines of one's hamlet were often quite limited, thus adding to the significance of festivals and other communal activities.

In the late 1960s, the skies of Cambodia clouded with B-52 bombers and F-100 fighter jets when the monsoonal rains abated. Five-hundred-pound Mark-82 bombs rained from the heavens, obliterating villages and evaporating people. A standard steel-encased Mark-82 contains approximately two hundred pounds of high explosives and produces a "kill zone" of approximately twenty-six thousand square feet upon detonation.[6] As an unguided "dumb bomb," a single Mark-82 has less than a 6 percent chance of hitting its target, thus requiring the release of hundreds of bombs during a single sortie. Writing in May 1973, Sydney Schanberg described the devastation inflicted on Route 30, south of Phnom Penh: "Ashes, broken cooking pots, shattered banana and mango trees, twisted corrugated iron roofing and sometimes the stilts of a house reaching toward nothingness—that is all that is left."[7] A farmer who returned to the place a village once stood said, "There was no sound. No people. No children. Not even a dog. It was all quiet. I wanted to cry. Everybody wanted to cry."[8]

Cluster bombs carried by AD-1 Skyraiders also plunged from the skies, maiming and killing Cambodia's men, women, and children as they abandoned their homes and fields and fled for safety. Cluster bombs (cluster bomb units, CBUS) consist of metal cases containing an approximate average of 650 bomblets, known as "bomb live units" (BLU). Each BLU, roughly the size of a tennis ball and weighing about one pound, contains upward of three hundred metal fragments. Dropped from an aircraft, the outer dispenser splits apart, releasing its contents. Some two hundred thousand metallic fragments are unloosed if all the bomblets detonate from a single CBU. When a high-velocity projectile, such as a steel pellet from a bomblet, passes through a human body, it pushes aside the soft tissues in its immediate path. These tissues, in turn, impart velocity to tissues farther away. A "temporary" cavity, several times wider than the wound track, is formed, and its rapid expansion crushes other organs and tissues, fractures bones, and damages nerves. Within a fraction of a second the fragmentation literally explodes within the body.[9]

Prior to the escalation of war by U.S. president Richard Nixon and the growing militancy of the Khmer Rouge, Cambodian society was already cracking under the pressures of a failing economy, widespread corruption, and alienation between the government and the people.[10] Myriad factors coincided to produce the violent conditions of famine experienced by Cambodia's people. In turn, famine contributed to the deepening of violent conditions associated with deprivation and desperation. As Ebihara writes, "The fabric of customary peasant life was already being seriously torn."[11] Indeed, by war's end, perhaps one-third of Cambodia's population was suffering from chronic hunger, malnutrition, and disease. Hundreds of thousands of people had been injured or killed; those who survived were often displaced and destitute.

Out of the rubble and ruins of war, the leadership of the Communist Party of Kampuchea (CPK) set out to rebuild Cambodia and Cambodian society. In less than four years—a duration shorter than the preceding civil war—the Khmer Rouge forcibly transformed the very being and meaning of the country: villages were reorganized into communes, subsistence farming rearranged as collectivized agriculture, and Buddhism banned and supplanted with secular "revolutionary" ethics and morals.[12] A new social fabric was to be spun, woven by men and women motivated by arrogance and anger. In this chapter I document the biopolitical and necropolitical technologies forwarded by CPK officials and their followers. In doing so, however, I underscore the fact that the famine dynamics of Cambodian genocide were conditioned by the preceding geopolitical violence sundering Cambodia's people from the land. In other words, the famine of 1975–1979 was not an aberration but instead a continuance of a famine facilitated by America's expansion of war into Cambodia.

This, in fact, was widely acknowledged by the Khmer Rouge. According to senior leaders of the CPK, the country had "just emerged from the massively destructive war and there [were] all kinds of shortages, everything from shelter, housings, food supplies, [and] the various means and tools from production."[13] Cambodia lacked cattle and buffalo, seeds, and—crucially—the discipline necessary to rapidly increase agricultural productivity and mitigate mass starvation. For senior Khmer Rouge cadres, urgent steps were necessary to provide famine relief. Hence, CPK officials implored their people to work harder, faster, and more efficiently to produce food. Their urgency motivated this June 1976 exhortation: "[The] Party's slogan is: Plant, plant, plant; plant everywhere, plant densely, plant until no land is left over; male youths, plant; female youths, plant; elderly and children, plant; both the able-bodied and the weak, plant; plant collectively; plant individually; plant farm fields; plant one or two clumps around the houses and around the worksites . . . and so on."[14] Materially, this translated to immediate resettlement of almost the entirety of Cambodia's population. Inhabitants were "to live in the countryside so as to be able to participate in the movement to increase production to sustain themselves and contribute to defending and building the country."[15] Subsequently, the Khmer Rouge leadership instructed the people of Cambodia to "go on the offensive" and plant "early season rice, mid-season rice, corn, beans, potatoes, and various vegetables."[16]

That said, the transformation of the nation's political economy was directed not toward the biopolitics of food provisioning but instead toward the accumulation of capital through the export of rice. Motivated to increase foreign exchange in order to (re)build a war-torn economy, CPK officials instituted ambitious production quotas with the goal of tripling rice production. From this vantage point, the imposition of food rations and the use of forced labor appear as necropolitical practices that "let die" hundreds of thousands of people in the service of capital.

Building Self-Reliance in Agriculture

The Khmer Rouge was not anomalous in its approach to development. As Michael Watts writes, "Food was very much at the forefront of development thinking in the 1970s."[17] And in this regard, the leading figures of the Communist Party of Kampuchea (CPK) were no different from the myriad international development agencies in operation. Such an assertion might seem odd, given the widespread belief that Khmer Rouge cadres withheld food from their people as a form of political control. However, documentary evidence suggests a different interpretation, one that aligns better with the ideological power struggles over food provisioning throughout the mid-twentieth century. Indeed, early planning documents prepared by the CPK leadership identify the interconnections of food, water, technology, and energy—that is, the need to expand the industrial production of generators and water pumps, tractors and other agricultural tools, fertilizers and pesticides, and hydroelectricity.

Geography figured prominently in the postwar policies of the CPK (figure 6). From 1975 onward, Democratic Kampuchea was partitioned administratively into several zones (Phumipeak). These zones were divided into regions (Damban), the regions into districts (Srok), and the districts into subdistricts (Khum), cooperatives (Sahaka), and villages (Phum).[18] Initially, the CPK divided Cambodia's nineteen provinces into five zones: the Northeast, North, Northwest, Southwest, and East. A "special zone" was also created to include the area around Phnom Penh. In the ensuing months, administrative divisions changed often, usually resultant from internal purges or power plays among CPK leaders. Toward the end of 1975 the Southwest Zone was split in two, forming a new West Zone and a smaller Southwest Zone. The Phnom Penh "special zone" was also dissolved, hereafter categorized as a distinct territory

FIGURE 6. Administrative boundaries of Democratic Kampuchea, circa 1976. Courtesy of Stian Rice.

not within the formal administrative structures. In 1976 two autonomous regions were formed: Region 106, consisting mostly of the former Siem Reap and Oddar Meanchey Provinces, and Region 103, composed of the former Preah Vihear Province. The port facility at Kampong Som was also organized as a separate entity. Finally, in 1977 a seventh zone was created when Regions 103 and 106 were merged to form the North Zone; the old North Zone was renamed the Central Zone.[19]

In their Four-Year Plan, developed between July 21 and August 2, 1976, senior leaders of the CPK identified two economic objectives.[20] The first proposed that the party would "serve the people's livelihood, and ... raise the people's standard of living quickly, both in terms of supplies and in other material goods."[21] A second objective was "to seek, gather, save, and increase capital from agriculture" to rapidly expand Cambodia's farming, industrial, and defense sectors.[22] The first aim can be understood as an attempt to respond to the immediate postwar crisis of insufficient food and other necessary supplies. The second directs attention to the broader structural transformations envisioned by the senior leadership.[23] As party secretary Pol Pot explained during an August 1976 planning session, "We must execute a plan that will enable us to build our country so as to advance swiftly and rapidly, and to strengthen ourselves." For the secretary, this strategy required effort to create "an economic base for the country in both the agricultural and industrial sectors so as to have a quantity of capital, quickly, ... to build the country and to solve the problem of the people's livelihood."[24] It is not coincidental that the meeting came just days after a historic assembly of member states of the Non-Aligned Movement (NAM).[25]

From August 16 to August 19, 1976, delegates from eighty-six member states of the NAM—including representatives from the newly formed Democratic Kampuchea—convened in Colombo, Sri Lanka.[26] A summary text of the conference was later published by the embassy of Democratic Kampuchea in Berlin, East Germany. According to this document, the conference "achieved brilliant victories," including a suite of resolutions that "reinforce the principles of non-alignment, enhance the role of this Movement and confirm the resolute solidarity of the non-aligned countries in the common struggle against imperialism, colonialism, neo-colonialism and ... the interferences, interventions, aggressions and ... expansionism of the rich great powers." The conference delegates also advocated "for independence, sovereignty, territorial integrity and the right of each people to determine the destiny of its nation by itself in full independence and sovereignty."[27]

The summary text continues, "The struggle to establish a new international economic order is a political struggle of far-reaching consequences and ... the great powers are entirely responsible for the grave situation existing in the development countries." Thus, "to bring about the establishment of a new international economic order, the non-aligned countries must therefore actively unite to wage a struggle against the aggressions and interferences, committed under whatever pretext, by the rich great powers. At the same time[,] they must undertake every effort to overcome all obstacles, build up their own national economy and strengthen their cooperation based on the principle of mutual respect."[28]

That senior leaders of the CPK aligned their state-building project with the Non-Aligned Movement is beyond doubt.[29] Indeed, they codified their adherence to the movement in the Constitution of Democratic Kampuchea. Of significance, these officials positioned their victory and subsequent government not as an aberration but as a defining moment in the broader anti-colonial movement. Certainly, words may ring hollow, and documentary evidence demonstrates that the rhetoric of the CPK often failed to match reality. Nevertheless, the argument holds that policies forwarded by the top echelons of the CPK adhered to the broad coordinates of the NAM. This is seen especially in numerous references in CPK documents calling for an economic agenda of independence, self-reliance, and self-mastery.

Frequently, scholars afford considerable weight to the bombastic claims of CPK spokespersons. Karl Jackson, for example, explains, "The Khmer revolutionaries were trying to establish total sovereignty and self-reliance in the cultural, economic, and political realms," and their "application of the doctrine of self-reliance led the revolutionaries to seal Cambodia off from all but a very few close allies."[30] Charles Twining likewise concludes that CPK leaders "wanted genuinely to create a country totally independent from every point of view. To achieve this state, Cambodia must be self-contained and self-reliant to the point of autarky."[31] On this point, scholars describe the Khmer Rouge as extreme, radical, and exceptional. Viewed within the context of the NAM, however, these conclusions come under question.

From the 1960s onward, leaders in myriad former colonies advocated national development programs informed by self-reliance and autonomy.[32] Here, self-reliance entails the "autonomy of decision-making and full mobilization of a society's own resources under its own initiative and direction."[33] Adherents to the Non-Aligned Movement also championed the idea of self-determination. In other words, leaders throughout the Third World demanded the right to determine participation in the global economy on their own terms. In practice, this meant that while many NAM member states sought to increase cooperative relations in and among Third World states, and to reduce their individual and collective dependence on the Western powers or the Soviet Union, other members could to align with either superpower.

In Democratic Kampuchea, senior leaders of the CPK advocated both self-reliance and self-determination, not in an effort to isolate their country from the wider global economy, but instead to participate in the global economy on terms of their own choosing. Party members affirmed that foreign aid might be accepted. However, such assistance would be refused if accepting it would impact commitment to political-economic independence and mastery.[34] Accordingly, domestic objectives, such as the raising of people's standard of living, elided structural objectives, such as the accumulation of capital. In theory, self-reliance affords primacy to the national objective of meeting basic human needs, including the provision of food, shelter, housing, education, health care, and jobs.[35]

For the CPK leadership, agriculture—not industry—would assume primary importance in the reorganization of Democratic Kampuchea's economy. Noting that some countries "place their confidence in heavy industry," Pol Pot demurred, explaining that if Democratic Kampuchea invested in heavy industries, such as large steel mills and chemical factories, it would do so at the expense of the people's livelihoods. On that point, the party secretary concluded that surplus capital derived from agriculture would be invested in light industry, including textiles, food production, and those "industries making tools useful in everyday life."[36] In a practical sense, CPK officials pursued an economic strategy advanced by other member states of the Non-Aligned Movement, namely import-substitution industrialization.[37] As Stian Rice explains, the capital growth called for by the CPK would be accomplished through an agriculture-led economic "takeoff." In accordance with this plan, agricultural products would be sold to other countries, and the foreign exchange obtained from these exports would be used to import necessary agricultural and industrial inputs.[38] The CPK articulated this arrangement clearly during a meeting held on May 8, 1976: "We will decrease importing items next year, including cotton and jute, because we are working hard to produce ours. We will import only some important items such as chemical fertilizer, plastic, acid, iron factory, and other raw materials."[39]

CPK officials premised that Democratic Kampuchea was brimming with "such things as land, livestock, natural resource[s], [and] water sources such as lakes, river[s,] and ponds," all of which afforded their country "great advantages compared with China, Vietnam, or Africa."[40] Likewise, in a document titled "Report of Activities of the Party Center According to the General Political Tasks of 1976" CPK representatives noted, "We can export and sell many products such as kapok, shrimp, squid, elephant fish, and turtles. All of these products can earn foreign exchange. There are great possibilities for exporting peanuts, wheat, corn, sesame, and beans. The objective would be to save up these products for export. Almost anything can be exported, so long as we don't consume it ourselves, but set it aside."[41] Among the myriad possibilities to generate foreign exchange, senior officials targeted rice as their country's primary comparative advantage. As the party detailed in the Four-Year Plan, "For 100,000 tons of milled rice, we would get [U.S.]$20 million; if we had 500,000 tons we'd get $100 million. . . . We must increase rice production in order to obtain capital. Other products, which are only complimentary[,] will be increased in the future."[42] Ultimately, rice exports were expected to make up 93 percent of foreign exchange by 1980, with a value upward of U.S.$1.2 billion.[43]

With the proposed transformation of Cambodia's economy, the conditions of famine changed dramatically, although the human toll remained. Fundamentally, Pol Pot introduced a crucial and fatal contradiction within Democratic Kampuchea's economy, in that rice would be produced exclusively for its exchange value. Programmatically, the CPK's Four-Year Plan to expand rice production was built on three objectives: to harvest two or more rice crops per year, to expand the area of cultivation through the conversion of nonagricultural land to rice fields, and to increase rice yields to a national average of three tons per hectare per harvest.[44]

More broadly, the strategy for increased rice production was predicated on the introduction of more "rational" and "efficient" agricultural techniques.[45] For example, the CPK classified rice fields in two categories: those harvested once a year and those harvested twice a year. Calculations made by the party indicate that by 1977 there would be an anticipated 2.4 million hectares of land suitable for rice production. Of these, 1.4 million hectares could sustain a single harvest per year; the remaining land would be conducive to two harvests. Over the next four years the land devoted to single harvests would remain constant, while the amount of double-cropped lands would progressively increase from 200,000 hectares in 1977 to 500,000 in 1980.[46] While augmenting rice cultivation, local officials were encouraged to prioritize those lands most suitable for expansion or intensification of harvests. As the CPK detailed in one planning document, "Throughout the country at each of the bases we must select the best and most favorable sites to work first. The difficult spots should be reserved for later. Doing it this way will lead to quick crop production and quick harvests."[47]

Here, it is necessary to consider more closely the CPK's stance on technology, for a common misperception is that senior leaders of the Khmer Rouge were anti-technology. This derives from the erroneous argument that CPK officials wanted to recreate "the greatness of the Angkor Wat civilization," when, in fact, these leaders from the beginning planned to rapidly modernize Cambodia's traditional farming sector.[48] On this point, CPK planners clarified that "viewing technology as more important than [one's] political and ideological stance" is a "wrong view."[49] They explained that "advanced scientific techniques should be available in order to build the country as fast as possible." But they also admitted, "[If] there is no correct revolutionary political and ideological stance, we can not build the country well and fast."[50]

Accordingly, within the "proper" framework, party members identified a number of "objective" problems that needed to be resolved, of which water was the most crucial. According to CPK leadership, "To master water for agriculture, the major thing is to solve paddy dikes, because these dikes are the dams holding back water at every location. Anyone can make them, make them by themselves, make them in large groups, make them by hand, by machines, etc." The leaders concluded, "If we have the paddy dikes we can also maintain soil fertility."[51]

The party stated in its Four-Year Plan, "[Cambodians will] increase the degree of mastery over the water problem from one year to another until it reaches 100 percent by 1980 for first-class rice land and reaches 40–50% for ordinary rice land."[52] CPK officials premised, "In order to gain mastery over water there must be a network of dikes and canals as the basis. There must also be canals, reservoirs, and irrigation pumps stationed in accordance with our strategy."[53] Simply put, irrigation was necessary for achieving both the seasonal yield goal of three tons per hectare and the goal of increasing the amount of land capable of two or more growing seasons.[54] Consequently, the party launched massive work projects—employing forced labor—to construct a network of dikes, canals, and reservoirs. In the end, approximately 7,000 kilometers of canals and dikes were constructed and over 350 reservoirs built.[55]

An essential material component—arguably, *the* essential component—in all storage and canal systems was concrete. Concrete was necessary for sluice gates and spillways, pump houses, dam foundations, and any location where moving water threatened the premature erosion of earthen structures. For that reason, the CPK ensured that cement production was one of the first domestic industries it restarted upon assuming power. In 1976, for example, the CPK imported industrial equipment to support the building of a cement factory at Châkrei Ting, with Chinese technicians assisting Cambodians in the construction and operation of the facility.[56] Similar demands were placed on steel production for rebar, gates, valves, pumps, and bridges.

CPK leaders planned to use existing machinery until they were able to build and operate their own light industries, notably in the production of tractors, water pumps, generators, and other items necessary for agriculture. In September 1975, for example, it was noted that cadres within Sector 25 were using "irrigation rigs with booms and fuel cans to pump water." From this observation, the CPK leadership determined, "We must make water pumps and mechanized equipment, semi-mechanized [equipment], [and be] inventive, becoming more and more modernized and improved." CPK officials understood that "industry [was] already working, but not yet in an industrial fashion." To remedy that problem, they concluded it would be necessary to develop the manufacturing capacity to build generators to expand irrigation systems: "Today we have the capability to make them, especially small electrical generators and small motors. We will buy just the wire and the carbon. If we gather up the old technicians to talk and draw experience, in combination with Chinese and Korean technicians, we can clearly do it, absolutely. We must set up shops to make machinery, and the technicians must be assembled to make calculations on these matters. Within two to three years, we can clearly do it."[57]

A similar unbridled optimism was apparent in the discussions to *manufacture* and *operate* tractors in agriculture. For example, the CPK leadership acknowledged that tractors from the previous regime were in (limited) use but that the machines would wear out within two or three years. While technicians were available to make repairs as needed, the main problem CPK officials identified was a shortage of components, such as gearboxes and bearings. Party members proposed to build tractor factories and related industries to furnish the necessary components. Indeed, officials acknowledged that efforts were already underway, with the assistance of the North Korean government, to reopen factories. The objective was for each zone to produce upward of 150 tractors by 1980. At this point, CPK representatives concluded, the country would "have machinery to assist the forces of the people and to replace manpower."[58]

The Four-Year Plan also called for the development of agricultural chemicals, such as synthetic fertilizers and pesticides, to increase yields.[59] Initially, CPK officers encouraged the use of traditional methods. For instance, the party's planners determined that the problem of fertilizer could initially be solved through natural means—that is, through the use of "manure, urine, leaves, ... water hyacinth, and water coconut plants, and human waste solids." The planning document states, "Urine must be saved, fish bones saved, fish entrails saved. Bran can be burned and made into good fertilizer. Silt can be used as fertilizer. We have the Mekong River and the Tonle Sap as sources which never dry up. If we place this silt on infertile soil ... we can change sterile soil to fertile soil."[60] However, officials concluded that modern forms of fertilizers would be required at some point in the future. They explained, "We must think about making agricultural chemicals ourselves and buying or bartering from other countries. There is a demand today for chemicals to defend against insect pests. We must research to find chemical technicians to help make them, and assign some of our youth to study overseas. We must make these chemicals to serve our agriculture."[61] In time, senior leaders of the CPK anticipated that Democratic Kampuchea would be self-sufficient in the manufacture of these inputs.

Beyond production considerations, CPK leadership anticipated difficulties in the transshipment of rice and other commodities. During five years of war, the roads, bridges, and other transportation networks were severely damaged, and Khmer Rouge officials initiated limited efforts to reopen highways and railways. However, from a fiscal standpoint, the CPK was sensitive to the added costs of overland transportation, especially the use of trucks. Khmer Rouge cadres concluded, "We will use more boats, ox carts and horse carts" to "reduce transport costs to a minimum and reduce the price of products."[62] This was no anti-technology ideology but instead a practice born of economic necessity. Trucks required petrol and spare parts—both of which were in short supply. "We have some capital," the Khmer Rouge explained in a September 1975 document, adding, "But we must make more river boats and ocean going vessels. We will use the waterways heavily in the future to move rice, corn, tobacco, rubber, etc. We will not use land routes as much because the expenses are great, both the cost of the vehicles and road making costs. In Phnom Penh we have some capital for building boats, and [North] Korea is helping to build another boat factor. The Zones must make large boats, 30–50 tons and 100–200 tons, for transport."[63]

In their totality, the production improvement strategies outlined in the Four-Year Plan were not new. As Rice explains, these plans aligned with development schemes articulated since the 1950s by Western experts, including U.S. advisers working to increase the agricultural productivity of the Lower Mekong River valley by improving irrigation and using "scientific" inputs. Indeed, in key respects the Khmer Rouge approach to rice production and water management echoed those of the French protectorate and the Sihanouk regime. Thus the CPK's Four-Year Plan was not fundamentally socialist or Communist but instead was a page out of the playbook of the green revolution. Simply put, CPK leadership would modernize Democratic Kampuchea's traditional farming sector using the best agronomic and scientific practices available.[64] In doing so, the party anticipated transforming the country's "backward" farming practices into "modern agriculture within ten to fifteen years."[65]

In their effort to secure foreign capital to (re)build a modern economy, Khmer Rouge cadres confiscated and exported substantial amounts of rice in exchange for capital; in turn, the party planned to funnel foreign earnings from the export of rice into Democratic Kampuchea's nascent industrial sector. Here, one is tempted to conclude that "surplus" capital was simply derived from increased rice production. In other words, it is tempting to conclude that "surplus" identified by the CPK was not "surplus" from a Marxist understanding but merely additional rice to be exchanged with foreign governments in return for other material goods. This interpretation is not so much incorrect as it is incomplete, for it is not just a matter of setting unrealistic quotas and confiscating excessive amounts of rice. Documentary evidence in fact suggests a different explanation. Indeed, an analysis of the CPK's Four-Year Plan provides insight into the economic calculus adopted by senior officials. Furthermore, such analysis better explains the logics of the party's agricultural policy. This is not to suggest that economic policies pursued by CPK leadership were either appropriate or effective—certainly, as starvation deepened throughout Democratic Kampuchea, the failings of the CPK strategy became all too apparent. Instead, CPK planning documents reveal the centrality of a necropolitical logic that was manifest socially, through the introduction of food rations as "compensation" for forced labor, and spatially, in the form of work-camps and communes.

The Sociospatial Organization of Famine Conditions

Throughout Democratic Kampuchea, food was not weaponized officially or explicitly as an instrument of submission and control—although terrified and traumatized people were cowed into compliance over time. From a policy perspective, documentary evidence suggests that food was deliberately withheld for monetary reasons in an effort to generate foreign revenue through the export of rice. Subsequently, when cadres brought forth evidence that standing policies were the cause of—and not the solution to—food insecurity, swift and brutal repression followed. The famine crime committed by senior leaders of the CPK was not so much a crime of commission as it was a crime of commodification. This truth is grimly encapsulated in a slogan introduced in March 1976: "Work more, gain more, but spend less capital."[66] Workers, simply stated, would be required to expend greater effort in the production of more rice but receive less in return.

Until the planned modernization of agriculture could take place, farming practices under the Khmer Rouge remained much as they had been prior to the revolution. The day-to-day activities of clearing lands, planting seeds, and harvesting rice were largely unchanged. Organizationally, however, senior leaders transformed the traditional rhythms of Khmer farming into a regimented agricultural system. Workers were to receive "three rest days per month" or "one rest day in every ten."[67] Pregnant women were allocated two months' rest (in confinement), and for "those under hospitalization," party officials would determine the duration of rest according to the "concrete situation."

CPK leaders further mandated that workers would use their leisure time in a productive fashion, explaining, "Resting at home is nominated and arranged as time for tending small gardens, cleaning up, hygiene, and light study of culture and politics."[68] Moreover, Khmer Rouge cadres closely monitored the *pace* of work performed. For the senior leaders of the CPK, it was imperative "to use [their] time effectively so that it [would] always benefit the works of the country building and defending."[69] Thus the people of Democratic Kampuchea were warned, "Even one day, one hour, one minute or one second, do not let the time go by uselessly, or use it to think about any difficulty or personal issues.... To save forces means knowing how to manage the available forces for the appropriate work in a very effective way."[70] Local cadres assigned men, women, and children daily quotas, and armed soldiers stood guard to enforce them. For those laborers who failed to meet expectations, punishment was often swift and severe.

CPK officials also restructured the social relations of traditional Khmer farming practices. As we have seen, prior to the revolution, both women and men engaged in agricultural work. Men typically plowed the fields, while women prepared nursery beds, transplanted seedlings, and harvested the crops. Daily life centered on the nuclear family, as families worked together. The Khmer Rouge not only altered daily routines, but they also sundered the fundamental social relations of family life, radically transforming society in the process. As Kalyanee Mam explains, "Before the [Khmer Rouge] regime, families worked together as an economic unit. Each family owned the modes of production as well as the fruits of their labor. Families were also social units that offered emotional support."[71] Following the revolution, however, cooperatives displaced the traditional family structure.[72] May Ebihara expounds, "The solidarity of the family as a primary social unit of economic cooperative and emotional bonds was shattered by communal organization into labor teams segregated on the basis of age and gender, dispersal of family members and kinfolk into different work groups and communes, and suppression of familial sentiments."[73]

The collectivization of agriculture and establishment of forced-labor camps was a necessary component of the CPK's rice production strategy. The decision of the CPK to organize peasant cooperatives *at a national level* apparently occurred on May 20, 1973, and was related directly to the ongoing effort "to launch military attacks against the enemies."[74] In addition, cooperatives screened and selected youths to send to the frontline battlefields, and they facilitated the support of base units by caring for the injured and transporting ammunition and other supplies. Crucially, these first collectives provided a necessary political lesson for new recruits. Through their formation, the "party was able to strengthen and extend its army[,] quickly emboldening its consciousness, politics and manpower." Cooperatives thus "were able to provide materials and supports to the livelihood and consciousness of families of the revolutionary soldiers and cadres."[75]

In effect, from 1973 onward, life in the liberated zones became increasingly harsh and rigid as Khmer Rouge cadres forcibly abolished landownership in the liberated areas, enforced complete collectivization, and demonetized the economy.[76] Efforts to "level" the population included confiscation of goods, relocation of villagers to new areas, and the incidence of dormitory living in some areas. Other such measures involved dictating standardized hairstyles for Muslim women, requiring that all people wear black clothing with no jewelry, and instituting rigid work schedules that would last from sunup to sundown. Survivors recall that deprivation of food and water was common, as were arbitrary arrests and imprisonment. Executions also occurred regularly.[77]

Ranging in size from several hundred people to several thousand, cooperatives were established after the war to facilitate the cultivation of selected crops. These associations grew rice, vegetables, fruits, and nonfood crops such as rubber, cotton, and jute. In addition, the collection and distribution of crops was centralized, with each cooperative chief responsible for meeting production quotas established by the Party Center. For senior leaders of the CPK, the establishment of agricultural cooperatives was paramount to the immediate provision of famine relief and the long-term economic strategies forwarded by the government. In the words of the party, "Cooperatives were on the offensive by solving a hundred thousand difficulties. The cooperatives resolved problems such as shortage of labor forces, cattle, plowshares, plows, rakes, hoes, knives, axes, the means of production, etc."[78]

"Concretely, it is imperative to strengthen and expand the cooperatives," CPK leaders concluded following a zone assembly held in August 1975. They continued, "[It is necessary to employ] the strength of the cooperatives as the core, making them the hard core for the absorption of the new people. The new people must be satellites of the cooperatives politically and economically. This is our orientation. The people will be firm only when the cooperatives are solid."[79] CPK officials additionally stated, "The cooperatives must be further strengthened and expanded. . . . In order to be able to effectively defend the country, the issue of people's living standards in the cooperatives must be resolved. We are striving to sort things out for the new people, too, to make them satisfied with the Revolution and make them see that this regime is one that belongs to them, so that they no longer desire to go anywhere else."[80] Thus, where the village or hamlet had constituted a fundamental sociopolitical unit in the old society, the cooperative under the Khmer Rouge became the organizational foundation of Democratic Kampuchea.[81]

Under the formal administration of the CPK, two broad forms of agricultural organization emerged: mutual-aid teams and solidarity groups. In the first type, families retained individual responsibility for all agricultural tasks—with the exception of harvesting, which was communal. Khmer Rouge cadres controlled all rice harvested, returning some to the villages while distributing the remainder elsewhere as needed to support the war effort.[82] Although private landownership continued, peasants were compelled to join cooperatives.[83] The second type of organization consisted of more formalized cooperatives involving communal landownership by interfamily groups, communal labor, and rice distribution. Trade within and between cooperatives was conducted largely through barter. Pol Pot referred to these cooperatives, which entailed the grouping of ten to twelve families, as collective mass organizations.[84] Notably, for the CPK, the word "cooperative" applied exclusively to agricultural groupings, including, whenever possible, persons experienced with blacksmithing, weaving, and other skills to make a unit self-sufficient. Persons working in factories and fishing, or in rubber or salt production, were not considered to be in cooperatives; they were known simply as factory workers and so forth, or as a group of factory or rubber workers.[85]

CPK officials expressed little doubt in their approach to agricultural collectivization. Indeed, as evidenced in various speeches, meeting minutes, and published commentaries, senior party representatives voiced a surety that frequently transformed into zealousness. Within cooperatives, the CPK leadership reasoned, "No one needs to think and worry anymore about their living and working. No one needs to borrow from someone else for living like during the time they lived in the private regime."[86] Within a Communist society, officials avowed, "the Party is in charge of promoting every aspect" of improving the people's livelihood and living standards. Senior CPK leaders noted, "We have distributed rice, clothing, salt, fish paste, plates, cooking pots, shelter and medicines to the people."[87] Indeed, party leaders were certain of collectives' primacy, concluding, "The power of the cooperatives is very mighty and indomitable."[88]

Concretely, the establishment of cooperatives, and the explicit goal of producing rice as a commodity to generate exchange value, constituted a radical transformation of traditional Khmer farming. This process was initiated under French colonial rule and sustained during the Sihanouk years. However, it was only under the Khmer Rouge that Cambodia's farming sector assumed the form of agrarian capitalism. In old-society villages, Ebihara explains, the means of production (land, oxen, plows, other agricultural implements) were individually owned, and the family served as the primary unit of production and consumption. In Democratic Kampuchea, the ownership of resources, production, and consumption became increasingly communal through time.[89] Farmers were effectively divorced from the means of production, and decision-making remained firmly held by only the most loyal and dedicated Khmer Rouge cadres. Moreover, life in Democratic Kampuchea was increasingly valued based on preference for one's capacity to labor and, consequently, to generate foreign revenue as a member of a productive work team. The Khmer Rouge inserted farmers more fully into the global economy than did either the French colonialists or the Sihanouk government, as production was predominantly destined not for individual consumption but to foreign markets.[90]

When the Khmer Rouge suspended currency, it did not sunder the basic form of productive activity among the peasantry. Farmers grew rice, and rice was collected by government officials, then exported to garner capital. What did change, however, was the social organization of laboring activities and the quest to accumulate capital through the export of commodified rice. In practice, this approach left unresolved the precise form and mechanisms of distributive efforts, and from the beginning, senior CPK officials wrestled with the proper allocation of resources to increase the people's livelihoods.

In early 1976, for example, CPK leaders acknowledged, "The forces of the people are a vast labor force, both mighty and enormous, both a physical force and a solid political force. But, if we cannot sort it out well or we do not figure out how to resolve the livelihood of the people, we will incur damages and losses of every kind, both physical losses and losses of manpower."[91] Indeed, the party determined, "We have huge resources in terms of means and material. We have a state authority that can manage all these affairs in order to figure out and resolve the livelihood of the people at all times, and also now, after this harvest season, we have sufficient rice and can distribute it to all the people to eat their fill, and so on." In the words of the CPK, all that was required was to calculate the proper allocation "to sort out the livelihood of our people appropriately, with everyone getting their fill."[92] On this point, senior leaders "sorted" people according to their standing in society. In other words, CPK officials engaged in a form of state racism, introducing political divisions into the population to separate those considered "pure" and welcome from those considered "impure" and so not.[93]

Much has been made of Khmer Rouge racism, nationalism, and xenophobia.[94] Ben Kiernan emphasizes the racist underpinnings of CPK ideology and highlights the party's engagement in violent persecution, especially of Cambodia's Muslim Cham, and of the country's ethnic Vietnamese minority populations.⁹⁵ However, the prejudice of the Khmer Rouge *leadership* is more properly understood as a form of state racism as articulated by Foucault. Thus, while the deeply entrenched and long-standing prejudices held by many Khmer Rouge officials and cadres cannot be denied, the key takeaway is that CPK officials exercised "the right to kill or the right to eliminate or the right to disqualify" grounded on particular calculations of potential worth.⁹⁶ As Michel Foucault explains, "The State is, and must be, the protector of the integrity, the superiority, and the purity of the race.... State sovereignty thus becomes the imperative to protect the race."⁹⁷ Here, racism encompasses a more expansive connotation than that forwarded by Kiernan, for the bigotry of the Khmer Rouge was not limited to perceived ethnic (or religious) divisions. Instead, there was necessarily a *political-economic* component to the state racism of CPK planning, a component that mediated one's exposure to premature death, either through direct physical violence or the indirect disallowing of life due to insufficient food, water, and medicine.

The most fundamental caesura introduced by Khmer Rouge officials was the distinction between "new" (or "April 17") people and "base" people. Base people were those individuals who lived in territories "liberated" by the Khmer Rouge during the civil war. In general, they were considered to be more loyal and trustworthy. New people were individuals who either did not live in liberated areas or did not support the Khmer Rouge. In concrete terms, new people were treated more harshly, received fewer material resources, and suffered considerably more than either base people or Khmer Rouge cadres. New people effectively were reduced to the status of *hominis sacer*: they could be killed or left to die, with their deaths having no meaning. Beyond this informal yet crucial distinction, other more codified political criteria were introduced. Among Khmer Rouge cadres—that is, members and potential members of the CPK—a tripartite classification of status was introduced: "full rights" (*penh sith*), "candidate" (*triem*), and "depositee" (*bannhau*). Full-rights status meant that members were permitted to "consider and discuss and join in decision making" on all party affairs, while candidate members and depositees were allowed only to participate in meetings, without the right of decision-making.⁹⁸ Notably, new people were prohibited from becoming party members.

All denizens of Democratic Kampuchea, regardless of political classification, were to serve the state and, by extension, the "building of socialism." However, it was the *capacity* to labor—not the laborer—that was of paramount consideration. Life-and-death decisions, notably the disbursement of food and other supplies, were strictly utilitarian: they were made based on their ability to produce for the state. Indeed, it was this logic that accounted for the attitudes of Khmer Rouge cadres toward ill and suffering workers. For example, the sick were considered to be shirking their duty. As Henri Locard explains, in the minds of Khmer Rouge cadres, "the sick could not be anything other than malingerers, because they could not or would not work, and therefore, were sabotaging the revolution. The following slogans capture these sentiments: 'We absolutely must remove [from society] the lazy; it is useless to keep them, else they will cause trouble. We have to send them to hell'; 'The sick are victims of their own imaginations'; and 'We must wipe out those who imagine they are ill, and expel them from society.'"[99]

Workers within Democratic Kampuchea were also classified according to their potential labor productivity. Thus, they were considered either *kemlang ping* (full strength) or *kemlang ksaoy* (weak strength), with the former category consisting of adults and the latter comprising small children and the elderly. This broad division was further separated into two subgroups, identified as *kemlang* 1 and *kemlang* 2. The first comprised young, single, able-bodied men and women who worked in mobile work brigades (*kong chhlat*) segregated by sex. Males belonged to *kong boroh*, and females belonged to *kong neary*. The second also consisted of young, able-bodied workers, but it included those who were married. These workers generally toiled closer to their home village or cooperative. Full-strength laborers, regardless of classification, performed the heaviest work details, including clearing forests; plowing fields; planting, transplanting, and harvesting rice; and digging or carrying dirt for irrigation projects.[100]

Elderly people, that is, those aged fifty years and above, formed work teams known as *senah chun*. Khmer Rouge cadres divided these teams according to sex as well, with men belonging to *senah chun boroh* and women to *senah chun neary*. Productive tasks for these working units included sewing, gardening, collecting small pieces of firewood, and caring for infants and young children. Depending on the conditions and the attitudes of the cooperative chief, some elderly workers might be required to labor in the rice fields or engage in other more strenuous work. Last, cadres assigned children fourteen years of age or younger to work groups known as *kong komar*, with boys and girls separated into *kong komara* and *kong khomarei*, respectively. Children were responsible for watching after cows and water buffalo, performing light digging in gardens and fields, collecting firewood, and gathering cow dung for fertilizer.[101]

Detailed work schedules were subsequently devised—although not necessarily implemented—that determined how many days of work were required, and for how many days, for society as a whole. In this way, party planners estimated an amount of surplus value required to plant and harvest rice. By extension, local cadres calculated work quotas specific to their cooperative or administrative unit, such as the amount of soil to excavate or the acreage of forest to clear.

For senior planners of the CPK, the "sorting out the livelihood of the people" centered on the notion of thrift. As the party announced in March 1976, "Thrift is an important factor for building the country."[102] CPK leaders explained, for example, "If we only strive to work, but we waste, damage, and leave the results carelessly everywhere, we will not be able to build socialism.... So, thrift is one of the determined factors in building socialism in our Kampuchea."[103] In practice, this meant the withholding and rationing of all products, but especially food. "We have to be thrifty with everything," party officials explained, including the consumption "of rice, salt, fish paste, preserved fish, meat and fish, [and] vegetables," but also "clothes, various tools, water and electricity, fuel, and even a string of thread, a nail, a piece of plywood or even a piece of firewood."[104]

With that goal in mind, party leaders developed a fourfold system to distribute food rations based on labor capacity.[105] Those workers classified in the No. 1 system would be allocated three cans of rice per day; those in No. 2, two and one-half cans; those in No. 3, two cans; and those in No. 4, one and one-half cans. This numeric system refers to the type of labor involved. In principle, those people performing the heaviest manual labor were to receive the highest rations. The lightest tasks, performed by the elderly or the sick, merited the smallest rations. Beyond the allocation of rice, workers were to receive daily two side dishes of soup or dried food and dessert.[106] Remarkably, CPK officials projected rice production to increase each year but planned to hold food rations constant.[107] Party leaders fixed the cost to reproduce labor from year to year, expecting workers to be more productive from one year to the next, but to live on the same food ration from year to year; in fact, the Four-Year Plan projected rations to remain constant from 1977 through 1980. As we saw earlier, party leaders demanded that citizens work more and gain more but spend (consume) less.

Given their determination that "from 1977, the ration for the people will average ... 312 kilograms of rice per person per year throughout the country," party members calculated the amount of surplus profits to be earned through the export of the crop.[108] This information appears as table 3 in the Four-Year Plan. CPK officials anticipated the production of 5.55 million tons of rice in 1977, with production increasing to 7.742 million tons in 1980. A footnote explains, "Total production for fields harvested twice per year is figured as 6 tons per hectare; ordinary fields harvested once per year is estimated at 3 tons per hectare."[109] Table 5 presents figures on capital expenditures and capital earned from the export of rice. Thus, of the target of 5.5 million tons of rice produced in 1977, the CPK determined that an equivalency of 3.2 million tons of rice be expended as capital (e.g., food rations, seeds, and "welfare"). Of the estimated 2.3 million tons of "surplus" rice, 1.3 million tons were to be exported. Based on an exchange rate of U.S.$200 per ton of rice, the party concluded that it would earn—in 1977—over U.S.$277 million. Subsequently, a seven-to-three ratio was calculated whereby 70 percent of the surplus would be spent for the "base" in order to build the zones, regions, and other units, while the remaining 30 percent would be set aside for the state to defend and build the country.[110] According to CPK calculations, earnings from rice were to increase each year between 1977 and 1980, with earning in 1980 anticipated at over U.S.$424 million.

Geographic organization was crucial to the economic planning of the CPK. For all administrative units, from the zone to the village level, party officials made separate calculations to determine the balance between surplus production and food rations. National planning, however, centered almost always at the zone level. In the Western Zone, for example, a senior party official explained how such calculations would be determined: "If the Zone has 600,000 people, they must eat 150,000 tons of [rice]. But we want more than this in order to locate much additional oil, to get ever more rice mills, threshing machines, water pumps, and means of transportation, both as an auxiliary manual force and to give strength to our forces of production. So we must not get just 150,000 tons of [rice]. We must get 300,000, 400,000, 500,000 tons just to break even and be able to build socialism."[111]

Despite attempts by the CPK to standardize the quantities of labor to be performed, in practice there was no uniform quota system. As Twining correctly identifies, whoever was in charge of a group of workers (for instance, one of the cooperative's team chiefs or the head of the village committee) determined the hours to be worked or the amount of labor to be performed in a day—for instance, the meters of irrigation canal to be dug or rice field to be cultivated.[112] Indeed, as Ebihara explains, "Local organization and conditions varied both regionally and through time, depending on such factors as ecological setting, ideological divergences and contention for power among factions of Kampuchean communists, stages of collectivization, and interpretations and implementations of policy by local cadres."[113] She continues, "Some communities had reasonable work requirements and adequate food, while others were subject to stringent discipline and starvation."[114] It follows that famine in Democratic Kampuchea was decidedly uneven, both socially and spatially. Far from a universal weaponization of food, Khmer Rouge policy and practice was manifest unequally throughout society, with one's vulnerability to premature death conditioned greatly by one's political standing.

Famine as Violent Condition

The political economy of Democratic Kampuchea placed the majority of the population between the teeth of two powerful forces: a demand for surplus rice and agricultural inputs that justified draconian labor policies, and a rationing system that winnowed away every excess grain of rice. For workers, the result was an institutional arrangement that could not (and would not) respond to deteriorating conditions. During a meeting held on March 8, 1976, for example, cadres acknowledged "the problems of many sick people in the work sites, [resulting in] a loss of 40 percent of the labor force," and yet concluded, "Expenditures for material purchases to solve the livelihood of the people are limited because we must purchase many other things as well." In the end, the committee at the meeting reiterated the two-can-per-day food ration.[115] The solution to the problem was greater "revolutionary zeal" among the workers, and those cadres not meeting expectations were, by the CPK's definition, traitors to both the state and the revolution.[116]

However, as people became weakened through malnutrition, starvation, and disease, their work productivity declined. When productivity declined, local cadres were forced to appropriate ever-greater quantities of rice to satisfy quotas established by officials at the upper echelons. Cooperative chiefs had to answer to district superiors; district secretaries had to answer to sector secretaries; and sector secretaries had to answer to zone secretaries. It was inevitable that "failures" occurring at one level would reverberate up and down the administrative hierarchy. The subsequent uneven conditions and mortality rates across Democratic Kampuchea reflect in part the varied responses of zone-, sector-, district-, and branch-level officials.[117]

The CPK central leadership avoided acknowledging its responsibility for famine and responded to reports of hunger and starvation with denial, blame shifting, and violent purges.[118] Frequently, CPK officials simply denied the existence of hunger or starvation; those who dared speak up most often met with swift and severe punishment. When irrefutable evidence of starvation did surface, the senior leadership blamed "traitorous" and "inept" cadres for undermining the food production apparatus. An article appearing in the November 1975 issue of *Revolutionary Flag*, for example, explained, "While our people were almost starving, some of our revolutionary male [and] female youths at certain offices, units, and ministries were living well, eating well, wearing flashy clothes, wasting things and having plenty.... At some places, they did not follow and apply the party food ration. They instead cooked rice excessively because they saw that there was plenty of rice in the warehouse." The article threatens, "These past wrong activities are very painful for all of our revolutionary male [and] female youths, so we must determine to eliminate them decisively so that they will not take place again in our view, stance, and application."[119]

Likewise, in a speech reprinted in the September 1977 issue of *Revolutionary Flag*, Pol Pot warned, "There are life-and-death contradictions owing to the presence of enemy agents, who belong to the various spy networks of the imperialists and international reaction and who secretly implant themselves to carry out subversive activities against our revolution."[120] He concluded, "Contradictions with these elements must be solved by the measures proper for enemies: separate, educate and win over the elements which can be won over; neutralize the elements which are wavering, preventing them from doing any damage to the revolution; and, finally, isolate and eradicate only the smallest possible number of those elements who are cruel and persist in acting against the revolution and the people, and collaborate with foreign enemies to destroy their own people and their own revolution."[121] Consequently, when hungry men, women, and children were suspected of, or apprehended while, stealing food, they suffered violent retribution.[122] On September 16, 1976, for example, a division chief reported that a man named Neak Loeung stole a haversack of rice. Khmer Rouge soldiers seized the man, but when he later tried to escape, cadres "shot him dead and did not get to interrogate him about anything."[123]

Confident in their actions, party leaders saw no need to rescind or modify policies that contributed to mass starvation. According to DeFalco, evidence "strongly suggests that the upper echelons of the CPK government expropriated and exported mass quantities of rice throughout the DK period with clear knowledge that this rice was coming at the expense of civilians."[124] Indeed, as conditions continued to deteriorate throughout Democratic Kampuchea, senior leaders made further demands on their citizenry. As late as April 1978, for example, Khieu Samphan, president of the Presidium of the State of Democratic Kampuchea, announced that the CPK "decided to export more rice than the previous year so that [Democratic Kampuchea] can accumulate more capital for national construction."[125]

In the end, the senior leadership of the CPK did not simply withhold or deny food from their subjects primarily as a weapon, for the key architects of Democratic Kampuchea's economy were quite clear in their motivation and resolve. Foodstuffs were provided in limited amounts to redress famine and jump-start a moribund economy devastated by war. The crime of the Khmer Rouge was neither a crime of omission nor one of commission, but instead an offense that combined both omission and commission. Upon learning of the inadequacies of the food provisioning system, CPK officials, on the one hand, refused to modify their rationing of rice. On the other hand, they violently suppressed accusations of mass starvation. The subsequent famine generated its own violent conditions, as zealous Khmer Rouge cadres arrested, detained, tortured, and executed men, women, and children framed as traitors to the party and its revolution.

Conclusions

In September 1976, senior leaders of the CPK stated that rice production should allow the people to "eat their fill and keep enough seed for next year." "If there is any remaining," the officials added, "we take some away to sell abroad."[126] The words of the CPK ring hollow when sounded against the concrete realities of famine during the Khmer Rouge period. To charge that party leaders were deceptive is an accurate but hardly remarkable conclusion. We readily see in Democratic Kampuchea a government prepared to "let die" hundreds of thousands of its subjects. But toward what objective?

In Democratic Kampuchea, the production of sufficient food was not the problem. Famine under the Khmer Rouge resulted primarily from the appropriation and uneven distribution of food. But this wasn't a "failure" of policy. Instead, the policies issued by the senior leadership of the CPK and carried out by local cadres worked precisely as intended. These measures appropriated a disproportionate share of rice harvests for export, and they allocated insufficient rations to the country's citizens based on calculations calibrated to ensure maximum returns through reductions in consumption. Simply put, every spoonful of rice consumed by workers in Democratic Kampuchea represented loss in potential earnings, a grim demonstration of the fatal contradictions inherent in Khmer Rouge bio(necro)politics. For the specific policies—displacement and dispossession, rationing of food, and self-sufficiency in medical care—were imposed paradoxically in a biopolitical attempt to *make life*. Accordingly, the deaths from exposure, starvation, and disease were not unintended side effects of poor research, poor planning, or poor implementation. Rather, they were the direct outcome of the CPK's necropolitical imperative to increase surplus capital through the implementation of subminimum wages (in the form of food rations) and, by extension, a pervasive indifference to life.

"The goal of our collectivism," Pol Pot explained in a CPK report, "is to raise the living standards of the people quickly and rapidly.... But an important point which must be discussed in a systematic way is whether we are to improve the people's living standards in the direction of individualism or in the direction of collectivism."[127] He concluded, "Our plan is to raise the living standards of the people quickly, in the direction of collectivism."[128] In actuality, deprived of adequate nutrition, exhausted from working long hours under adverse conditions, and denied access to effective medical care, hundreds of thousands of men, women, and children succumbed to premature death. That the CPK did not work to end the famine—indeed, that it punished those who acknowledged the famine conditions—is an extreme example of sovereign violence, an example whereby a government deliberately disallows life to millions of its citizens for political-economic gain.

CHAPTER 4

Another Cambodian War

> A generation of Cambodian children is in danger of being lost.
> —Rosalynn Carter

At midnight on December 24, 1978, approximately 150,000 troops of the People's Army of Vietnam (PAVN), together with several thousand Cambodian members of the United Front for the National Salvation of Kampuchea (known by its French acronym, FUNSK), moved into Democratic Kampuchea.[1] Hastily formed throughout late 1978, the Salvation Front was a motley assembly of Khmer Rouge deserters and Cambodian refugees. Their unity was found not in ideology but in lived experience. As Nayan Chanda explains, it was common hatred for the Pol Pot regime that had brought together under Vietnamese guidance the disparate collection of survivors. Indeed, many of the men and women who joined or supported the Salvation Front harbored grave doubts about the Socialist Republic of Vietnam's (SRV's) ulterior motives, but they saw no other alternative in seeking help to fight the murderous Pol Pot regime.[2]

For senior leaders of Vietnam, the invasion was an attempt to resolve long-standing grievances with Pol Pot and his inner circle. From the 1940s onward, Vietnamese Communists allied—albeit uneasily—with their Cambodian counterparts, a task made difficult by the various factions of Communists in Cambodia, and by the antagonistic personalities of many of the Khmer Rouge leaders. After the CPK secured victory in 1975 and Pol Pot solidified his preeminent position within the party, the strained relationship unraveled entirely. The proximate spark was territory—notably, disputed claims along Cambodia's southeastern border with Vietnam. The irredentist claims of the Khmer Rouge were twofold. On the one hand, Pol Pot and other high-ranking officials intended to recover lost territories of the ancient Khmer empire, and to "liberate" the Khmer people living under Vietnamese control. On the other hand, the disputed areas of southern Vietnam, known as Kampuchea Krom to the Cambodians, consisted of fertile agricultural lands that could contribute to Democratic Kampuchea's rice-based, export-oriented economy.

During the early months of the territorial dispute, diplomatic solutions were sought. However, from May 1976, negotiations between representatives from Hanoi and Phnom Penh bogged down, and Khmer Rouge forces launched a series of assaults against Vietnamese forces just across the border. For Pol Pot, buoyed by his belief that his military forces had single-handedly defeated the United States, war with Vietnam was welcomed.[3] In early 1977 Khmer Rouge raids on Vietnam began in earnest, and within the year fighting escalated into full-scale conflict, providing Hanoi sufficient justification for armed intervention.[4]

Now, within days of Vietnam's military offensive in late 1978, key provincial towns fell, including Kratie, Stung Treng, and Kompong Cham. Equally important, vital agricultural regions also came under Vietnamese control. By January 6, 1979, Vietnamese forces crossed the Mekong at Neak Luong—the site of ferocious fighting four years earlier—and made their way to the capital. On the following day Phnom Penh was captured, and on January 11 officials in Hanoi installed Heng Samrin, a Khmer Rouge defector, as head of state of the new People's Republic of Kampuchea (PRK).[5] Fierce fighting would continue until August 1979, by which time the remnants of the Khmer Rouge had been driven across or close to the Thai border to regroup as a guerrilla force.[6]

Officials in Hanoi anticipated international pushback for their military actions. Sensitive to previous accusations by the Chinese of "expansionism and hegemonism," the Vietnamese attempted to garner international support through repeated condemnations of the "genocidal" Khmer Rouge. For example, during a broadcast delivered on June 20, 1978, Hanoi Radio declared, "The Pol Pot-Ieng Sary clique have proved themselves to be the most disgusting murderers in the latter half of this century.... The Pol Pot-Ieng Sary clique are only a cheap instrument of the bitterest enemy of peace and mankind. Their actions are leading to national suicide. This is genocide of a special type. Let us stop this self-genocide! Let us stop genocide at the hands of the Pol Pot-Ieng Sary clique."[7] Predictably, though, China and several Western governments, including that of the United States, framed Hanoi's "liberation" of Democratic Kampuchea as an "invasion." Vietnam's military aggression thus constituted an unlawful infringement on the territorial integrity of Democratic Kampuchea and violated international norms. Indeed, many officials in the United States publicly denied the existence of genocide, knowing full well the Khmer Rouge committed numerous atrocities.[8] Instead of being recognized by the international community for removing the Khmer Rouge—a political party Henry Kissinger described as "murderous thugs" in 1975—Hanoi officials were met with international scorn and condemnation.[9]

When the Khmer Rouge members retreated to the jungles along the Thai-Cambodian border, they did so intending to continue their armed struggle to retake the capital and once again rule Democratic Kampuchea. This objective was aided by the international condemnation of Vietnam. For example, in response to the establishment of Heng Samrin's government and the formation of the PRK, representatives of China and the United States sought—and received—international recognition at the United Nations for the exiled Khmer Rouge.[10] Ultimately, it was this geopolitical context that formed the contours of Cambodia's third famine.

Famine in 1979 was not inevitable; nor was it merely the continuation of famine into the following year. Indeed, Cambodia's third famine of the 1970s supports the thesis that serial famines, at least in this case, are both discrete and continual. This apparent paradox is resolved when one considers concretely the different policies and practices put forward by successive regimes. Under the Lon Nol regime, famine was conditioned by declines in food production and availability; during the Khmer Rouge regime, however, food production increased but famine persisted, primarily because of the export of rice for surplus gain. In fact, by 1977 Democratic Kampuchea was producing enough rice to feed its population. This was made possible in part because of the CPK's draconian policies of assembling people into agricultural cooperatives, and in part through the forced construction of myriad irrigation projects across the country. Malnutrition and starvation persisted in Democratic Kampuchea through 1978 not because of a failure of food production but instead because of the regime's policy to withhold rice for export. Therefore, when the CPK government collapsed in January 1979, so, too, did the agricultural cooperatives. Cambodia's third famine emerged against this backdrop.

The Unfolding Conditions of Famine

If the Vietnamese had not expected the swift collapse of the Khmer Rouge resistance, they also were not fully prepared for what awaited them.[11] After years of civil war and Khmer Rouge brutality, Cambodia was not just a land without money, markets, a postal system, or schools; it was a land littered with mass graves and filled by a traumatized people. And while Vietnam had couched its invasion of Democratic Kampuchea in terms of a humanitarian intervention, it was not immediately prepared to supply the Cambodian people with the large-scale stocks of food and medical supplies they so desperately needed.[12] In part, this is because Vietnamese strategists *anticipated* that adequate foodstuffs and other provisions would be available.

Throughout the Indochina Wars, military operations frequently were launched to coincide with the monsoons; that is, major operations began with the cessation of rains. For Vietnamese strategists in 1978, the liberation of Democratic Kampuchea was timed to concur with the late-season rice harvest. This meant that the Vietnamese troops and the Cambodian people would have the maximum amount of rice available for emergency consumption. With this accomplished, the Vietnamese plan was seize the rice warehouses and redistribute the supply to a hungry and malnourished populace, thereby winning their immediate goodwill. In addition, the captured food supplies would support Vietnamese soldiers as they scoured the countryside to annihilate the remnants of the scattered and defeated Khmer Rouge army. If all went according to plan, by the time the next planting season began in April 1979 the rice fields would be secure, and the people organized sufficiently to begin agricultural production.[13]

The senior leaders of the CPK were sensitive to the possibility of a Vietnamese invasion. And for that reason, throughout November and early December, Khmer Rouge cadres pushed their people to harvest and gather as much rice as quickly as possible, in part for their own consumption, but also to deny supplies for the expected invading Vietnamese forces. In some villages, the plan was to stockpile bags of rice, along with salt, meat, and medicines, to be carried away by oxcart in the event of a Vietnamese onslaught. Elsewhere, rice and other supplies were stockpiled in prearranged base camps, often located deep in surrounding forests and other defensible positions. What the Khmer Rouge could not carry or stash away, they destroyed: tons of seed rice, seed corn, and seed tuber; carts and draft animals; and agricultural tools. Some villages were completely laid to waste, and in the market towns, countless bags of rice were burned in place.[14]

From January onward, weary and beleaguered Khmer Rouge cadres made their way to the temporary camps established in the mountainous regions of north and northeast Cambodia; as these camps fell, tens of thousands of hungry and malaria-ridden black-clad Khmer Rouge soldiers, their families, and base people crossed into Thailand, most in desperate need of food and other forms of humanitarian aid.[15] Mason and Brown describe the conditions in which these individuals existed:

> They wore the traditional Khmer Rouge clothing of loose black pajama shirts and pants, and sandals made from the rubber of tires. They walked silently to the villages, rarely speaking or looking at others. Their eyes and cheeks were sunken, their bodies ravaged by disease and lack of food. Many of the soldiers were mere boys and teenagers, and they looked frightened as they approached the Thais for help. The women and children had endured the hardships since all available food supplies had been allotted first to the guerrilla soldiers. Women carried their weightless babies in stick-thin arms; their elbows and knees looked grossly enlarged by comparison. Most of the children were malnourished and showed the symptoms of kwashiorkor—reddish hair, balding, large listless eyes.[16]

For the base people who chose to remain in situ, hunger arrived quickly. The scorched-earth campaign of the Khmer Rouge left behind a wake of devastation. Many villages had been laid to waste. Most foodstuffs and agricultural implements had been taken away; that which remained was destroyed by retreating Khmer Rouge forces. According to Heder, more than half of all villages throughout Cambodia were simply deserted. Abandoned rice stalks grew overripe and fell to the ground, sometimes sprouting into new seeds but most often being devoured by birds and rodents. Storehouses of rice likewise mildewed or were eaten by rats and field mice. Heder estimates that more than one-third of the 1978–1979 rice crop was simply lost.[17] The few supplies that the people retained soon ran out. Unable to cultivate rice, they lived on meager stocks of maize and manioc.[18]

Vietnamese officials assumed, perhaps naively, that they would be welcomed most of all by the former new people, who had suffered the most under the Khmer Rouge for years. And to a degree, the Vietnamese were welcomed. As Heder explains, for the new people, the Vietnamese invasion initially carried high hopes, only to be followed by great disappointment. Many survivors believed, often quite correctly, that the arrival of the FUNSK and PAVN forces saved them from eventual premature death by execution or by overwork combined with starvation rations; however, conditions for many did not readily improve, and often actually worsened.[19]

Initially, the newly installed PRK government renounced the previous Khmer Rouge restrictions on mobility. No longer forced at gunpoint to live in agricultural cooperatives or mobile work camps, the erstwhile new people were free to search for lost family and relatives or return to their former homes, whether in rural villages, provincial towns, or Phnom Penh. Others made the dangerous journey to Thailand. There, they hoped to find temporary relief from chronic hunger before returning to their villages or continuing to an unknown foreign destination—hopefully beyond the reach of the remnant Khmer Rouge or the Vietnamese-backed PRK government.

Those survivors who stayed in Cambodia met with disappointment in their attempt to return home and start life again. Many individuals found their homes destroyed, in disrepair, or occupied by other people who were also desperate to restart their lives. In the more rural areas, fields were uncultivable due to neglect or damage. Little rice was available, and still less of the rice seed so vital for the upcoming planting season.[20] Most tragically, husbands and wives, mothers and fathers, sons and daughters, and aunts, uncles, brothers, sisters, and cousins were nowhere to be found, having been killed or left to die at the hands of the Khmer Rouge. Rare was the individual who didn't suffer personal, profound, and irreparable loss.

Within weeks, two distinct famine geographies materialized. First, there were the hundreds of thousands of refugees concentrated within Thailand or along the border. Many of these exiles were former members of the Khmer Rouge; and of these, many hoped to continue the fight against the Vietnamese. Other refugees joined, or supported the creation of, "liberation" militias pledged to fight both the Khmer Rouge and the Vietnamese occupying forces. Most evacuees, however, simply tried to stay alive. A second and more dispersed famine geography consisted of the millions of Cambodians who remained in the countryside or had made their way to the provincial capitals and Phnom Penh. Unable to provide adequate food, medicine, and shelter for these individuals, PRK officials initiated a series of programs that exacerbated the mounting crisis in key respects. To begin, for many functionaries, the urban-based refugees constituted nothing more than "a mass of underemployed persons draining an already severely overtaxed urban and semi-urban economy and contributing little to the immediately much more crucial agricultural sector."[21] Consequently, in February and March 1979, in a process eerily similar to that ordered by the Khmer Rouge four years earlier, Vietnamese and PRK officials ordered the evacuation of provincial market towns. Their decision echoed that of the ousted and detested Khmer Rouge: to relieve the population pressures, to encourage rural farming, and to regain some semblance of control.

Compounding the problem within Cambodia was the fact that rice was being exported to facilitate the rebuilding of war-torn Vietnam. In addition, Vietnamese officials in Phnom Penh continued to requisition food stocks to feed the city's occupying forces. In anticipation of the war, Vietnamese troops were expected to feed off captured rice stocks; they had entered the country with only about one month's rations. Consequently, as the weeks dragged into months, more and more rice was diverted from the hungry and malnourished Khmer people to feed garrisoned troops at a ration of seven hundred grams per day. What little remained was often distributed, first to cadres of the Salvation Front. The vast majority of Cambodians in the countryside and the cities were left to scavenge for themselves.[22]

Throughout much of Cambodia during the 1979–1980 growing season, agricultural production came to a standstill. In some places, only between 10 and 20 percent of rice fields that had been cultivated in 1978 were under the plow in 1979. Elsewhere, circumstances were marginally better. Indeed, the conditions experienced by the Khmer people varied greatly. In the more secure districts, upward of 70 percent of the rice fields were cultivated, thus providing much-needed, albeit still insufficient, resources locally. Overall, for many survivors, there was no one to turn to for assistance. Ten years of war, famine, disease, and genocide left behind many orphaned children, widows, and elderly people without relatives. The traditional sources of support had long been destroyed. Beyond the dissolution of the extended family, the Buddhist wats, traditionally a source of social welfare for the poor and suffering, had been destroyed.[23] An estimated 12,500 monks were believed to have been executed by Khmer Rouge cadres, and many thousands more who were forced to work in the rice fields, clear forests, or dig canals died of disease, malnutrition, and starvation.[24]

And throughout 1979, as famine swept across the country, the newly installed PRK government proved unable or unwilling to provide sufficient assistance. Blame, however, is capacious, and Cold War ideologies provided the necessary geopolitical context that unnecessarily prolonged the suffering of the Cambodian people.

The Necro-Geopolitics of Famine Relief

The deepening humanitarian crises both within the PRK and along the Thai-Cambodian border were not inevitable. Rather, they were the manifestation of combined negligence and malfeasance. On the one hand, all parties wielded the existence of famine as political propaganda; on the other hand, all parties openly weaponized the distribution of food in an attempt to subdue their respective enemies. Cold War ideologies provided the fulcrum for the crisis.

Both PRK and Vietnamese officials, for example, dismissed initial claims of widespread food shortages as propaganda intended to destabilize the new government; indeed, throughout all of 1979 officials would downplay reports of mass starvation. Thus, speaking before the United Nations in October, a Vietnamese spokesperson brushed off reports, explaining, "This so-called famine is a trap, a Chinese plot.... The West is playing it up to supply food and ammunition to the Pol Pot forces."[25] Behind the public facade, however, government officials both in Phnom Penh and Hanoi sensed the gravity of the situation and permitted the distribution of aid from the Soviet bloc. By the end of October, Vietnam had delivered 120,000 tons of food to the PRK, with an additional 30,000 tons provided by the Soviet Union.[26] Western officials, notably those in Washington, similarly downplayed or dismissed reports of famine.[27] Such denials were not grounded on concrete evidence but instead based on geopolitical calculations mediated by shifting Cold War alliances.

Soon after its proclamation, the PRK was accorded diplomatic recognition by the governments of Vietnam, the Soviet Union, and its allies. The Treaty of Peace, Friendship, and Cooperation was concluded between the PRK and Vietnam. Yet member states of the Association of Southeast Asian Nations (ASEAN), however, refused to recognize the PRK; in turn, they supported efforts forwarded by the United States and China to acknowledge the ousted CPK government of Pol Pot as the rightful sovereign authority of the country. Relief agencies rightfully expressed concern that the geopolitical struggles would result in a humanitarian crisis for the Cambodian people. Of critical importance was the disruption of the rice harvest as a consequence of Vietnamese military operations and the attendant upheaval and insecurity. The necessary planting of rice for the next harvest was seriously jeopardized, as a shortage of rice seed and draft animals was compounded by the movement of hundreds of thousands of people.[28]

In the days following the overthrow of the Khmer Rouge, representatives from the International Committee of the Red Cross (ICRC) and the United Nations Children's Emergency Fund (UNICEF) began making formal requests to enter Cambodia to provide assistance. Both the ICRC and UNICEF are bound to help all civilians in distress on a nondiscriminatory basis, and they are also obliged to ensure adequate monitoring of the distribution of relief supplies. However, the Heng Samrin government refused initial overtures. In part, both Hanoi and Phnom Penh insisted that the international position of the Heng Samrin government not be undermined by any relief aid agreement that formally conceded international relief agencies' right to supply aid to the Khmer Rouge. It would take several months before international aid organizations were allowed into the country, and still more months before a permanent presence could be established.[29]

Immediately after the Vietnamese overthrew the Pol Pot regime and installed the Heng Samrin government, American officials initiated an international campaign to punish Vietnam.[30] This, in turn, was predicated on Chinese-led efforts to restore the fighting capabilities of the Khmer Rouge to oppose the newly installed PRK government. President Jimmy Carter made the U.S. position clear in a February 14, 1979, letter to Australian prime minister Malcolm Fraser: "Since the Vietnamese attack on Cambodia, we have moved together with other governments, including your own, to isolate the Vietnamese diplomatically.... Other governments, including yours, have agreed to suspend future bilateral and multilateral economic assistance so long as Vietnamese aggression continues. We have also stressed the importance of withholding legitimacy from the Vietnamese-installed government in Phnom Penh."[31] Carrying out these plans meant denying famine relief supplies to the Cambodian people, for any extension of aid could be seen as a legitimation of Vietnam's actions.

From the outset, rebranding, rebuilding, and recycling the Khmer Rouge became the shared objective of China and the United States. Effectively, as "Beijing concentrated on the military side of this enterprise, Washington worked publicly on the diplomatic front, while ensuring adequate material supplies were delivered."[32] Indeed, during the early months of 1979, Carter and members of his cabinet negotiated at length with their Chinese counterparts to determine the most effective means of funneling military and financial aid through Thailand to the Khmer Rouge.[33] U.S. officials' overarching concern was to avoid a widening "Sino-Soviet confrontation over Indochina."[34] This called for a delicate balancing act that required both undermining the new government in Phnom Penh and humiliating and isolating Vietnam, all without unduly antagonizing the Soviet Union. However, the political response of Thailand was crucial to achieving these objectives. From an operational standpoint, China promised the exiled Khmer Rouge leaders arms, ammunition, and massive financial assistance; fulfilling this commitment required that Thai territory be used as a "pipeline for arms and other equipment destined for Pol Pot's army."[35] As expressed in a State Department telegram, the "resupply of a guerrilla [Khmer Rouge] campaign would almost certainly require an agreement between China and Thailand to permit overland transit through Thailand of Chinese aid."[36]

Although the Thai government expressed initial concern about Vietnamese intentions, the consensus apparently was that the threat of Vietnamese forces marching across Cambodia's western border into Thailand was virtually nonexistent. That said, American officials hoped to capitalize on the *perceived* danger to Thailand's sovereignty and territorial integrity. U.S. ambassador to Thailand Morton Abramowitz observed, "The Thais are deeply disquieted and concerned, but not panicked. They recognize that Vietnam's course in Kampuchea was motivated by special circumstances which do not necessarily apply to Thailand. They do not now see the Vietnamese as marching across the Kampuchean border into Thailand, although they are fretful about the long run."

Consequently, Abramowitz advised the U.S. State Department, "We should preemptively respond to inevitable questions about our security commitment by declaring flatly that we regard ourselves as continuing to have a valid treaty obligation with Thailand." The intent was "not [to] resurrect dominoes," he cautioned; official statements on Cambodia "should play down worry about the threat posed to Thailand or about Thailand's future." Rather, the ambassador said, the U.S. position should "impress on Hanoi the force of our international condemnation of its actions. Despite our distaste for the Pol Pot government, we must continue to loudly and roundly condemn this act of external aggression." In other words, U.S. officials wanted to downplay the atrocities of the ousted regime, instead refocusing the geopolitical spotlight on Vietnam. Abramowitz continued, "From behind the scenes we should encourage the Thais and other like-minded states within the grouping to produce an ASEAN condemnation of Hanoi and its violation of its peaceful intent. We should urge others to contribute to this effort and we must consider whether we want to get others to suspend aid to Vietnam." Notably, Abramowitz saw "no advantage in attempting to preserve a Pol Pot regime in exile and [believed the United States] should therefore refrain from getting involved in a credentials or any other legalistic struggle on its behalf."[37]

Yet the specter of Pol Pot's brutality could not but figure into the geopolitical calculations of the United States and other interested parties. As detailed in a briefing memorandum, U.S. officials concluded, "[The] Vietnamese government will certainly lose no time in reestablishing the façade of Cambodian sovereignty under new management. The latter, to justify itself, will most probably throw part of its energies into exposing the depredations of the Pol Pot government against the Cambodian populace. Both Hanoi and the new Phnom Penh will make reassuring approaches to the ASEAN states about pacific intentions." This placed the United States in a difficult position, for in order to challenge the legitimacy of Vietnam's offensive, it was necessary to deny or dismiss claims of genocide and other crimes against humanity committed by the "obnoxious Pol Pot regime."[38]

Carter's concern with human rights led him to condemn the Khmer Rouge, calling its members the "worst violators of human rights in the world."[39] However, the ousted Pol Pot government was allied with China, which the United States fully supported.[40] To that end, according to Michael Vickery, "concern with human rights or atrocities was of secondary importance to considerations of international power politics; and [while] no one was willing to suddenly declare Pol Pot a bulwark of the Free World against Godless Communism, the atrocities over which he had presided tended to be implicitly forgiven as his role in an anti-Vietnamese coalition was emphasized."[41] As Kenton Clymer reasons, "In all of this, there was almost no thought given to what was best for the Cambodian people—those who had suffered so severely under the Khmer Rouge and who were now (for the most part) free of that scourge."[42]

As the famine unfolded, the United States continued to work the diplomatic front. As counseled by national security adviser Zbigniew Brzezinski, it was necessary to "continue to keep the international heat on Vietnam and to discourage all aid to donors to Vietnam from giving aid until Vietnam withdraws its forces from Cambodia." Furthermore, Brzezinski advised, "[The United States should] indicate to the Chinese that our common approach in the U.N. and our efforts to persuade others not to give aid to Vietnam are proving successful, that we have indicated to the Soviets our expectation that they will not make use of any opportunities to establish military bases in Vietnam, and that Chinese military action against Vietnam would jeopardize the gains we are making in isolating Vietnam in the international community."[43] As Fawthrop and Jarvis conclude, "This meant holding the Cambodian people hostage, sweeping aside all considerations of human rights, the interests of Cambodian survivors and international humanitarian law."[44] In short, the geopolitical calculations of the United States carried a significant necropolitical dimension—the withholding of famine relief from approximately 80 percent of Cambodia's people.

In February 1979 the International Committee of the Red Cross (ICRC) offered medical assistance to the new government in Phnom Penh; the organization was met, however, with stony silence.[45] Distrustful of Western aid agencies, both Vietnamese and PRK officials continued to dismiss reports of famine. Effectively, the Heng Samrin government expressed concern, legitimately so, that international aid and famine relief was being directed toward the border in support of the remnant Khmer Rouge forces. To this end, authorities in Phnom Penh were outspoken in their opposition to any offers proposing relief to the entirety of the country—including the Khmer Rouge sanctuaries along the Thai-Cambodian border. From their vantage point, any assistance to the Khmer Rouge was an implicit recognition and legitimation of the former government. In addition, PRK officials voiced outrage over the military implications. By this point, the Vietnamese had succeeded in isolating and weakening the Khmer Rouge forces; indeed, the Vietnamese military was effectively starving them into either submission or annihilation.[46]

However, as the weeks passed, members of the Heng Samrin government acknowledged that upward of *four million* people would face serious food shortages by the end of the year, and that many parts of the country would lack food entirely.[47] The food provisioning system was effectively broken, and rationing had already been imposed; indeed, with deteriorating health and nutritional conditions, mortality in many places was rising.[48] Subsequently, when representatives of UNICEF and ICRC made a joint appeal to break the impasse, PRK officials allowed a two-person delegation into the country for exploratory talks. Yet no agreement was reached, and famine relief for the Cambodian people remained largely out of reach.

Deteriorating conditions inside Cambodia contributed to ongoing refugee flows to the Thai border, and by June this growing stream became a major concern to the Thai government. Indeed, in an effort to halt the flow, Thailand's military used force to drive tens of thousands of starving Cambodians back into their home country. In response, UNICEF authorized the expenditure of U.S.$200,000 from its Emergency Reserve Fund to purchase food, medical supplies, and material for temporary shelters for the individuals seeking safety along the border. An additional U.S.$60,000 was allocated for relief and rehabilitation of Thai villages evacuated from the border region. It was hoped that Thailand's refugee policies would be more lenient if its government received international support. However, at the end of June, the nation's prime minister, Kriangsak Chomanan, announced the forced repatriation of several thousand Cambodians seeking refuge. This time, UN secretary-general Kurt Waldheim interceded and offered U.S.$500,000 in aid for the exiles.[49] Only then did the Thai government accede to global demands to provide relief along the border.[50]

However, famine aid in the area was slow in coming, and many members of the Khmer Rouge, their dependents, and former base people were starving. Thus, when Khmer Rouge leaders learned of the efforts of UNICEF and ICRC officials to provide relief to Phnom Penh, they protested vehemently.[51] Still claiming to possess the rightful sovereign power of Cambodia, Khmer Rouge officials were adamant that any international assistance to the PRK government would legitimize Vietnam's invasion and occupation of Democratic Kampuchea.

As a result, on July 25, Democratic Kampuchea's permanent representative to the United Nations, Ambassador Thiounn Prasith, denounced the UNICEF offers of aid to the Heng Samrin government. He declared that any relief provided by Western donor states should be directed toward the Khmer Rouge, as the group remained the officially recognized sovereign member of the United Nations. Thiounn Prasith forwarded four reasons supporting this argument: To start, any offer of aid to the PRK constituted an implicit recognition of the illegitimate Heng Samrin regime. Furthermore, support would not be distributed to the starving and malnourished Cambodian children but would instead be used for the benefit of the "aggressors"—the Salvation Front and the Vietnamese army. In addition, the only effective way to provide relief to the children would be to stop Vietnam's "imperial quest for control and extinction of Kampuchea." Finally, the CPK government, as the only legal and legitimate representative of the country, was ready to accept and distribute any aid destined for Cambodia's children.[52]

For their part, international aid agencies understood that geopolitics greatly conditioned their ability to respond to the disparate geographies of famine. Delegates of the ICRC and UNICEF recognized that any chance to provide relief *inside* Cambodia risked their ability to provide relief *along the border*.[53] Likewise, efforts to assist refugees in the Thai-Cambodian borderland precluded attempts to help those under the purview of the PRK government. Overtures to Khmer Rouge leaders along the border and to officials in Phnom Penh entailed political risks, with Cambodians poised to suffer the most. In August, Khmer Rouge officials met with delegates of the ICRC and UNICEF to request the delivery of famine relief to the Thai border areas adjacent to Khmer Rouge populations. A tentative agreement was reached, and both ICRC and UNICEF began limited operations, remaining acutely sensitive to public appearances for fear of upsetting negotiations with the government in Phnom Penh.[54] Sure enough, when delegates of the ICRC met with government officials in Phnom Penh, representatives of both the PRK and Vietnam complained bitterly about the international aid agencies' apparent duplicity. Simply put, the Heng Samrin government would only allow global relief organizations to operate in the PRK if no assistance was given in the border camps.

UNICEF and the ICRC were not the only international agencies involved in famine relief. In August Oxfam dispatched an assessment mission to Phnom Penh, headed by Jim Howard, the association's disaster response coordinator. Howard spent two weeks inside the PRK evaluating conditions in and around the capital and southwest of it. He reported that in the countryside, "the villages all contained starving people," most of whom "couldn't possibly survive more than several months on what they had available."[55] In response, Oxfam organized a multiagency consortium that would eventually comprise twenty-seven agencies providing U.S.$40 million for Cambodian relief.

Unlike officials of the ICRC and UNICEF, Oxfam representatives were willing to accept the conditions imposed by the Cambodian government; they therefore agreed to work only in areas under the Cambodian administration's control.[56] As Charny explains, this decision violated a fundamental principle of humanitarian response, that of impartiality. However, by expressly agreeing to work with only one group of suffering Cambodians, those under the control of the PRK government, Oxfam was making a partisan choice. The first shipments of relief supplies the organization provided to the PRK arrived in October. These included much-needed food and medicine, as well as agricultural goods hand tools, seeds, twine, and spare parts for a fishnet factory in Phnom Penh. According to Charny, "The focus on industries that produced basic goods for agricultural producers and consumers was probably Oxfam's most significant contribution to the early phase of the overall relief and rehabilitation effort."[57]

Oxfam's decision had a ripple effect on international aid agencies—most of the other major organizations, notably the ICRC and UNICEF, were steadfast in their demand to provide aid to the entirety of Cambodia, including the refugee populations in Thailand and along the border. Oxfam's decision, however, was not without merit. According to most estimates, upward of two million people *within* the PRK were at risk of premature death from famine conditions. And the needs of the people remaining inside the country—as opposed to the roughly half a million refugees inside Thailand or along the border—far exceeded the international assistance that was likely to be available to them.[58] Indeed, as Mason and Brown explain, the condition of the Cambodian refugees had shocked the world, as photographs of emaciated and deathly ill exiles were splashed across newspapers. In turn, huge sums of money poured in for their relief, and large numbers of aid personnel arrived at the border to help.[59] No such help was likely forthcoming for the hundreds of thousands, if not millions, of Cambodians wholly dependent on the willingness or capability of the Heng Samrin government. It was all too apparent that the PRK leadership had left the vast majority of Cambodians to solve their own problems.[60]

By September UNICEF/ICRC officials estimated that 80 percent of the children within the PRK were starving.[61] Indeed, in many places, famine conditions under the new government were *worse* than they had been under the

Khmer Rouge. As a result, UNICEF and ICRC decided to downplay their commitment to the principle of aid to both sides of a conflict. The outfits realized that famine relief from other agencies was forthcoming for the refugees in and around the Thai-Cambodian border. However, hardly any assistance was expected for the millions of Cambodians held hostage by Phnom Penh. By mid-October ICRC and UNICEF officials proposed a compromise whereby the bulk of famine relief would be channeled through Phnom Penh, while low-level assistance would be provided along the border. In order to minimize the political consequences, the parties involved agreed not to give interviews or make public statements to the media with respect to border aid. In this way, by maintaining a small relief effort at the border, ICRC and UNICEF would keep their promise of providing "aid to all sides." But by keeping the aid level low and keeping the press quiet, they hoped to convince the PRK government of their commitment to Phnom Penh.[62]

U.S. officials were also confronted with difficult choices. As the months wore on, the Carter administration found itself boxed in by its Janus-faced response to the famine. On the one hand, Cold War ideologues such as Brzezinski continued to push for Vietnam's isolation and the support of Khmer resistance forces against the Heng Samrin government. This meant backing efforts to provide famine relief exclusively to the border. On the other hand, several U.S. officials also worried that humanitarian aid provided to refugees along the Thai-Cambodian border—including sizable numbers of "Pol Pot soldiers"—risked a military response by Vietnam.[63] Ambassador Abramowitz effectively summarized the ongoing dilemma of the Carter administration: "The U.S. wants to get SRV out of Kampuchea, but we find other policy interests and constraints precluding us from trying to do so. We appear contradictory.... We have no significant dialogue with the PRC on their support for Pol Pot, and there is no political solution possible with Pol Pot on the scene. We have generated no focus for pressure toward a political solution.... At the same time we have given not insignificant material aid to the Thais, but our help has been less than spectacular (especially in comparison to the Soviet flood of materials into Vietnam)." Abramowitz added, somewhat despondently, "I assume recognition of Pol Pot is too damaging to our position in the area at this time."[64]

As the humanitarian crisis deepened, a growing number of U.S. politicians pressured the Carter administration to do more to help the refugees. In October, for example, Brzezinski and special representative for economic summits Henry Owen informed Carter of "a growing desire [on behalf of key members of Congress] to see the United States make a generous response." They explained, "We are being asked why Congress had not yet been asked for funds or support."[65] Indeed, following a fact-finding mission to Phnom Penh, Senator John Danforth (R-Mo.) gave a "chilling report" to his colleagues about conditions inside the PRK, recalling that his delegation saw Cambodians "literally dying before [their] eyes."[66] Nevertheless, even with enthusiastic public support for humanitarian aid, just how forthcoming the United States would be about distributing funds within the PRK remained uncertain. As Clymer writes, politics still mattered.[67]

Consequently, in an effort to provide a modicum of famine relief, plans were developed in September to provide for "a one-time airdrop of supplies to needy refugees in Western Kampuchea." However, a plan of this nature "must be weighed against anticipated benefits." As Secretary of Defense Harold Brown explained to Carter, "Such an operation might be misconstrued by [Vietnam] as an effort by the Thais with our connivance (or vice versa) to supply Pol Pot. In that case it might precipitate Vietnamese retaliation in Thailand; and it would probably provoke strong criticism of U.S. actions from international relief agencies; and it might enable Hanoi to shift the focus of international attention away from their genocidal policies to allegations of U.S. intervention in Cambodia."[68] This last concern is particularly noteworthy. Throughout 1979 U.S. officials played up the deleterious conditions within the PRK as supposed evidence of Vietnam's genocidal campaign to exterminate the Khmer. Indeed, as Vickery documents, ongoing CIA efforts were explicitly concocted to "put the pro-Vietnamese Heng Samrin regime in the worst possible light." Ironically, this entailed representing the previous Pol Pot administration as having achieved "steady progress interrupted only by the Vietnamese invasion and the change of regime." Based on this framing, it was because of Vietnamese aggression that "Cambodia was in danger of extinction."[69]

Between November 8 and November 10, First Lady of the United States Rosalynn Carter visited a handful of refugee camps being hastily built along the Thai-Cambodian border. Since mid-October, Thailand had announced a major policy change regarding the Cambodian exiles. For "humanitarian" reasons, officials agreed to accept Cambodians within Thailand's border, but these "refugees" were not granted official refugee status. They were instead called illegal immigrants. In addition, Thai officials agreed to the construction of "holding centers" (as opposed to "refugee camps") by the United Nations High Commission for Refugees (UNHCR).[70] Within days, the Sa Keo holding center was built. As Mason and Brown describe, "No advanced plans or preparations had been made; sufficient construction materials and experienced builders were lacking; no drainage or sewage systems had been planned; no water sources or wells existed. Yet, a small city of small huts and improvised shelters was built for 32,000 refugees in a matter of days. A corps of backpackers, seasoned relief workers, former Peace Corp volunteers, and a host of others pitched in with the dazed Khmer to create an urban haven where before there had been barren rice land."[71]

Following the establishment of the Sa Keo holding center, UNHCR officials were able to better plan and design the construction of subsequent holding centers. A larger camp designated Khao I Dang was soon developed. Unlike Sa Keo, Khao I Dang was an orderly community with latrines, hospitals, feeding centers, a water supply, and a network of laterite roads. Within two months, its population surpassed 150,000.[72] However, tens of thousands of Cambodians continued to live outside any formal camp system. It was among these camps that First Lady Carter witnessed, in her words, "incredible starvation, disease, dislocation and suffering," and "observed overcrowded and humiliating conditions which refugees awaiting final processing for emigration must endure." "The plight of the children is particularly distressing," the First Lady said, also noting that famine relief was desperately needed—and effective. "I held one infant," she elaborated, "who had survived despite malnourishment because aid was available."

However, Mrs. Carter also lamented, "As bleak as these conditions were ... they pale in horror by comparison to those which must be experienced by those still living in Cambodia." Unable to travel within the PRK, the First Lady explained that she "was informed that nearly a quarter of a million [refugees] gathered near Sisophon close to the Thai Border [faced] the most desperate situation." In a plea directed toward the international community, Mrs. Carter declared, "We must not allow others to die because our assistance was either too little or too late."[73]

Faced with mounting pressure, the Carter administration decided to undertake a major effort on behalf of the suffering Cambodians. Apart from U.S.$7 million already authorized, Carter asked Congress to make an additional $30 million available for famine relief. This amount would include $20 million in commodities to Cambodia, $3 million in aid to UNICEF and the ICRC, and another $9 million for Catholic Relief Services and United Nations programs that were assisting Cambodian refugees in Thailand.[74] In turn, however, key U.S. officials—notably Brzezinski and Mondale—hoped to exploit the ongoing humanitarian crisis to their advantage. In December, members of the Carter administration concluded that "the more food [was] getting into Cambodia[,] the less the danger of mass influxes of refugees pouring into Thailand and causing further instability [would be]." On this point, it was agreed that support for anti-Vietnamese resistance groups was desirable, and that support for the growing number of humanitarian-based refugees was not. That said, the highly visible presence along the border of refugees fleeing the PRK government could prove politically invaluable. With this understanding, U.S. officials determined, "More must be done to get food to the Cambodians through all routes, and to dramatize and publicize both those efforts and Vietnamese/Cambodian poor performance in distributing food."

Effectively, the Carter administration countenanced a reversal in policy, concluding that a greater commitment to relief programs could be spun as an explicit condemnation and delegitimation of an incompetent government (the Heng Samrin regime) and its belligerent sponsor (Vietnam). To present that argument, the White House actively sought to increase "food supplies to Cambodia via Thailand and [to find] ways of dramatizing these increases."[75] At this point the geopolitics of U.S. famine relief pivoted from a position of necropolitics to one of biopolitics. The end game, however, remained the same: to isolate and punish Vietnam and, with any luck, facilitate the downfall of the Heng Samrin government.

Having recalibrated their options, the Carter administration forwarded a publicity campaign that accused Vietnam of famine crimes. In November the NSC drafted a militant statement accusing Vietnam of "conducting a war of conquest" in Cambodia with Soviet backing, a war designed "regardless of human cost" to put its "puppet regime" in control "of the entire country." Because they were denying the relief agencies access to hundreds of thousands of Cambodians, the Vietnamese would "carry a heavy burden before history for this callous and inhuman disregard of human life, bringing a new version of genocide to their tragic victims."[76] Effectively, the United States, under Brzezinski's guidance, mounted an international disinformation campaign whereupon the Vietnamese government was accused of waging a war of extermination against the Cambodian people; in the process, the exiled Khmer Rouge was portrayed as an effective anti-Vietnamese fighting force. Within a month, Brzezinski directed the CIA "on an urgent basis" to disseminate as widely as possible reports of Vietnam's alleged "starvation policy."[77]

U.S. intelligence agencies responded quickly to Brzezinski's fictitious "Vietnamese Starvation Policy in Kampuchea." By December 11, according to CIA director Stansfield Turner, fifty stations with media assets or potential media assets had followed through on the national security adviser's directive to "urgently publicize the Vietnamese starvation tactics in Kampuchea." Three stations in East Asia had distributed twenty-four stories and editorials on Vietnam's alleged famine crimes, and a station in Africa placed "an editorial on death and starvation in Kampuchea." According to Turner, a story in a "prestigious newspaper based on a fact sheet sent out some weeks ago" that highlighted "the Vietnamese starvation policy and war of genocide in Kampuchea, as well as the magnitude of Soviet aid to Vietnam," was expected to appear soon. In addition, he noted that "some good film footage of Vietnamese atrocities in Kampuchea" was set to be televised within two weeks.[78]

Although slow in coming, famine relief did begin to arrive both along the Thai border and throughout the PRK. Now, the problem shifted toward distribution. Within the refugee settlements, rice and other commodities often went directly to camp leaders who sold or bartered them, instead of giving them away as donors intended.[79] In addition, the distribution of rice in the border regions encouraged informal trade among the Khmer Rouge, Thai merchants, and even Vietnamese soldiers. By the end of 1979, Gottesman describes, Thai border towns contained huge open-air markets where Cambodians bought dishes, forks and knives, bottles, cloth, string, shoes, matches, candles, alcohol, cigarettes, prescription drugs, cosmetics, radios, cameras, guns, mechanical parts, soap, shampoo, toothpaste, and canned food.[80] All was for sale, to be paid for in rice or gold.

Within the PRK, food and other relief supplies remained largely unavailable to those people most in need. Here, the problem was structural and underscores the cumulative aspect of serial famines. Without a functioning economy, paper currency, or any actual assets, the PRK government had no way of paying its employees. Consequently, government officials were compelled to pay civil servants and military personnel in rice that had been donated as famine relief. In doing so, the PRK administration initiated policies mirroring those of the Khmer Rouge. In Democratic Kampuchea, rice was rationed in an effort to increase exports for capital gain; now, however, imported rice was rationed in order to pay workers. In Phnom Penh, for example, civil servants and their families received allocations of thirteen kilograms for adults, with half that amount for children, in lieu of monthly salaries. Very little food aid was actually distributed to the countryside; and that amount was frequently as meager as it was irregular.[81] Most often, though, relief aid was simply not distributed. Within Phnom Penh, many government officials displayed a combination of indifference and political obstinacy in their inability or unwillingness to redistribute aid. Consequently, food piled up in warehouses as people continued to go hungry.

Reorganization of the Rural Economy

After Cambodia's liberation in January 1979, the first fragile steps were taken in setting up a new government. The new administration faced immense structural constraints given the massive destruction of the country's infrastructure during the civil war (1975-1979), and the subsequent inability and unwillingness of the CPK to make necessary repairs during its reign.[82] The newly installed government was, as Fawthrop and Jarvis describe, "a government that lacked everything."[83] In Phnom Penh, officials "faced monumental shortages of everything from food and shelter, to trained staff, to a simple lack of typewriters and paper. Vietnamese, and later Russian, engineers and plumbers arrived to wrestle with the long-neglected water supply and the power station in an attempt to restore basic services."[84] And beyond Phnom Penh and other provincial towns similarly attempting to recover, residents in the myriad hamlets and villages also tried to retrieve a semblance of their former life—often with little to no assistance from the overburdened government.

Adding to the problems facing the Heng Samrin government was the decision to grant the former Khmer Rouge regime diplomatic recognition by seating it at the UN. This choice had a determining effect on immediate famine relief efforts and the long-term rebuilding of Cambodia. As Orlin Scoville explains, both the ICRC and UN relief agencies could legally provide aid to governments not recognized by the UN only if the purpose was humanitarian relief to suffering people. On that point, there is a continuum from simple relief to development assistance, and establishing guidelines for relief to the PRK was fraught with difficulties. Tractors and bulldozers or animal-breeding programs, for example, were considered developmental aid and could not be sent as contributions from the UN or U.S. sources.[85]

Inside the PRK, these material conditions placed severe constraints on the new leadership. As Quinn-Judge details, the Heng Samrin government, with minimal assistance, had to reorganize a country whose educated population had been decimated. For example, of the 450 medical doctors in Cambodia before 1975, only 45 remained in the country in 1979. Of the estimated 20,000 teachers, only 7,000 could be found. Draft animals had been reduced from 1.2 million head in 1967 to only 768,000 by 1979; those that remained were mostly weakened and diseased. There was no infrastructure to speak of and no currency; nor were there financial institutions, a public transport system, and telephones. Most of the physical infrastructure—the bridges, highways, and railways—was destroyed or so damaged as to be unusable.[86] In addition,

Cambodia's four rice-research stations were completely demolished under the Khmer Rouge, along with records and germplasm collections. Some deep-water rice varieties, traditionally important to areas flooded by the Tonle Sap Lake, were deliberately eliminated during the Pol Pot regime, which thought it unnecessary to grow rice in flooded areas. In addition, as Mysliewic finds, prior to 1976 approximately 1,600 people had been employed in the agricultural sector as planners, technicians, or policy makers; by 1980, only 200 remained, of whom only 10 were university graduates. Only one licensed veterinarian and a handful of veterinary technicians were known to have survived.[87]

International aid donors responded also to the short-term production challenges facing Cambodia's agricultural sector. In 1979–1980, over 1 million hoe heads, 5,000 small irrigation pumps, 1,300 power tillers, 55,000 tons of rice seeds, and many thousands of tons of fertilizer were imported. However, rebuilding efforts would require long-term assistance, including the training of agricultural and veterinary personnel, the repair of irrigation systems, and the development of animal health and vaccination programs. Similarly, resources were needed to restore agriculture-related industries—mainly the production of jute, cotton cloth, and fishnets—and to rebuild industries that could provide other basic necessities, such as soap, textiles, and plastics. In addition, foundries had to be equipped for making agricultural implements and spare parts for machinery; and communication networks had to be completely rehabilitated, roads and bridges repaired, and river transport restored.[88]

Beyond these stopgap measures, the PRK government initiated programs to promote long-term economic stability and turned to the problem of landownership and property rights.[89] In doing so, however, government officials had to walk a fine line. Committed to a socialist economy, state planners in Phnom Penh envisioned a society of cooperatives and collectives. And yet, given the brutality and terror associated with the former CPK government, members of the Heng Samrin administration were sensitive to the trepidation expressed by the Cambodian people.[90] Consequently, the key strategy adopted toward increased food production was the "solidarity group," or *Krom Samaki*.[91]

Under the new government, agricultural land was the property of the state but was distributed to each family within the group according to the number of active laborers. Land was allocated to the solidarity group on the basis of approximately one to two hectares per family, depending on the availability and quality of the property. In key respects, therefore, solidarity groups were built on the traditional system of mutual aid at planting and harvesting time, and they recalled the traditional Khmer tenure system whereby peasants could possess (but not "own") a plot of land simply by working it. This was a crucial consideration, given that records of landownership titles were largely destroyed under the Khmer Rouge. Consequently, solidarity groups enabled a weakened labor force to restore land's productivity to mitigate chronic food shortages, and to facilitate the organization of the rural population for special tasks, including forest clearing, the repair of irrigation systems, and craft production.[92]

The area of land distributed to families depended on both the total land available in any given village and the total number of families. Given that there were no mechanisms of compensation *between* villages, landholdings allocated to families could be very different. In locations of relatively low population densities, families might, on average, receive considerably more land than families of comparable size elsewhere. In addition, the bureaucratic implementation of land reform contributed to inequities in ownership. For example, general rules of distribution were dictated by the central party of the Heng Samrin government but implemented locally by the group chief. This meant, in practice, that the interpretation of rules was contingent on the discretion of the local authorities.[93] Even if land had been redistributed equitably, however, an estimated one-third of the rural families in Cambodia would have been unable to survive as private farmers because of a lack of tools, draft animals, and male workers. Thus, the Krom Samaki system provided many vulnerable households a much-needed safety net, as the introduction of solidarity groups afforded a degree of security especially to widows, orphans, and families lacking labor power.[94]

In practice, agricultural activities, including the preparation of fields and the planting, maintenance, and harvesting, were to be conducted communally. The equipment and draft animals used in this work were either collectively owned, or privately owned but collectively shared with the group. The harvest was collected by the group chief and redistributed to the people according to a system of labor points distinguishing between the main labor force, auxiliary labor, and dependents. Notably, given that tools and draft animals were recognized as privately owned, owners were recompensed for making them available to the collective.[95]

Beyond the redistribution of land during the PRK government, collectivization was in principle to be applied to all means of production, including draft animals and farm equipment. However, as Diepart and Sem detail, due to the de facto reappropriation of animals and tools in 1979, officials were reluctant to confiscate what was already in the hands of the people. Accordingly, the families who could reappropriate cattle received more land than others, in that one buffalo was equivalent to one full active laborer.[96] Notably, the Krom

Samaki was not restricted to farmers' groups; it included all types of production sectors, such as fishing and craftwork.[97] Throughout the 1980s, peasants collectively restored thousands of kilometers of small canals, dikes, and reservoirs, reconstructed several dams, and repaired a number of pumping stations; in doing so, they revived upward of 250,000 hectares of irrigated land to facilitate double-cropping.[98]

In time, many families were able to acquire additional land beyond that allocated to them through the Krom Samaki system. Throughout the 1970s, considerable tracts of land, especially those not conducive to rice production, were abandoned and became overgrown with shrubs. The PRK provided no guidelines for the redistribution of this property, and so appropriation depended either on families' labor capacity and initiative to expand their agricultural holdings, or on families' privileged relationships with the group or village chief.[99] In addition, whenever and wherever possible, Cambodian peasants freely appropriated natural resources from traditional commons—a practice prohibited under the Khmer Rouge. The forests provided wild fruits, vegetables, and game animals; local streams and ponds provided fish and crustaceans.[100]

Remarkably, even in areas not directly under the administration of the Heng Samrin government, villagers organized their food provisioning and distribution systems in ways similar to those initiated and enforced by the Khmer Rouge. As Heder explains, villagers reasoned that "the starvation or sub-starvation communal ration system of the Democratic Kampuchea period was ... after all better than no ration system at all. The Vietnamese and Salvation Front policy of 'solving your rice problem your own way,' which had originally implied family farm self-reliance and meant eating freely what the Democratic Kampuchea cadre would have strictly rationed, now took on a sinister and cynical coloration: it simply meant that the Vietnamese were not going to help you, but would leave you to your own devices in an impossible situation."[101] Thus, it was not that the Cambodian people yearned for a return to Khmer Rouge governance. Rather, a pragmatic calculation that "the use of a universal ration system—however flawed, however inegalitarian, however oppressive—to deal with a situation of famine and political upheaval" was Cambodians' most rational course of action in the short term.

By 1980, there were about eighty thousand farm production groups; but while agricultural productivity steadily increased, so, too, did conflicts within the Krom Samaki system.[102] In areas with low productivity, for example, a directive stipulated that households needed to show solidarity and distribute the harvest equally according to consumption needs. Consequently, as Diepart and Sem explain, in these areas conflicts occurred when hardworking families believed they were working for the benefit of lazy ones. Accordingly, in 1982 the government reorganized the Krom Samaki model to differentiate among three forms of collective organization. Level one comprised the collective organization of the labor force by groups or teams. Farmland was collectively held and worked by small groups of families, and the harvest was divided among the group or team members according to the labor each had provided. In level-two systems, labor remained organized collectively, but the agricultural land was divided into individually held plots and privately farmed. Under this guise, a system of mutual aid organized by the group chief allowed families to manage peak labor needs. Level-three systems were the least collectivized form of Krom Samaki, whereby draft animals and land were allocated to families as private possessions, and each family was permitted to manage its production individually. Any collective activities, such as mutual planting or harvesting practices, were arranged by the families themselves.[103]

Although imperfect, as Diepart and Sem conclude, the contribution of Krom Samaki was far from insignificant. Given the widespread prevalence of famine conditions throughout the PRK, the system allowed a quick recovery of agricultural production in regions heavily destroyed by war or neglected under the Khmer Rouge. As a decentralized mode of production, the Krom Samaki afforded considerable flexibility to identify and adjust land tenure regimes that were socially acceptable and economically sound.[104]

Conclusions

By the end of 1980, international aid, combined with the resilience and resourcefulness of the Kampuchean people, and the prospects of a rice harvest, dispelled the threatening clouds that had hung over the country in 1979.[105] By 1982–1983 famine conditions receded throughout the entirety of Cambodia.[106] However, while famine did not reappear, the possibility of hunger and malnutrition remained. As Jenny Smith explains, even after the harvest and supply crisis of 1979–1980 had passed, the PRK was forced to depend on outside aid for food, other consumer goods, and a variety of heavy industry, especially trucks and construction equipment. Notably, Smith concludes, this was a situation Heng Samrin's government did not create, but also a circumstance officials took few steps to reduce or eradicate.[107]

This is not to say that the PRK government was entirely indifferent to or reckless about the plight of its people. Rather, in many instances, administration officials were mostly unable to provide the means necessary to rebuild the economy and mitigate chronic vulnerabilities to hunger and malnutrition because of outstanding obstacles to international aid. As the Khmer Rouge continued to represent Cambodia at the United Nations—and the Vietnamese remained a pariah in the eyes of the international community—there was only a minimal UN presence within Cambodia to administer emergency relief.[108]

When the food emergency was declared over in 1983, a U.S.-led embargo on development aid was implemented.[109] This meant, in practice, that limited food supplies were permitted to enter Cambodia to meet localized shortages but that the necessary technical and material inputs for rebuilding the shattered country were prohibited.[110] Effectively, the PRK remained starved of key production materials, including irrigation pumps, tractors, shovels, and hoes.[111] Moreover, the international boycott of Heng Samrin's Cambodia was extended to Vietnam, taking the form of an embargo on most multilateral and unilateral development assistance until 1991.[112] Vietnam's international isolation then compounded problems inside the PRK, for the Heng Samrin government was heavily dependent on Vietnam.[113]

Recurrent famine was prevented in Cambodia, but vulnerability to chronic hunger remained, conditioned in part by the deliberate indifference of the international community. Certainly, Cambodia was devastated by the violence enacted by the Khmer Rouge. However, throughout the 1980s the majority of member states of the United Nations allowed the Khmer Rouge to retain its seat at the General Assembly. In doing so, the international community failed to permit development aid to assist in the rebuilding of Cambodia, and thus circumscribed efforts to promote long-term stability. Indeed, the United States—under Presidents Jimmy Carter and Ronald Reagan—would provide political support and material aid, directly and indirectly, to the Khmer Rouge *after the humanitarian crisis had passed.*

Under the pretext of famine relief, U.S. officials not only permitted the Khmer Rouge to use refugee camps in Thailand as a base for its war against the new government in Phnom Penh, but they also helped fund and train the Khmer Rouge guerrilla forces throughout the 1980s.[114] On the one hand, the United States supported the Chinese, who in turn provided weapons and other supplies to the Khmer Rouge. Speaking in 1981, Brzezinski explained, "I encouraged the Chinese to support Pol Pot." The United States, he added, "winked publicly" as China sent arms to the Khmer Rouge.[115] On the other hand, under the guidance of Michael Eiland, working in partnership with the CIA and other intelligence agencies, the United States established the Kampuchea Emergency Group (KEG). With the group's major operations based along the Thai-Cambodian border near the town of Aranyaprathet, U.S. operatives ensured that humanitarian aid went directly to Khmer Rouge enclaves in the refugee camps. Yet the primary objective of the KEG was not to coordinate famine relief for refugees. Instead, the organization focused on gathering intelligence from the hundreds of thousands of Cambodians who had fled to the border with Thailand seeking food, shelter, and news of their relatives. The U.S. refugee assistance program was staffed by a number of intelligence operatives who had long been involved throughout Indochina.[116]

By the end of 1980, note Mason and Brown, the health of the Khmer Rouge had improved, and the group began actively fighting the Vietnamese. Aid organizations considered support for the guerrillas inconsistent with their humanitarian goals and proposed to terminate famine relief to the Khmer Rouge. However, the U.S. government, which by this point was funding the bulk of relief operations in Thailand, insisted that the Khmer Rouge be fed.[117] By 1986, an estimated U.S.$85 million was redirected to the guerrilla forces of Pol Pot.[118] This aid, John Pilger explains, "helped restore the Khmer Rouge to a fighting force, based in Thailand, from which it destabilized Cambodia for more than a decade."[119] Consequently, because of these covert activities, throughout the 1980s U.S. officials routinely rejected efforts to describe the violence enacted by the Khmer Rouge as genocidal. Chinese and U.S. actions facilitated the continuation of the Khmer Rouge insurgency throughout the 1980s and into the 1990s. In turn, the prospect of famine remained ever present, as much-needed international assistance was prevented from reaching the Cambodian people. Effectively, the international community sustained those conditions that made future famines possible—that is, a state-induced condition of potential famine.

EPILOGUE

> We will face more malnutrition and illness.
> —Phat Phalla
>
> We are farmers, but if we don't do farming, what do we have to eat?
> —Laing Thom

Hidden among the gentle hills of Kampot Province, approximately sixty kilometers south of Phnom Penh, one can find an utterly unremarkable earthen structure. Spanning some twelve kilometers in length, fifteen meters in height, and 20 meters in width, what remains of the Koh Sla Dam seems at peace among the short grass and scrub. Crisscrossed by narrow footpaths, the embankment connects myriad stilt houses, rice paddies, and fishponds. Landscapes lie, however, and the stillness of this earthwork conceals a much darker past. Under the vegetation that covers its arched form is a story of pain and suffering. Constructed by forced labor beginning in 1973, Koh Sla Dam is one of thousands of irrigation schemes built under the watchful eye of the Khmer Rouge. Conditions were horrendous, with countless men, women, and children dying of exposure, disease, and starvation. The colonial myth that "no one starves in Cambodia" was put to rest in the graves of millions of Cambodians, and food insecurity for millions of Cambodians remains to the present day.

The Koh Sla Dam remains solidly on the landscape, and for those familiar with its horrific history, it provides a tangible connection to Cambodia's past famines. To walk its length is to be reminded of the draconian policies initiated by the Communist Party of Kampuchea, of the indifference to life evidenced by a governing power that was willing to sacrifice its people in the name of development. The dam *should* also remind us that the policies and programs of the Khmer Rouge did not materialize in a vacuum. The modernist aims of the CPK leadership were not aberrations in the historical transformation of Cambodia's political economy but instead the latest reconfiguration of the country's agrarian foundation. That the actions of the Khmer Rouge occurred within the context of a much wider proximate war fought among several sovereign states is a significant but insufficient factor when interpreting the famines that gripped Cambodia in the 1970s. Indeed, the Koh Sla Dam imparts two key lessons.

First, it is a mistake to interpret Cambodia's famine as *exclusively or even principally* a byproduct of civil war or the Khmer Rouge genocide. That armed conflict disrupted Cambodia's food provisioning systems during the 1970s is not subject to debate. From the sustained aerial bombing campaigns unleashed by the United States, through the mass executions committed by the Khmer Rouge, to the scorched-earth campaigns of the Khmer Rouge in 1979, warfare led to the loss of land under cultivation, the destruction of landesque capital and draft animals, the displacement (and killing) of farm labor, and the breakdown of distribution systems through the destruction of the transportation network. And yet the violence of the Khmer Rouge is only one part of the story. The genocide and famine that marked Democratic Kampuchea were no more foundational than the bombing and denial of aid during the U.S.-supported Lon Nol regime or the UN-supported economic embargoes of the People's Republic of Kampuchea.

Second, it is a mistake to limit our understanding of state-induced famines and famine crimes to the vantage point of the states in which famine occurs. Again, what happened in the 1970s is inseparable from the machinations of the Communist Party of Kampuchea. However, it is mistaken to restrict study of Cambodia's famine to the state-sanctioned policies of the CPK, for the maneuverings of the CPK were themselves inextricable from a broader geopolitics that includes but is not limited to French colonialism and U.S. imperialism. Indeed, the state-induced violence of armed conflict, the deliberate withholding of famine relief, and the imposition of international trade embargoes underscore a more complex geopolitical context that mediated the activities of the Khmer Rouge both prior to and subsequent to the establishment of Democratic Kampuchea.

This is not to excuse the Khmer Rouge or to condone its policies and practices. Rather, it is to call for a more capacious reinterpretation of famine that is inclusive of myriad foreign state actions and inactions that contributed to the violent conditions manifest in Cambodia throughout the 1970s and into the 1980s. Between 1970 and 1975, the United States in particular withheld or manipulated the provision of food for geopolitical concerns that bore minimal relation to the violent conditions experienced by Cambodia's people. Similarly, in 1979 Vietnam, China, and the United States worked to prevent famine relief from reaching selected populations in need of it. Notably, the United Nations—influenced to a considerable degree by the United States—continued to deny adequate resources to the people of Cambodia and thus kept them in a perpetual state of famine vulnerability. On that point, the withholding of food in the form of rations by the Khmer Rouge differs little from the deliberate denial of famine relief during civil war, or the prohibition of imported supplies necessary for the rebuilding of a postgenocide society. In other words, states may and do commit famine crimes through both acts of commission and omission directed toward other states.

Famine in Cambodia was not determined by civil war and genocide; rather, it emanated from myriad geopolitical, biopolitical, and necropolitical practices. In the 1970s these practices coalesced in catastrophic ways, and the social, economic, and political consequences remain, not unlike the remains of Koh Sla Dam. These ruins carry the burden of the dam's past, and the men, women, and children who built it remain buried in its soil. State-induced famine can return to Cambodia not because of any possible return of the Khmer Rouge but precisely and paradoxically because the threat of civil war or foreign aggression is so small. Indeed, the risk of future state-induced famines remains because of the authoritarian character of Cambodian politics and the likelihood that geopolitical, biopolitical, and necropolitical practices can once again coalesce into something unimaginable. And if famine does reappear, it will not appear in the guise of black-clad teenage boys and girls wielding AK-47s. Indeed, state-induced famine need not appear so visibly in the form of carpet bombings, scorched-earth campaigns, and deficient food rations. If state-induced mass starvation does reappear in Cambodia, it is because the geopolitical, biopolitical, and necropolitical practices that make such famishment possible exist, albeit in forms different from those found in the 1970s. It remains the focus of this epilogue to consider how future famines may manifest in Cambodia.

The Politics of Postconflict Cambodia

From 1979 onward the ruling party of the People's Republic of Kampuchea initiated policies that find resonance with previous regimes, from those of the French colonialists through the governments of Sihanouk, Lon Nol, and Pol Pot. As Cambodia is a predominantly agrarian country, rice remains its stalwart crop for economic development. However, the concrete form agriculture assumes is mediated by political processes both internal and external to Cambodia. Throughout the 1980s, the socialist PRK leaned heavily on the Krom Samaki system. In some regions, rice production increased appreciably, and the conditions of acute hunger lessened; overall, however, as Jenny Leigh Smith explains, there remained significant and telling indications that all was not well in the PRK, and that food insecurity might continue to plague the country. During the 1980s, for example, the PRK needed between 900,000 and 1.5 million tons of milled rice to meet basic subsistence years. Yet throughout the decade, annual harvests continually fell short of these goals. Smith details that in no year did the harvest exceed one million tons. In 1982, spring floods destroyed much of the young paddy rice, and droughts in 1985 also contributed to shortfalls. Consequently, the PRK government was routinely asking for food aid to cover harvest deficits and prevent the return of widespread famine.[1]

By the beginning of 1989, Viviane Frings explains, the leaders of the PRK came to admit that the system of landownership they tried to promote did not adequately respond to the economic or social needs of the country. To that end, tentative steps toward land reform, including modifications of the constitution, were introduced. These allowed for a greater privatization of land, thereby serving as an incentive to increase productivity. That said, according to Frings, boosting agricultural production was not the main aim; instead, the principal aim was political.[2]

Here, the geopolitical context is important. The Vietnamese invasion in 1979 realigned forces in the region. Member states of the Association of Southeast Asian Nations (ASEAN), previously most fearful of Chinese expansionism, now joined forces with China and the United States to oppose what they perceived as Vietnamese aggression in the region. To that end, ASEAN both supported efforts to rearm the Khmer Rouge insurgents in their struggle to overthrow the PRK government, and backed U.S.-Chinese efforts to retain the Khmer Rouge as the rightful claimant to Cambodia's seat at the United Nations.

Sensitive to the bad optics of supporting the Khmer Rouge, however, China, the United States, and ASEAN endorsed the formation in 1982 of the Coalition Government of Democratic Kampuchea (CGDK). More performative than substantive, the CGDK was an uneasy alliance composed of the Khmer Rouge and two non-Communist resistance groups opposed to Vietnamese occupation: the United National Front for an Independent, Neutral, Peaceful, and Cooperative Cambodia (FUNCINPEC in its French acronym), which was a royalist grouping led by Prince Norodom Ranariddh, and the Khmer People's National Liberation Front (KPNL). From 1982 until 1991, the CGDK occupied the Cambodian seat at the UN, retained diplomatic missions around the world, controlled some territory in western Cambodia, and successfully prevented international recognition of the People's Revolutionary Party of Kampuchea (renamed the Cambodian People's Party, CPP, in 1991).[3]

For ten years, the pro-Vietnamese government of the PRK and the Khmer Rouge–led insurgents engaged in a low-intensity but no less violent protracted war that, in certain respects, was nothing more than the dying embers of the Cold War. After enduring decades of war and being hamstrung by U.S.-led trade embargoes, Vietnam struggled in its own efforts to rebuild. It was simply unable—and to a degree unwilling—to invest in the military defense and economic development needed in the PRK. In addition, the Soviet Union—Vietnam's primary ally—was itself mired in a disastrous war in Afghanistan, and was in no position to assist either Vietnam or the PRK. On the other hand, neither China nor the United States had any desire to get bogged down in another ground war. They thus maintained their support indirectly, sending material aid to the Khmer Rouge insurgents and providing diplomatic support of the CGDK at the UN. Consequently, without sufficient military support from their principal backers, neither the Khmer Rouge nor the PRK could make substantial progress in defeating the other.

In 1989, with the imminent collapse of the Soviet Union, officials in Hanoi withdrew all Vietnamese forces. With no international backing, the PRK government was forced to negotiate with the CGDK to resolve the military stalemate. Informal talks led to formal negotiations, and a political settlement was reached two years later with the signing of the Paris Peace Accords in 1991. Notably, this agreement mandated the establishment of an interim government, the United Nations Transitional Authority in Cambodia (UNTAC), which was to supervise the Cambodian authorities in four areas of sovereign activity—defense, finance, foreign affairs, and public security.

Indeed, as Jeldres describes, the postconflict reconstruction effort was unprecedented in the UN's history. In concrete terms, the effort involved a U.S.$2 billion budget and the deployment of 16,000 peacekeeping troops, over 3,000 police officers, and 3,000 civilian officials. This massive infusion of money, material, and manpower was intended to verify the complete withdrawal of foreign forces from Cambodia; to supervise and monitor a cease-fire; to canton and disarm the armed forces of the four Cambodian factions; to supervise the detection and removal of the estimated 1 million land mines sowed throughout the country; to coordinate the repatriation of refugees from camps in Thailand; and to foster an environment of respect for human rights. In practice, UNTAC's most notable and contentious achievement was the holding of national elections in 1993 to determine the sovereign leadership of the country.[4]

With a mandate from the Paris Peace Agreements, the UNTAC coordinated and supervised national elections held between May 23 and May 28. In the months leading to the elections, 29 political parties registered to compete during the elections, including the CPP, FUNCINPEC, and the Buddhist Liberal Democratic Party (BLDP). And from the vantage point of the UN, the staging of peaceful and democratic elections was a remarkable success. The UN trained about 50,000 Cambodian poll watchers and established upward of 1,400 polling stations throughout the country. Ultimately, upward of 90 percent of Cambodia's electorate voted. For many observers, however, the elections—and, indeed, the entire UNTAC transitional period—were anything but a "free and fair" democratic process implemented to bring peace and democracy to Cambodia. Instead, as Simon Springer explains, the UNTAC mission effectively solidified and expanded a series of neoliberal reforms initiated by the ruling CPP in the late 1980s.[5]

In response to the emerging sea change in global geopolitics, the Cambodian government introduced a number of economic reforms in 1989: changes to land tenure, tax, and marketing policies; a new investment law designed to attract foreign capital; and a separation of the state from production through the reduction of subsidies and the privatization of state-owned businesses.[6] According to Springer, the timing of these measures was deliberate. The collapse of the Soviet Union and the imminent withdrawal of Vietnamese troops signaled to Cambodian elites that the Communist era had ended, leaving autarky or the free-market economics of the West as the two remaining options.[7] For astute politicians such as Hun Sen, the cultivation of Western international backers was key to retaining power and increasing personal wealth. Thus the UNTAC mission did not end the civil war; nor was its primary objective to promote postconflict justice or reconciliation. Rather, the Paris Peace Agreements and subsequent elections were engineered to restructure the political economy of Cambodia in line with free-market economics.

From the outset of the UNTAC period, the UN and most Western governments favored Hun Sen and the ruling CPP. This support marked a decisive geopolitical shift; no longer was the regime in Phnom Penh viewed as a pariah in the international community. As Springer writes, for the international community, Hun Sen was not required to act democratically as the country emerged from years of isolation under the Khmer Rouge and then as a Vietnamese client state; all that mattered was that his government remained committed to further neoliberalism.[8] To that end, the power grabs of Hun Sen and the CPP were conveniently overlooked in the months leading up to the elections. To begin, the campaign was marred by assassinations, harassment, intimidation, and general violence; and while the CPP did not have a monopoly on violence, it was well positioned to benefit the most.[9] This followed from the failure of UNTAC to disarm the warring factions, including the Khmer Rouge.

Initially, the Khmer Rouge was a signatory of the peace agreements. However, Khmer Rouge leaders soon rejected the plan and resumed guerrilla activities when they realized that they would be unable to attain political power through democratic means. Consequently, the Khmer Rouge refused to disarm, and other factions, including the CPP, refused to disarm in turn. Failed disarmament subsequently had detrimental effects on the creation of a neutral political environment, as the continued strength of the military, and its control by the CPP, made it impossible to disentangle CPP from the state apparatus.[10] The CPP did everything it could to sabotage the attempt to enforce democratic political and judicial reforms, strengthening its grasp on the population by reorienting state administrative structures to party-building tasks.[11] Indeed, the party-state apparatus of the Hun Sen regime, which controlled the largest swath of territory and the most extensive set of administrative structures, enjoyed a huge unfair advantage stemming from its near-total control of the media.

Despite the violence, intimidation, and fraud committed by the CPP, the elections brought about a surprising victory for FUNCINPEC. Consequently, the CPP again turned to force and fraud in an effort to overturn the election results and remain in power. Refusing to accept the outcome, the CPP threatened the secession of all lands east of the Mekong River and the resumption of civil war. The UN, for its part, had declared the elections "free and fair" yet soon capitulated to the strong-arm tactics of the CPP. On this point, UN representatives underscored their inability to confront the CPP militarily and hope to avert civil war, thus upsetting the peace process.

Springer forwards a more skeptical view for the UN's unwillingness to challenge the CPP's refusal to accept the outcome. Given the neoliberal imperative of the UNTAC process, Springer suggests, the mission can be interpreted as an exercise in realpolitik intended to confer legitimacy on Hun Sen's regime, as CPP offered the best prospect for electoral victory. More importantly, the party offered the best prospect for market security.[12] From this vantage point, the surprise victory of FUNCINPEC threatened to overturn broader economic reforms that were years in the planning. As Springer concludes, "FUNCINPEC could not offer the same degree of political-cum-economic stability, and accordingly the will of the Cambodian people was disrespected in favor of an authoritarian regime seen as the best chance of both commitment to, and capacity for, neoliberalizing Cambodia."[13]

In the aftermath of the elections, and with UN approval, FUNCINPEC and the CPP formed a coalition led by Randariddh and Hun Sen as co–prime ministers. The political amalgam was fraught from the beginning, and it not unexpectedly ended with the usurpation of power by Hun Sen and the CPP in 1997. From that point onward, Cambodia has been locked in the grips of an authoritarian state that routinely places its own power and prestige over the needs of the Cambodian people.

According to Croissant and Lorenz, the long-term control of the CPP rests on four pillars. The first is the CPP's firm command over the electoral process, from the preparation of the polls to the postelection phase. Second, the ruling party uses its control over the state apparatuses to co-opt strategic groups, such as the business sector, into the regime coalition by allocating posts and material and immaterial rewards in exchange for loyalty. Effectively, the CPP functions as a kleptocracy, where "legitimacy" and "power" are conferred and disbursed through partisan control of the military, a quasi-legal framework with a thoroughly corrupt judiciary, and a complex system of patronage extending to the lowest levels of government.[14] That said, this system of patronage depends on profits from the extraction of rural resources; state officials and the business elite are given access to lucrative contracts, such as Economic Land Concessions (ELCs) and logging and mining licenses, in exchange for their loyalty. In the process, rural areas are rendered as "sacrifice zones" for the enrichment of the elite.[15]

Notably, there is a substantial geopolitical component to this second pillar. As Caroline Hughes points out, since the arrival of UNTAC, the donors, international organizations, and international nongovernmental organizations have had a major impact on Cambodian politics. Hughes explains that international actors, operating in conjunction with Cambodia's elite, have focused on the promotion of stability rather than the empowerment of the poor. This emphasis emerges from neoliberal approaches favored by dominant actors in the international system, including the World Bank and the International Monetary Fund. More precisely, these actors forward an agenda of so-called poverty reduction and economic progress, both concepts predicated on a model that regards economic growth as the key to development. In practice, this approach guarantees stability for capital accumulation and the deepening of patron-client relations that suffuse Cambodian economics and politics. Indeed, as Springer highlights, the limited state provisions and benefits of development that do trickle down to rural areas are not considered as sourced from the state. Instead, they are deemed benevolent favors extended by Hun Sen personally and the CPP more generally.[16]

A third pillar of CPP control is direct violence, as co-optation and personalization are mediated by the brutal suppression of opposition politicians, journalists, and activists. Indeed, conditions of patronage engender considerable violence, as those Cambodians without its protections are frequently forcibly removed from their lands when and where speculation determines a monetary value. In turn, those individuals who speak out against the deleterious effects of widespread dispossession and displacement are met with arbitrary arrest, detainment, and even murder.[17] This circumstance quite literally bleeds into the fourth pillar, whereby the regime attempts to legitimate its claim to power to both its citizens and the international community. On the one hand, Hun Sen stylizes himself as the only person able to guarantee economic development and social peace. Here, Hun Sen frequently invokes the specter of the Khmer Rouge, promoting himself as the best hope to prevent the return of material deprivation and armed conflict. On the other hand, combining democratic forms with autocratic substance and playing the game of free-but-unfair multiparty elections legitimates the regime vis-à-vis international donors and Western governments.[18]

The current Cambodian state is a state indifferent to the needs of its people. The biopolitics of providing the basic material necessities that make life possible are routinely, expressly, and purposefully cast aside in order to accumulate power and prestige. Central to the current political dominance of the ruling CPP is its ability to maintain a strong patronage network. This system's monopoly over the national and local state apparatuses allows it to command patronage-based loyalty through the allocation of resources, government positions, and lucrative business licenses to key segments of the political, military, and business elite.[19] The embeddedness of these elements prevents democracy from consolidating. As Kheang Un explains, consolidation requires the establishment and strengthening of myriad "accountability" institutions, notably anticorruption laws and bodies, an independent and effective judicial system, and civil-society organizations such as a free press.[20] Without these safeguards, Cambodia's kleptocracy will continue to precipitously increase the vulnerability of the country's marginalized citizens, exposing them to greater corruption, coercion, and violence.

The international community not only turns a blind eye to the corruption and violence sutured into Cambodia's political economy, but it also tacitly approves of such actions. This circumstance only compounds the desperate plight of Cambodia's populace. As Springer notes, although the country's donor community is very vocal about democracy promotion, it generally accepts the perceived need for "order" and "security" at face value. This is precisely because the donor community shares the same concern with order as necessary for promoting economic liberalism. That is to say, the international community in general welcomes the authoritarianism of the Cambodian state, for the "periodic lamentations of donors represent a convenient political tool, as they encourage us to focus our view inward on Cambodia's democratic shortcomings."[21] Through political inaction, sovereign states and international donors habitually condone the Cambodian state's imposition of violent conditions that provide context for land grabs and forced evictions.

For heuristic purposes, we can presuppose that sovereign states under the current world order are obliged to promote positive and negative rights. Positive rights permit or compel action, whereas negative rights permit or compel inaction. To promote positive rights is to actively intervene, to create those conditions that allow people to participate fully in society. To promote negative rights, conversely, is to ensure that people are not denied the right to participate within society. For a state to provide food—a positive right—requires many material resources and many different types of policy interventions, all oriented toward the establishment of food provision systems and related distribution systems. However, the state's obligation to protect access to food is partly a negative right, in that it requires that the state not prevent its citizens from accessing food that is otherwise available to them.[22] From this vantage point, the imposition of political and economic reforms, including land grabs and other practices of displacement and dispossession, constitutes failure on the part of the sovereign state to ensure people's ability to secure adequate food. This allows for a more capacious understanding of famine crimes.

State-induced famines may result from the deliberate and intentional disruption of food provisioning systems and the withholding of famine relief. This is most readily understood in the context of armed conflict, whereby food is weaponized in an effort to subjugate an enemy population. State-induced famines may also result from the indifference or incompetence of a government. In this situation people have little access to adequate and sufficient food, although the government's principal motive is not to disrupt the food provisioning system. And it is this form of state-induced mass starvation that is most likely to occur in Cambodia in the near future. In the following section, I broadly chart the coordinates of such an occurrence, with a focus on two development-mediated forms of possible state-induced famines: land grabs and hydropower development.

Necropolitical Land Grabs as Precursor to State-Induced Famines

The term "global land grab" is a well-known catchphrase denoting the contemporary phenomenon of transnational commercial land investments involving the production and selling of food, biofuels, mining activities, and conservation programs.[23] Conceptually, land grabbing refers to a process variously termed "primitive accumulation" or "accumulation by dispossession." As Derek Hall explains, there are substantial tensions and ambiguities over the meaning(s) of both primitive accumulation and accumulation by dispossession; and the terms are used to mean quite different things.[24] For my present purposes, however, I follow Wendy Wolford and others and use the terms interchangeably in reference to those processes "whereby direct producers [are] separated from the means of production, common property rights [are] privatized and non-capitalist modes of production [are] either harnessed or destroyed."[25] This definition, however, risks overshadowing the more salient point underscored by Fred Magdoff: in human terms, land grabs mean real people and families are dispossessed. Simply put, when people lose access to their land, they often lose their means to obtain food.[26]

Land grabbing and dispossession involve a range of actors, including those benefiting from the change of land access and use, and those affected by it, regulating it, and supporting or challenging it.[27] However, the role of the sovereign state is necessarily at the core of global land grabs.[28] For Philip Hirsch, states play a role in dispossession in three main ways. First, the state claims ownership of, or rights to manage, large portions of territory. Second, some land is repossessed under the principle of eminent domain—that is, land reclaimed because it is needed for the wider public good. Third, myriad apparatuses of the state are responsible for the actual transfer of ownership and the subsequent dispossession of communities.[29] The centrality of the sovereign state, we will see, mediates the possibility of state-induced famines through accumulation by dispossession.

To further clarify the role of the sovereign state in land grabs, Wolford and her coauthors forward four key arguments. To begin, states are not simply passive victims in these social and structural arrangements; they are not necessarily coerced into accessing foreign capital by selling off pieces of their territory to more powerful economic or political players. Instead, states are often active, calculative partners in land deals, negotiating the costs and benefits in order to maximize returns on what are considered marginal lands or marginal communities.[30] This is not to discount the very real inequalities between sovereign states but rather to underscore the complexities of decision-making within the global economy. In an approach similar to our broader conceptualization of state-induced famines, it is necessary take seriously the intricate ways in which geopolitical relations mediate how sovereign states provide or deny the availability and accessibility of food and other necessary resources.

Second, states do not divide neatly into those acquiring land and those "giving up" land.[31] In other words, it is too simplistic to conclude that *a priori* state actions are coherent and unified. Composed of myriad actors, often with contradictory and conflicting agendas, the sovereign state is more appropriately understood as a site of contestation. This is to say, different groups and representatives may either work together on or compete over land deals. In part, this dynamic stems from state efforts to satisfy two often contradictory objectives—namely, the accumulation of capital and the legitimacy of rule.[32] Third, sovereign states are not static in their responses to land grabs and dispossessions.[33] For example, some of them may initially support such processes but later impose more stringent regulations to temper the deleterious effects of displacement. Conversely, states may embrace large-scale land deals and harshly quell any attempt to regulate or challenge such arrangements. Notably, the pendulum swings of state support for land grabs may be in response to the aforementioned contradictory goals of accumulation and legitimacy.

Fourth, it is important to highlight the different forms of power available to the sovereign state: for example, the police, the courts, and various "shadowy elements," including paramilitary forces, militias, or criminal syndicates.[34] These latter elements are particularly important when land grabs include illegal activities, such as poaching or illegal logging. Overall, the myriad legal, quasi-legal, and illegal forms of power at the disposal of the state can be, and frequently are, deployed in response to challenges put forward by those adversely harmed by land grabs.

Global land grabs located in or facilitated by sovereign states have increased precipitously in recent decades.[35] That said, the acquisition and control of land and resources by central authorities, including but not limited to states, has a long history. Examples include royal appropriations of timber and game on private and communal lands, allocation of lands to commodity producers in the colonial era, and postcolonial land reforms.[36] The current global "rush" for large-scale land deals is motivated by the combined effects of global climate change, agro-industrial development, natural-resource extraction, neoliberal austerity policies, and rapid urbanization.[37]

The increase in land grabs in Cambodia is part of a broader embrace of capitalism since the early 1990s, motivated by the neoliberal agendas of international donor agencies and of the country's ruling elite. However, as Alice Beban and Courtney Work rightfully argue, more frequent dispossession also is part of a longer history of vast social, economic, and environmental destruction.[38] caused by years of "progress" and conflict, initiated under French colonial authorities and maintained in different guises under the regimes of Sihanouk, Lon Nol, Pol Pot, Heng Samrin, and Hun Sen. In other words, the past century has witnessed a steady deterioration in the economic and political security of most of Cambodia's population, spurred in large part by the ongoing displacement and dispossession of individuals and communities because of uncontrolled land grabs.[39] Related to this point, the famines that affected Cambodia in the 1970s occurred within a longer historical arc of agrarian and land-use changes set in motion decades earlier. Cambodia's contemporary political-economic regime and development of a concession economy are in this way properly tied to the country's postsocialist, postwar trajectory of a state-managed transition to capitalism. Even so, these efforts must also be seen as an attempt to restart the earlier land reform efforts of both the colonial and Sihanouk regimes.[40] Indeed, existing programs forwarded by the Hun Sen regime build on those policies initiated by the CPK and continued by the PRK regime; but these measures were enacted largely in response to structural changes introduced by the French.

In the early 1990s, large-scale acquisition of forestlands and resources took place through the forest concession system. A law passed in 1992 stipulated that all land belonged to the state and that all Cambodians had possession rights; however, the act was in key respects ambiguous. On the one hand, it prohibited the private ownership of agricultural land. On the other hand, though, it established the conditions for someone with a possession certificate to become the actual owner of the property. In doing so, the law failed to reconcile three disparate landownership systems inherited from the past: the traditional acquisition "by the plough," private ownership initiated by the French, and state ownership introduced under the CPK and PRK governments.[41] Consequently, the law facilitated the large-scale seizure of land and the subsequent dispossession of peasant families.

In the context of postwar struggles between different political factions, the CPP effectively used Cambodia's natural resources—including land—to create a patronage network traversing the party and state apparatus.[42] During this period, Cambodia exported an estimated U.S.$2.5 billion worth of timber, which at one point accounted for about 43 percent of the country's export earnings. This recomposed concession system, based on resources extraction, benefited from strong support from international organizations, namely the World Bank. It also became the main tenure system for natural-resources management in Cambodia throughout the 1990s.[43] Concurrently, the CPP was able to consolidate its dominant position by drawing the wealthy business community into its patrimonial networks, and by strengthening relations with powerful provincial families and military commanders.[44]

These early land concessions contributed to massive and illicit acquisitions in Cambodia and to the de facto privatization of state resources. The corollary, however, was a decrease in access to the common-pool resources, which had a profoundly negative impact on rural livelihoods and contributed to the vulnerability of the peasantry. Materially, private enclosures of the commons—resultant from land concessions—constrained the everyday production strategies of those farmers who depended most on common-pool resources to compensate for low rice production. In turn, the decline in common-pool resources placed additional strain on rice production, for a series of bad harvests could portend mass starvation.[45]

Under pressure from international donors, notably the Asian Development Bank, in 2001 the Cambodian government passed a new law establishing a relatively comprehensive legal framework for land tenure and administration. The 2001 Land Law also introduced a number of significant reforms that effectively increased commercial pressure on land speculation and acquisition.[46] In concrete terms, the legislation formalized the procedures to grant concessions for social and economic purposes; particularly important were Economic Land Concessions (ELCs), long-term leases allowing the beneficiary to clear land in order to develop industrial agriculture.[47]

At first blush, the 2001 Land Law appears as a biopolitical imperative, a concerted effort to liberalize the food provisioning systems and thus secure the condition to "make life" possible through the reduction of future famines. To achieve this goal, ELCs have been granted across Cambodia for various agro-industrial purposes, including raising animals, building agricultural processing plants, and establishing plantations for the cultivation of monocultural crops, including rubber, sugar, cassava, palm, cashews, teak, and acacia.[48] In practice, however, the 2001 Land Law solidified further the "violent accumulation" of wealth, power, and prestige for Cambodia's elites.[49] Crucially, the statute mandated that people who were unable to prove that they had worked their land for five years could be evicted—in order that more "productive uses" of the land be developed.

Indeed, according to Pou Sovachana and Paul Chambers, land developers possessed enormous advantages over poor farmers whose right to till their holdings could be legally disputed. Facilitated by greater education, better finance, a partisan judicial system, beneficial corruption, and advantageous connections to senior CPP officials, these entrepreneurs were able to secure the necessary documentation to obtain titles for land speculation, acquisition, and development.[50] To this end, granting concessions for agribusiness, resource extraction, and urban development projects has been, and continues to be, an important part of building and maintaining relationships with powerful actors. In turn, such influential individuals have an interest in maintaining existing power arrangements.[51] It should not go unmentioned that these practices continue the extractive politics of the Khmer Rouge insurgents who, throughout the 1980s and 1990s, generated revenue primarily through granting concessions to Thai interests for the exploitation of timber and gems.[52]

Since the passage of the 2001 Land Law, the territory domestic and foreign corporations acquire through land concessions has increased immensely. According to government sources, by 2014 a total of 122 companies had been granted ELCs covering a total land area of 1.3 million hectares; nongovernment organizations, however, place the figure at more than 2 million hectares. The discrepancies result in part from the charge that many concessions have been granted in violation of the law. For example, a number of concessionaires who have used the grants to cut trees have failed to cultivate the land, or encroached on land beyond concession boundaries, or left parts of the concession vacant in order to sell to third parties. In addition, a large number of ELCs have been linked to serious land conflicts, destruction of indigenous community land, and blocking access to natural resources for use by local communities.[53]

In sociospatial terms, Cambodia's land-grabbing policies have contributed to severely unequal land concentration and a consequent increase in landlessness and poverty. Within ten years of the passage of the 2001 Land Law, as much as 30 percent of Cambodia's land was owned by only 1 percent of the population; moreover, around 60 percent of the country's arable land was held under concessions. At the same time, 29 percent of rural households were recorded as landless, while 27 percent owned less than one hectare.[54] The benefits of Economic Land Concessions promised by the government, such as job creation, poverty reduction, and improved welfare, have not materialized; nor were they ever really intended to.

Agriculture remains a central pillar of the Cambodian economy, accounting for more than a third of the country's gross domestic product. And while the agrarian contribution to the national economy has decreased in recent years, it still provides the main source of employment for a majority of the total labor force. Indeed, while only about half of Cambodia's sixteen million people are engaged full time in agriculture, upward of 85 percent of Cambodian households participate in some form of agricultural activities.

Landholdings are relatively small; the average farming household owns just 1.6 hectares of agricultural land. Consequently, many rural households rely on other types of economic activities, including access to common-pool resources, wage labor, and self-employed nonfarm jobs. That said, many of Cambodia's rural households are impoverished, with almost three million people classified "poor" and an additional eight million considered "near poor." Demographic pressures contribute to economic precarity. With an estimated 220,000 to 300,000 new entrants to the labor force each year, the agricultural sector is no longer able to absorb farmworkers. Given these trends, the rising incidence of landlessness and land concentration, as well as the decline in landholding size per household, portends serious challenges in the coming years.[55] Given these trends, the rising incidence of landlessness and land concentration, as well as the decline in landholding size per household, portends serious challenges in the coming years.

Since 2000, approximately 850,000 people, or 6 percent of Cambodia's population, have been adversely affected by land conflicts, often in violent circumstances. Through displacement and dispossession, people are left bereft of sustenance and livelihood, with little or no compensation.[56] Indeed, land grabs have greatly decreased many rural Cambodians' food security. In the absence of government assistance, their plight foreshadows the prospect of mass starvation. However, given the willful disregard of abuses perpetrated in the name of "development," it is highly doubtful relief will be forthcoming when needed. Bluntly stated, the government is committed to permitting domestic and foreign corporations, often backed with foreign investment, to profit from seizing land for minimal cost, and with minimal regard for the rights of the poor who rely on it for their homes, livelihoods, and survival.[57] State-induced famines need not occur in the context of armed conflict; and the crime of starvation can arise through necropolitical negligence when the accumulation of capital takes precedence over social justice.

This is not to say that rural people have remained passive. Indeed, as Alice Beban, Sokbunthoeun So, and Kheang Un report, people have responded to the spread of land concessions and elite land capture with grassroots resistance, increasingly using translocal mobilization to bring together community activities and domestic and international nongovernmental organizations.[58] Struggle, though, is dialectic, and the ruling state has responded in kind, often violently.[59] That said, the fact remains that rural households dispossessed by land concessions have been forced to find alternative income sources and encroach on marginal lands.⁶⁰ For Arnim Scheidel and his coauthors, this constitutes a process of "increased livelihood diversification *by necessity*" that may become a central feature of Cambodia's rural economy in the coming years. Simply put, for Cambodia's rural families, lacking access to land not only decreases food security and farm-income generation, but it may also simultaneously increase expenditures due to growing dependency on food from the market. Accordingly, land-poor households face a potential lack of access to food and income in the short term, as well as a lack of productive resources and an ability to sustain stable livelihoods over the long term.⁶¹ To the extent that the Cambodian state remains indifferent to the growing desperation of its citizenry, there exists the all-too-real likelihood of future mass starvations.

Under the CPP, land reform has never been biopolitical in the sense of truly providing for the people of Cambodia. Indeed, the CPP has capitalized on its hegemonic position to further consolidate its power and to accumulate wealth for Cambodia's elite. Effectively, the party has proved more than willing to subject its citizenry to a precarious existence, including the vulnerability to premature death. Andrew Cock is blunt in his assessment: "The Cambodian state is a set of predatory mechanisms for the private exploitation and accumulation of the country's human, natural and financial resources. The discriminatory enforcement of laws and regulations, discretionary provision of monopoly franchise, concessions and contracts, and the diversionary collection of public revenues and disbursement of state lands, funds and employment have served as essential instruments of this state-based predation."⁶² To that end, economic development under CPP-controlled Cambodia remains necropolitical in concrete form.

Hydro-Necropolitics as Precursor to State-Induced Famines

The possibility of famine in Cambodia is conditioned also by the ongoing transformation of the county's socionatural processes, notably the violence being done to the Mekong River and its tributaries. The Mekong is a transboundary river whose main stem and extensive network of tributaries support the livelihoods of tens of millions of people in China, Myanmar, Laos, Thailand, Cambodia, and Vietnam.⁶³ From its source in the Tibetan Plateau, the Mekong River courses nearly 3,000 miles through six countries before entering the South China Sea. With a catchment area of approximately 307,000 square miles, the Mekong Basin is slightly larger than the country of Turkey. Ranked by mean annual flow, the Mekong ranks tenth among the world's great rivers.

The Greater Mekong Basin can be divided into two main parts: the Upper Basin in China (where the river is called the Lancang Jiang), and the Lower Mekong Basin stretching from Yunnan Province downstream to the South China Sea. The Upper Basin makes up 24 percent of the total catchment area of the Mekong and contributes 15 to 20 percent of the water that flows into the Mekong River. Known as the Yunnan Component, this volume of water plays an important role in the low-flow hydrology of the lower mainstream during the dry season. Indeed, as far south as Kratie, the Yunnan Component accounts for almost 30 percent of the average dry-season flow. The Upper Basin is also important for its contribution to the overall sediment load of the Mekong. In this region, the topography is steep and rugged; tributaries are short and narrow. Consequently, soil erosion is significant, and approximately 50 percent of the sediment in the Lower Mekong comes from the Upper Basin.[64]

By the time the Lancang reaches southern Yunnan's border with Laos, having dropped some fifteen thousand feet in elevation, the Mekong enters the Lower Basin, where it is joined by several major tributaries. These systems are frequently classified as either tributaries that contribute to the major wet-season flows, or tributaries that drain low-relief regions of lower amounts of rainfall. The rivers in the first group, notably the Nam Khan, Tha, and Nam Ou, drain the high-rainfall areas of Laos, while those in the second group, including the Mun and Chi Rivers, drain the low-relief areas of much of northeast Thailand.[65]

The Mekong enters Cambodia at the Khone Falls, a series of falls and rapids that are impressive not for their height but rather their width. Indeed, the mainstream divides into seven main sections, making the Khone Falls the widest in the world. By this point, as the Mekong enters Cambodia, over 95 percent of the flows have already joined it. The main hydrological components to the Mekong inside the country originate from the Se Kong, Se San, and Sre Pok catchments. Combined, these rivers make up the largest hydrological subcomponent of the Lower Basin, accounting for over 25 percent of the mean annual flow volume at Kratie.[66] Downstream of Kratie, at Phnom Penh, the reach includes the hydraulic complexities of the Cambodian floodplain, the Tonle Sap River, and the Tonle Sap (or Great Lake). Phnom Penh also marks the beginning of the delta system of the Mekong River as the river bifurcates, with the Bassac River separating from the mainstream. From here, the Mekong and Bassac Rivers further divide into a complex, increasingly controlled, artificial system of branches and canals in southern Vietnam.[67]

At the confluence of the Mekong and the Tonle Sap Rivers, key conditions of hydrology shift from an accounting of water discharge to the assessment of water level, overbank storage and flooding, and the hydrodynamics that determine the timing, duration, and volume of the seasonal flow reversal into and out of the Great Lake.[68] As indicated in chapter 1, the Tonle Sap is the largest body of fresh water in Southeast Asia and forms a key part of the Mekong hydrological system. Differences between the water levels in the Great Lake and the Mekong account for the seasonal reversal of the Tonle Sap River and the cyclical flooding of Cambodia's central plain. During the flood months, usually beginning around May, water flows up the Tonle Sap from the Mekong River into the lake; in late September, as the water level in the mainstream subsides, water flows out of the lake and back into the Mekong. On average, the reversal lasts 120 days and sends upward of 10 cubic miles of water flooding into the lake.[69] Consequently, the mean surface area of the Great Lake varies from approximately 1,300 square miles during the dry months (January to May) to upward of 6,000 square miles during the rainy season. Likewise, the mean depth of the lake changes throughout the year, from a low of about 1–2 feet to a maximum of nearly 30 feet. As such, the amount of water stored in the lake changes seasonally, ranging from 0.5 cubic mile to 20 cubic miles.[70]

The Tonle Sap River and Great Lake System represents one of the world's most productive ecosystems. However, this high biological productivity depends on the transfer of floodwater from the Mekong during the wet season. On this point, the lake retains about 80 percent of the sediment and nutrients carried into it by the flow reversal, and this annual natural fertilization of the floodplains has been—and remains—a key factor in thousands of years of successful wet rice cultivation. In addition, the flooding of vast tracts of forest provides an abundant food source for fish. Indeed, this river-lake system supports the world's largest freshwater fishery and directly or indirectly provides a livelihood for most of Cambodia's population.[71] Indeed, farmers and fishers of Cambodia have developed cultural and economic practices based on the Mekong River's dependable dry- and wet-season patterns, as well as the aquatic species that have adapted to the river pulse and the unique habitats it spawns.[72]

Cambodia's unique flood-pulse system, however, is under threat, in large part because of global climate change. Temperatures recorded in the country have increased appreciably, and precipitation events have departed substantially from long-standing patterns. Overall, the immediate impact for Cambodia's millions of smallholder farmers and fishers is an increase in extreme weather events, notably floods and droughts, and more erratic patterns of weather in general.[73] For example, climate data indicates that the long-standing bimodal pattern of rainfall, with peaks in July and September, is increasingly becoming monomodal, with a single peak in September. This poses considerable problems. For farmers who rely exclusively on rainfall, the shift toward a monomodal precipitation pattern severely limits the scope for double-cropping, thus greatly diminishing overall annual harvests.[74]

Yet climate change is not the only threat to Cambodia's rural farmers and fishers who depend on the falling rain and flowing rivers. Indeed, while the climate crisis intensifies food insecurities in the country, scientists have been sounding alarm bells for decades. The greatest threat arises from the environmental degradation of the Mekong, born of large-scale hydropower development programs that now encompass the entirety of the river and its tributaries. Indeed, this is not a new threat; efforts to harness the Mekong have ebbed and flowed throughout the twentieth century. What is new is the scale and scope of current plans, as hydropower development schemes have been folded into the violent accumulation strategies of neoliberalism. Concerns about dams blocking annual upstream fish migration, submerging critical fisheries' breeding habitats, and changing the flood pulse that supplies nutrients and sediments into the Tonle Sap are critical issues that underpin the very real threat of future famines.[75]

Regional plans for the harnessing of the Mekong River are geopolitical in origin, derived from Cold War ideologies and modernist development thinking. In 1957, the Mekong Committee was established under the auspices of the United Nations; in actuality, it operated under the patronage of the United States. As Philip Hirsch explains, during the Cold War the United States initiated an ambitious development plan to impound the Mekong River into a stepped series of lakes stretching from northern Laos to the head of the delta in central Cambodia. These plans were part of an even broader geopolitical project to preempt Communism and enhance American influence in Cambodia, Laos, South Vietnam, and Thailand through economic growth.[76]

In the main, the grandiose schemes of the United States failed to materialize, as the conflict around the Second Indochina War precluded any large-scale investment or construction.[77] That said, limited development did occur, with both Thailand and Laos constructing dams along key tributaries of the main river in the 1960s and early 1970s. In 1966, the Nam Pung Dam was built in northeastern Thailand, followed by the Nam Pong Dam, the Ubol Ratana Dam, and the Lam Pao Dam. The first large dam in Laos, the Nam Ngum Dam, was completed in 1971. However, with the deepening armed conflict throughout Vietnam, Laos, and Cambodia, hydropower dam development halted, only to resume in earnest in the 1990s.[78] Indeed, the ending of the Cambodian conflict with the signing of the Paris Peace Accords in 1991 helped facilitate the transformation of the region from "battlefield" into "marketplace."[79]

Construction of the Pak Mun Dam, located on the Mun River, the most important Mekong tributary in Thailand, began in 1990. The government of Thailand also started developing other medium and large irrigation dams associated with the Khong-Chi-Mun Scheme, a development project designed to promote irrigated agriculture by withdrawing water from the main channel of the Mekong River.[80] In Laos, construction began on multiple dams, including the Houay Ho Dam and the Theun-Hinboun Dam. Vietnam joined the development onslaught when it began construction on the Yali Falls Dams. In 1992, China commissioned the Manwan Dam, the first of six large hydropower dams built on the Lancang.[81] Following a brief hiatus in dam construction triggered by the 1998–1999 Asian financial crisis and a subsequent decline in market demand for hydropower energy in the 2000s, hydro-development projects resumed with alacrity in the 2010s. In Laos, for example, sixty-one hydropower dams were in operation by 2019, with an additional thirty-six dams either planned or under construction.[82]

China has continued its development along the Lancang. Indeed, according to Carl Middleton and Jeremy Allouche, China's construction on the Lancang River has largely heralded a new era of regional hydropolitics. These dams, together with dam construction on the Lower Mekong mainstream and tributaries, are rapidly and irrevocably transforming the river's hydrology and ecology, resulting in severe implications for rural livelihoods.[83] As of 2020, there were eleven dams on the Upper Mekong, two on the Lower Mekong, and more than one hundred on the Lower Mekong's tributaries; in addition, more than two hundred dams were either planned or under construction (figure 7). Already, these structures have reduced the downstream flow, blocked the pathways of migratory fish, and prevented the invaluable, nutrient-rich sediment from reaching the floodplains.[84]

As Karen Bakker explains, unlike other cash-generating modes of resource exploitation, such as logging and gem mining, hydropower development almost always requires foreign capital and expertise.[85] Until the 1990s, most dams in the Lower Mekong states were public investments based on loans from the World Bank and the Asian Development Bank. More recently, the geo-economics and, by extension, the geopolitics have shifted to China. Now, most dams are commercial projects for which the Chinese government provides necessary support. Indeed, China is the world's preeminent promoter of large dam schemes abroad, with Chinese companies involved in more than

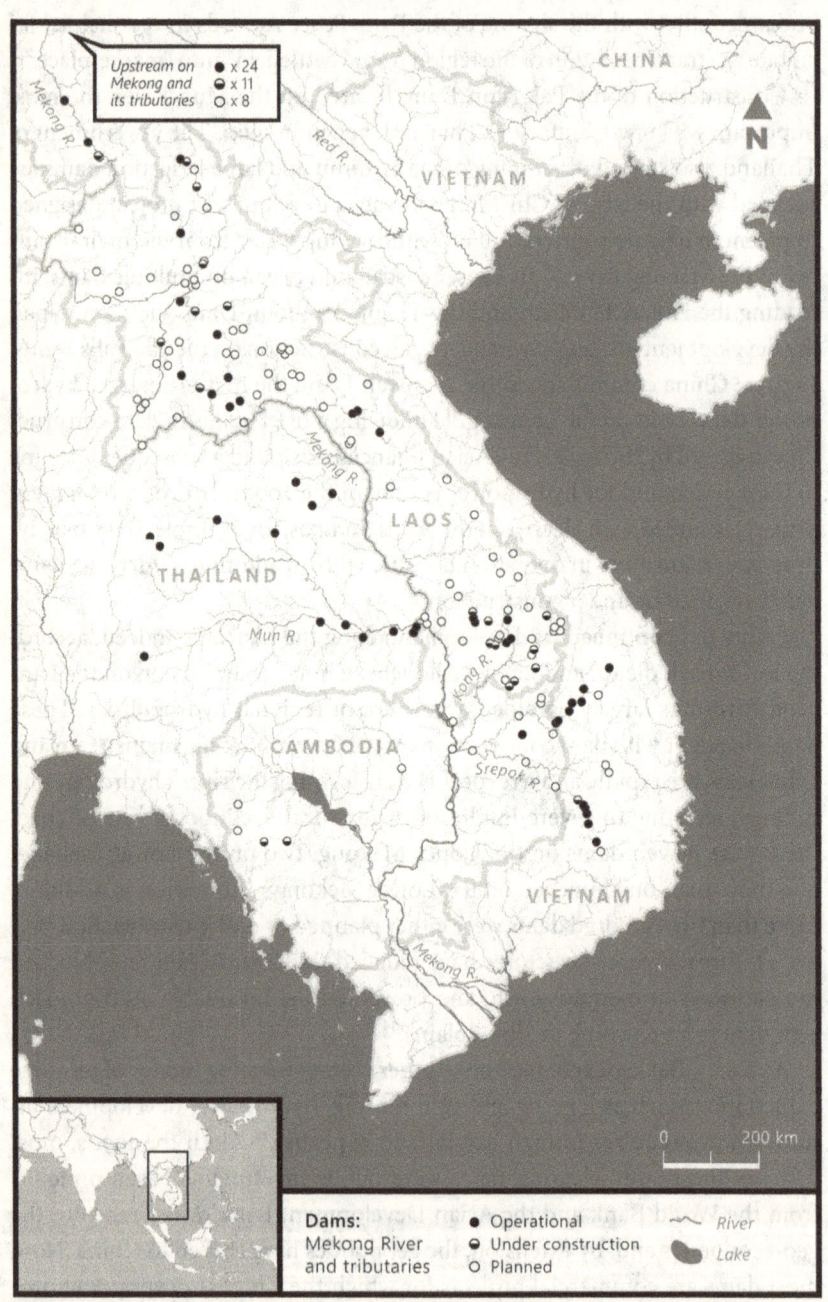

FIGURE 7. Actual and proposed dams along the Mekong River and tributaries. Courtesy of Stian Rice.

360 dams in 74 countries.[86] Within the Mekong Basin, an estimated 40 percent of the proposed tributary and mainstream hydropower development projects in coming years will be constructed by Chinese firms.[87]

The environmental economics around downstream dams on the Lancang and Lower Mekong is intricately bound up in a wider world of geopolitical relations.[88] This circumstance suggests that food provision systems, including fishing and agriculture, within downstream countries such as Cambodia are necessarily transnational. In other words, the livelihoods of rural households are enmeshed in capacious geopolitical relations that include myriad states, international donors, and corporations. That is to say, the possibility of decreased food security in Cambodia resultant from hydropower maldevelopment exists precisely because of necro-geopolitics that routinely place profits over people. These conditions, coupled with the environmental impacts of climate change, mean that the outlook is dark. In 2019, for example, a prolonged drought affected much of the Lower Mekong Basin. With the onset of monsoon rains delayed, rice farmers were unable to plant their main crops when they normally would; this, in turn, contributed to a diminished harvest. And yet during the planting season, Chinese authorities intentionally withheld water for their own economic needs, thus increasing the vulnerability of downstream farmers in Cambodia.[89]

It would be disingenuous, however, to focus the spotlight exclusively on the Chinese government, thereby allowing other key actors to remain hidden. For example, the ruling party in Cambodia also contributes to the increased vulnerability of the country's citizens. Since the 1980s, the CPP has remained the party most experienced and skilled at harnessing foreign donor-funded infrastructural development aid. It does so not to benefit Cambodia's poor and marginalized but to serve its own narrow interests, both as a political party and in terms of individual economic advancement.[90] CPP members routinely benefit from control of the most lucrative and influential government bureaucracies, including those for agriculture, forestry, and water resources. Thus the CPP profits handsomely from myriad development ventures, including land grabs, but also from irrigation schemes and other water-management projects connected with the exploitation of the Mekong and its tributaries.

Indeed, according to David Blake, irrigation projects are invariably considered an integral component of politicians' electoral strategy to incentivize rural people to vote for them. In addition, these projects are a means for elites to reward loyal bureaucrats, contractors, party members, and politicians through mutual rent-seeking opportunities during the scheme's construction.[91] As Blake details, having de facto control over much of the bureaucracy has allowed the CPP to exercise control over water flows, people, and development funds (whether domestic or international aid), all while taking little interest in questions of equity, sustainability, or the environment.[92]

Notably, Hun Sen has in recent years become a vocal champion of Mekong hydro-development projects. Previously, and at least rhetorically, he expressed mild opposition toward large-scale dams upstream on the Mekong, including those in China. From the early 2000s, however, Hun Sen has reversed course—not unlike the Tonle Sap. No doubt changing in response to regional geopolitical currents, Hun Sen and the ruling CPP now back the development of hydropower projects along the Mekong and its tributaries almost without exception. To this end, Cambodia has become a near-model client state for China, both in terms of facilitating Chinese investment in Cambodia and supporting its foreign policy goals in Southeast Asia.[93] As Sreang Chheat explains, Chinese capital dominates the textile and garment industry, the biggest earner of foreign exchange for the country, which employs more than seven hundred thousand workers; in addition, China is the largest foreign investor in the energy sector and is the major sponsor of Cambodia's dam-construction projects.[94]

Effectively, China's hydro-diplomacy and Cambodia's kleptocracy have become inextricably linked.[95] For Blake, an important aspect of this deepening geopolitical relationship is mediated by Cambodia's emergence as a satellite hydraulic state of China, as evidenced by the numerous hydropower and irrigation schemes appearing throughout Cambodia.[96] Unsurprisingly, many of these projects have dovetailed with the rapacious land grabs and subsequent resettlement programs.

The social, economic, and environmental impacts of hydropower development projects throughout the Mekong Basin, including those affecting rural households in Cambodia, are well documented.[97] From a physical standpoint, there are disturbing signs that the Tonle Sap River will, in the foreseeable future, cease to reverse its flow. In 2019, according to the Mekong River Commission, the usually monomodal reverse flow into the Tonle Sap occurred twice. In the first instance, the reversal began on July 5 and ended July 13, with only negligible contributions to the Great Lake. In the second instance, the reversal began on July 30 and ended on September 26, lasting for less than two months. Overall, the total inflow volume for the year was substantially less than the average inflow. In 2020, a similar pattern was observed, as the onset of the reversal was again delayed and its duration decidedly less than normal. Reverse flows into the lake again occurred twice, but only briefly and with extremely low volumes that were difficult to observe. Indeed, many local residents maintain that there was no reversal. Estimates from the Mekong River Commission conclude, however, that two minuscule reversals took place, first between July 7 and July 15 and again *for just three days* in late July.[98]

The Mekong–Tonle Sap flood-pulse system serves a vitally important resource for the whole of Cambodia. Yet the damaging impacts associated with hydropower development—in addition to those resultant from climate change—will reduce the ecosystem's productivity, thereby leading to potentially catastrophic famine conditions.[99] In many parts of the country, the ongoing development-induced displacement connected with dams and other irrigation schemes has already deepened poverty and increased vulnerabilities among Cambodia's rural population. Most pressing, disruptions in the Mekong–Tonle Sap ecosystem portend chronic food insecurities. In the Tonle Sap region, for example, annual fish catches total more than 235,000 tons, and more than 1.2 million people depend almost exclusively on fisheries for food security and supplemental income.[100] And yet, as Sneddon reminds us, fish production in the Tonle Sap is almost entirely dependent on the magnitude and timing of annual floods. However, the flooding of the Tonle Sap is in turn dependent on the collective flows of the entire Mekong drainage basin upstream of the confluence of the Mekong and Tonle Sap Rivers.[101]

Still, the socio-nature relationship is even more complex than this simple description implies. According to Sneddon, the ecohydrological characteristics of the Tonle Sap, its fisheries production, fish migration patterns, and fish species diversity, are linked to fishery practices in various ways. By way of illustration, the diversity of fish in the Tonle Sap contributes to the sustainability of the fisheries and the participation of large numbers of small-scale fishers. This diverseness serves as a "safety valve" whereby the decline of one species in a given season—for example, through overfishing or disease—is compensated for by increased fishing of species occupying similar ecological niches. Also, the diversity of species, the range of habitats, and the variation in catches over time and space permit a range of livelihood strategies for Cambodia's rural population, including those households in which fishing is the main source of food and income, and those individuals who supplement their primary economic activities through fishing.

Given this link between biodiversity and participation, Sneddon concludes, any development projects that degrade the ecological integrity of the flood-pulse system and reduce the ecosystem or species diversity will lead to diminished opportunities for participation and potential loss of livelihood.[102] This, in fact, is already occurring, as a growing number of rural households are experiencing acute food shortages and hunger. Kim Rai, a thirty-three-year-old fisherman who lives on the Tonle Sap about thirty miles upriver from Phnom Penh, explained, "We have gone out to fish nearly 10 times but we could not catch anything."[103]

Abby Seiff is blunt in her assessment, writing, "With the rapid expansion of hydropower dams along the Mekong and its tributaries, the Tonle Sap lake has been doomed for years now, but the pace at which it is dying has taken fishers by surprise." She explains that the last five years have been the five warmest on record, and that repeated El Niño weather conditions have led to multiple devastating droughts in Southeast Asia. Any chance of the lake's recovery from the changing climate has been obliterated by the influx of dams on the Mekong and its tributaries. Seiff concludes that China is "effectively starving its downstream neighbors of their river."[104] In fact, it is not simply the direct producers—the farmers and fishers of Cambodia and Vietnam—who are at risk. The vast and growing urban populations reliant on the rice, fish, and other foodstuffs made possible by the seasonal flooding of the Tonle Sap are also in danger. To that point, if China's necro-hydropolitics "lets die" the seasonal reversal of the Tonle Sap River, the entire ecological system will be irreparably harmed. If that happens, and if no substantial international relief efforts are available, there exists the possibility that millions of people throughout the whole of the Lower Mekong Basin will starve.

Conclusions

Capitalist accumulation in Cambodia has been dominated by a relatively small elite characterized by large-scale land concentration. This accumulation has been driven by the appropriation of natural resources within the country and an influx of foreign capital from outside. Consequently, rural livelihood strategies have eroded for millions of Cambodians; formerly communal land that provided much-needed resources for poorer rural villagers through fishing, foraging, and cultivation has been privatized. In turn, rural households are shifting to new forms of farming and other economic activities.[105] Coupled with these structural transformations spurred principally by land concessions are broader environmental shifts wreaked by climate change and development-induced displacements. Simply put, Cambodia's rural population is increasingly caught in the vises of parallel threats that—if left unchecked—foreshadow a catastrophic future that would dwarf the country's famines of the 1970s.

For many, the possibility of future famines will be framed as the tragic outcome of a revanchist nature, the cataclysmic consequence of uncontrolled climate change. And there will be a kernel of truth to these claims. The climate change–induced floods and droughts will severely and adversely affect food production in Cambodia. As Yang Saing Koma explains of climate change, "It is an excuse just to blame nature."[106] To this point, the proximate threat of malnutrition and mass starvation will be the inability of farmers and fishers to adapt their livelihoods to the changing climate. However, the root cause of any approaching famine will be anthropogenic—not in the sense that climate change is human induced, which it is, but because the willful necropolitical negligence of state and corporate actors who routinely and deliberately place profits over people. Indeed, as Paula Nuorteva, Marko Keskinen, and Ollis Varis document, in the Tonle Sap area, farmers and fishers are generally well adapted to seasonal changes; however, this capacity is undermined by governmental policies that actually reduce resilience. The government maintains existing power imbalances, denying particularly the poorest citizens and ethnic minorities equal access to common resources, and to the decision-making processes at the village and commune levels.[107] To this end, future mass starvation in Cambodia will constitute state-induced indirect famines, a manifestation of a calculated indifference that disallows life through the unintended disruption of food provision systems.

NOTES

INTRODUCTION

The epigraph is from Achille Mbembe, *Necropolitics*, translated by Steven Corcoran (Durham, N.C.: Duke University Press, 2019), 80.

1. Document No. E3/160, archived by the Extraordinary Chambers in the Courts of Cambodia (ECCC) at https://www.eccc.gov.kh/sites/default/files/documents/courtdoc /00143036-00143459_E3_160_EN.TXT.pdf.

2. On famine under the Khmer Rouge, see Randle C. DeFalco, "Accounting for Famine at the Extraordinary Chambers in the Courts of Cambodia: The Crimes against Humanity of Extermination, Inhumane Acts and Persecution," *International Journal of Transitional Justice* 5, no. 1 (2011): 142–158; Randle C. DeFalco, "Voices of Genocide: Justice and the Khmer Rouge Famine," *Searching for the Truth* (First Quarter, 2013): 29–32; Randle C. DeFalco, "Justice and Starvation in Cambodia: The Khmer Rouge Famine," *Cambodia Law and Policy Journal* 2 (2014): 45–84; James A. Tyner and Stian Rice, "To Live and Let Die: Food, Famine, and Administrative Violence in Democratic Kampuchea, 1975–1979," *Political Geography* 52, no. 1 (2016): 47–56; and Stian Rice and James A. Tyner, "The Rice Cities of the Khmer Rouge: An Urban Political Ecology of Rural Mass Violence," *Transactions of the Institute of British Geographers* 42 (2017): 559–571. For useful introductions to the traumatic legacy of the genocide and famine, see Estelle Bockers, Nadine Stammel, and Christine Knaevelsrud, "Reconciliation in Cambodia: Thirty Years after the Terror of the Khmer Rouge Regime," *Torture* 21, no. 2 (2011): 71–83; Beth Van Schaack, Daryn Reicherter, and Youk Chhang, eds., *Cambodia's Hidden Scars: Trauma Psychology in the Wake of the Khmer Rouge* (Phnom Penh: Documentation Center of Cambodia, 2011); Devon E. Hinton, Alexander L. Hinton, Kok-Thay Eng, and Sophearith Choung, "PTSD and Key Somatic Complaints and Cultural Syndromes among Rural Cambodians: The Results of a Needs Assessment Survey," *Medical Anthropology Quarterly* 26, no. 3 (2012): 383–407; and Devon E. Hinton, Ria Reis, and Joop de Jong, "Ghost Encounters among Traumatized Cambodian Refugees: Severity, Relationship to PTSD, and Phenomenology," *Culture, Medicine, and Psychiatry* 44 (2020): 333–359.

3. Chanthou Boua, "Development Aid and Democracy in Cambodia," in *Genocide and Democracy in Cambodia: The Khmer Rouge, the United Nations and the Interna-*

tional Community, ed. Ben Kiernan (New Haven, Conn.: Yale University Southeast Asia Studies, 1993), 273–283, at 277.

4. For a critique of this trope, see Simon Springer, "Culture of Violence or Violent Orientalism? Neoliberalisation and Imagining the 'Savage Other' in Post-Transitional Cambodia," *Transactions of the Institute of British Geographers* 34, no. 3 (2009): 305–319.

5. For a notable exception, see Meng-Try Ea, "War and Famine: The Example of Kampuchea," in *Famine as a Geographical Phenomenon*, ed. Bruce Currey and Graeme Hugo (Hingham, Mass.: Kluwer Academic, 1984), 33–47.

6. Alex de Waal, *Famine Crimes: Politics & the Disaster Relief Industry in Africa* (Bloomington: Indiana University Press, 1997); Jenny Edkins, "Mass Starvations and the Limitations of Famine Theorizing," *IDS Bulletin* 33, no. 4 (2002): 12–18; Rhoda E. Howard-Hassmann, "State-Induced Famine and Penal Starvation in North Korea," *Genocide Studies and Prevention* 7, nos. 2–3 (2012): 147–165; Alex de Waal, "Ending Mass Atrocity and Ending Famine," *Lancet* 386 (2015): 1528–1529; Alex de Waal, *Mass Starvation: The History and Future of Famine* (Medford, Mass.: Polity, 2018); Alex de Waal, "The End of Famine? Prospects for the Elimination of Mass Starvation by Political Action," *Political Geography* 62 (2018): 184–195.

7. Chris Philo, "Less-Than-Human Geographies," *Political Geography* 60 (2017): 256–258.

8. David Nally, "The Biopolitics of Food Provisioning," *Transactions of the Institute of British Geographers* 36 (2011): 37–53, at 38 and 49.

9. de Waal, *Mass Starvation*, 9.

10. James C. Welling, "The Law of Malthus," *American Anthropologist* 1, no. 1 (1888): 1–24, at 3.

11. Stian Rice, *Famine in the Remaking: Food System Change and Mass Starvation in Hawaii, Madagascar, and Cambodia* (Morgantown: West Virginia University Press, 2020), 2.

12. Amartya Sen, "Famines as Failures of Exchange Entitlements," *Economic and Political Weekly* 11, nos. 31–33 (1976): 1273–1280; Amartya Sen, *Poverty and Famines: An Essay on Entitlement and Deprivation* (Oxford: Clarendon, 1981).

13. Stephen Devereux, "Sen's Entitlement Approach: Critiques and Counter-Critiques," *Oxford Development Studies* 29, no. 3 (2001): 245–263, at 246.

14. Amrita Rangasami, "'Failure of Exchange Entitlements' Theory of Famine: A Response," *Economic and Political Weekly* 20, no. 42 (1985): 1797–1801; Peter Bowbrick, "The Causes of Famine: A Refutation of Professor Sen's Theory," *Food Policy* 11 (1986): 105–124; Alex de Waal, "A Re-Assessment of Entitlement Theory in the Light of the Recent Famines in Africa," *Development and Change* 21, no. 3 (1990): 469–490; Michael Watts, "Entitlements or Empowerment? Famine and Starvation in Africa," *Review of African Political Economy* 51 (1991): 9–26; and Peter Nolan, "The Causation and Prevention of Famines: A Critique of A. K. Sen," *Journal of Peasant Studies* 21, no. 1 (1993): 1–28.

15. Devereux, "Sen's Entitlement Approach," 256.

16. Edkins, "Mass Starvations," 13.

17. Devereux, "Sen's Entitlement Approach," 256. See also Stephen Devereux, *Famine in the Twentieth Century*, Working Paper 105 (Brighton: Institute of Development Studies, 2000).

18. David P. Nally, *Human Encumbrances: Political Violence and the Great Irish Famine* (Notre Dame, Ind.: University of Notre Dame Press, 2011), ix.

19. Joanna Macrae and Anthony B. Zwi, "Food as an Instrument of War in Contemporary African Famines: A Review of the Evidence," *Disasters* 16, no. 4 (1992): 299–321; René Provost, "Starvation as a Weapon: Legal Implications of the United Nations Food Blockade against Iraq and Kuwait," *Columbia Journal of Transnational Law* 30, no. 3 (1992): 577–640; David Keen, *The Benefits of Famine: A Political Economy of Famine and Relief in Southwestern Sudan, 1983–1989* (Princeton, N.J.: Princeton University Press, 1994); de Waal, *Famine Crimes*; Gesine Gerhard, *Nazi Hunger Politics: A History of Food in the Third Reich* (Lanham, Md.: Rowman & Littlefield, 2015); Rhoda E. Howard-Hassmann, *State Food Crimes* (Cambridge: Cambridge University Press, 2016); Randle C. DeFalco, "Conceptualizing Famine as a Subject of International Criminal Justice: Towards a Modality-Based Approach," *University of Pennsylvania Journal of International Law* 38, no. 4 (2017): 1113–1187; Bridget Conley and Alex de Waal, "The Purposes of Starvation: Historical and Contemporary Uses," *Journal of International Criminal Justice* 17 (2019): 699–722; Carlisle Ford Runge and Linnea Graham, "Hunger as a Weapon of War: Hitler's Hunger Plan, Native American Resettlement and Starvation in Yemen," *Food Policy* 92 (2020): 101835.

20. Meredith Woo-Cumings, *The Political Ecology of Famine: The North Korean Catastrophe and Its Lessons* (Manila, Philippines: Asian Development Bank Institute, 2002); Jamey Essex, "The Work of Hunger: Security, Development, and Food-for-Work in Post-Crisis Jakarta," *Studies in Social Justice* 3, no. 1 (2009): 99–116; Jamey Essex, "Idle Hands Are the Devil's Tools: The Geopolitics and Geoeconomics of Hunger," *Annals of the Association of American Geographers* 102, no. 1 (2012): 191–207.

21. David Marcus, "Famine Crimes in International Law," *American Journal of International Law* 97, no. 2 (2003): 245–281. See also de Waal, *Mass Starvation*, 106–108.

22. Establishing intent and culpability is not straightforward, for in many famines there are overlapping and contradicting plans, policies, and practices that create, sustain, or mitigate famine conditions. See de Waal, *Mass Starvation*, 107.

23. Marcus, "Famine Crimes," 247.

24. de Waal, "The End of Famine?," 193.

25. de Waal, *Mass Starvation*, 107.

26. Marcus, "Famine Crimes," 246.

27. de Waal, *Mass Starvation*, 106.

28. Stephen Devereux, *Theories of Famine* (London: Harvester Wheatsheaf, 1993).

29. Rhoda E. Howard-Hassmann, "Faminogenesis: State Policies That Undermine the Right to Food," *Netherlands Quarterly of Human Rights* 29, no. 4 (2011): 560–590, at 561.

30. Milla Emilia Vaha, "Duties of Whom? States and the Problem of Global Justice," in *New Waves in Global Justice*, ed. Thom Brooks (New York: Palgrave Macmillan, 2014), 48–72, at 51.

31. Vaha, "Duties of Whom?," 50.

32. Peter Ronayne, *Never Again? The United States and the Prevention and Punishment of Genocide since the Holocaust* (Lanham, Md.: Rowman & Littlefield, 2001).

33. Ramesh Thakur, "Intervention, Sovereignty and the Responsibility to Protect: Experiences from the ICISS," *Security Dialogue* 33, no. 3 (2002): 323–340, at 331.

34. Michel Foucault, *"Society Must Be Defended": Lectures at the Collège de France, 1977–1978*, trans. David Macey (New York: Picador, 2003), 240. See also Michel Foucault, *The History of Sexuality: An Introduction*, trans. by Robert Hurley (New York: Vintage Books, 1990).

35. Foucault, *"Society Must Be Defended,"* 240.

36. Michel Foucault, *Discipline and Punish: The Birth of the Prison*, trans. Alan Sheridan (New York: Vintage Books, 1977), 26.

37. Paul Rabinow and Nikolas Rose, "Biopower Today," *BioSocieties* 1 (2006): 195–217.

38. Claire Blencowe, "Foucault's and Arendt's 'Insider View' of Biopolitics: A Critique of Agamben," *History of the Human Sciences* 23, no. 5 (2010): 113–130, at 122.

39. Foucault, *"Society Must Be Defended,"* 62.

40. Gavin Rae, *Critiquing Sovereign Violence: Law, Biopolitics, Bio-Juridicalism* (Edinburgh: Edinburgh University Press, 2021), 134.

41. Rae, *Critiquing Sovereign Violence*, 135.

42. Foucault, *"Society Must Be Defended,"* 254.

43. Foucault, *"Society Must Be Defended,"* 256.

44. Achille Mbembe, "Necropolitics," trans. Libby Meintjes, *Public Culture* 15, no. 1 (2003): 11–40, at 12.

45. Mbembe, "Necropolitics," 12.

46. Jamie Allinson, "The Necropolitics of Drones," *International Political Sociology* 9, no. 2 (2015): 113–127, at 118.

47. de Waal, *Mass Starvation*, 23.

48. Giorgio Agamben, *Homo Sacer: Sovereign Power and Bare Life*, trans. Daniel Heller-Roazen (Stanford, Calif.: Stanford University Press, 1998), 1; Jenny Edkins, *Trauma and the Memory of Politics* (Cambridge: Cambridge University Press, 2003), 179.

49. Agamben, *Homo Sacer*, 144; Edkins, *Trauma and the Memory of Politics*, 179.

50. Edkins, *Trauma and the Memory of Politics*, 180.

51. Edkins, *Trauma and the Memory of Politics*, 179–180.

52. Agamben, *Homo Sacer*, 15.

53. Agamben, *Homo Sacer*, 15.

54. Daniel McLoughlin, "The Fiction of Sovereignty and the Real State of Exception: Giorgio Agamben's Critique of Carl Schmitt," *Law, Culture and the Humanities* 12, no. 3 (2016): 509–528, at 516.

55. Edkins, *Trauma and the Memory of Politics*, 181.

56. Giorgio Agamben, *State of Exception*, trans. Kevin Attell (Stanford, Calif.: Stanford University Press, 2005), 1.

57. Rae, *Critiquing Sovereign Violence*, 150.

58. Edkins, *Trauma and the Memory of Politics*, 181.

59. Edkins, *Trauma and the Memory of Politics*, 182.

60. Nally, "The Biopolitics of Food Provisioning," 38.

61. Mbembe, *Necropolitics*, 38.

62. Watts, "Entitlements or Empowerment," 9, 16.

63. Michael Watts, "Heart of Darkness: Reflections on Famine and Starvation in Africa," in *The Political Economy of African Famine*, ed. Roger E. Downs, Donna O. Kerner, and Stephen P. Reyna (Philadelphia: Gordon, 1991), 23–71, at 25.

64. Essex, "Idle Hands," 195.
65. Nally, *Human Encumbrances*, 3.
66. Ea, "War and Famine," 33–47, at 44.

CHAPTER 1. NO ONE STARVES IN CAMBODIA

The epigraph is quoted in David Chandler, *A History of Cambodia*, 3rd ed. (Boulder, Colo.: Westview, 2000), 147.

1. Michael J. Watts, *Silent Violence: Food, Famine, and Peasantry in Northern Nigeria*, with a new introduction (1983; reprint, Athens: University of Georgia Press, 2013), 119.
2. William E. Willmott, "Cambodia," *New Left Review* 25 (1964): 33–38, at 36.
3. Kate G. Frieson and Pech Sithan, "Social Landscapes and Rural Livelihoods in Transition," in *Social Landscapes and Rural Livelihoods: Cambodian Communities in Transition*, ed. Kate G. Frieson (Phnom Penh, Cambodia: Learning Institute, 2010), 31–44, at 32.
4. Watts, *Silent Violence*, 13.
5. Kent Helmers, "Rice in the Cambodian Economy: Past and Present," in *Rice Production in Cambodia*, ed. Harry J. Nesbitt (Manila: International Rice Research Institute, 1997), 1–14, at 1.
6. Helmers, "Rice in the Cambodian Economy," 1–14, at 1.
7. Helmers, "Rice in the Cambodian Economy," 2.
8. Henry J. Nesbitt and Chan Phaloeun, "Rice-Based Farming Systems," in *Rice Production in Cambodia*, ed. Harry J. Nesbitt (Manila: International Rice Research Institute, 1997), 31–37, at 31. See also E. L. Javier, "Rice Ecosystems and Varieties," in *Rice Production in Cambodia*, ed. Nesbitt, 39–81.
9. Stian Rice, *Famine in the Remaking: Food System Change and Mass Starvation in Hawaii, Madagascar, and Cambodia* (Morgantown: West Virginia University Press, 2020), 143.
10. Nesbitt and Phaloeun, "Rice-Based Farming Systems," 33.
11. Nesbitt and Phaloeun, "Rice-Based Farming Systems," 33.
12. Javier, "Rice Ecosystems and Varieties," 44.
13. Javier, "Rice Ecosystems and Varieties," 63.
14. Javier, "Rice Ecosystems and Varieties," 75–76.
15. Jean-Christophe Diepart, *The Fragmentation of Land Tenure Systems in Cambodia: Peasants and the Formalization of Land Rights* (Paris: Technical Committee on "Land Tenure and Development," 2015), 6.
16. Jean-Christophe Diepart and Thol Sem, *Cambodian Peasantry and Formalization of Land Right: Historical Perspectives and Current Issues* (Paris: French Technical Committee on Land Tenure and Development, 2018), 9.
17. Diepart, *The Fragmentation of Land*, 6.
18. Diepart, *The Fragmentation of Land*, 6; Diepart and Sem, *Cambodian Peasantry*, 12.
19. Diepart, *The Fragmentation of Land*, 6–7.
20. Diepart, *The Fragmentation of Land*, 7.
21. Richard A. Engelhardt, "Two Thousand Years of Engineering Genius on the Angkor Plain," *Expedition* 37, no. 3 (1995): 18–30; Roland Fletcher, Christophe Pottier, Da-

mian Evans, and Matti Kummu, "The Development of the Water Management System of Angkor: A Provisional Model," *Indo-Pacific Prehistory Association Bulletin* 28 (2008): 57–66; Brendan M. Buckley, Kevin J. Anchukaitis, Daniel Penny, Roland Fletcher, Edward R. Cook, Masaki Sano, Le Canh Nam, Aroonrut Wichienkeeo, Ton That Minh, and Truong Mai Hong, "Climate as a Contributing Factor in the Demise of Angkor, Cambodia," *PNAS* 107, no. 15 (2010): 6748–6752; Damian Evans, "Applications of Archaeological Remote Sensing in Cambodia: An Overview of Angkor and Beyond," in *Space, Time, Place: Third International Conference on Remote Sensing in Archaeology*, ed. Stefano Campana, Maurizio Forte, and Claudia Liuzza (Oxford: Archeaopress, 2010), 353–366; Miriam T. Stark, Damian Evans, Chhay Rachna, Heng Piphal, and Alison Carter, "Residential Patterning at Angkor Wat," *Antiquity* 89, no. 348 (2015): 1439–1455; Terry Lustig and Eileen Lustig, "Following the Non-Money Trail: Reconciling Some Angkorian Temple Accounts," *Journal of Indo-Pacific Archaeology* 39 (2015): 26–37; Damian Evans, "Airborne Laser Scanning as a Method for Exploring Long-Term Socio-Ecological Dynamics in Cambodia," *Journal of Archaeological Science* 74 (2016): 164–175; Alison Carter, Piphal Heng, Miriam Stark, Rachna Chhay, and Damian Evans, "Urbanism and Residential Patterning in Angkor," *Journal of Field Archaeology* 43, no. 6 (2018): 492–506; Cristina Cobo Castillo, Martin Polkinghorne, Brice Vincent, Tan Boun Suy, and Dorian Q. Fuller, "Life Goes On: Archaeobotanical Investigations of Diet and Ritual at Angkor Thom, Cambodia (14th–15th Centuries CE)," *Holocene* 28, no. 6 (2018): 930–944; Cristina Cobo Castillo, Alison Carter, Eleanor Kingwell-Banham, Yijie Zhuang, Alison Weisskopf, Chhay Rachna, Piphal Heng, Dorian Q. Fuller, and Miriam Stark, "The Khmer Did Not Live by Rice Alone: Archaeobotanical Investigations at Angkor Wat and Ta Prohm," *Archaeological Research in Asia* 24 (2020): 100213; and Mitch Hendrickson and Stéphanie Leroy, "Sparks and Needles: Seeking Catalysts of State Expansions, a Case Study of Technological Interaction at Angkor, Cambodia (9th to 13th Centuries CE)," *Journal of Anthropological Archaeology* 57 (2020): 101141.

22. Hendrickson and Leroy, "Sparks and Needles."

23. Engelhardt, "Two Thousand Years," 22.

24. Engelhardt, "Two Thousand Years," 19.

25. Fletcher et al., "The Development of the Water Management System," 57.

26. Engelhardt, "Two Thousand Years," 22.

27. Chelsea Fisher, "Archaeology for Sustainable Agriculture," *Journal of Archaeological Research* 28, no. 3 (2020): 393–441, at 415.

28. Kenneth R. Hall, "Eleventh-Century Commercial Developments in Angkor and Champa," *Journal of Southeast Asian Studies* 10, no. 2 (1979): 424.

29. John Tully, "Cambodia in the Nineteenth Century: Out of the Siamese Frying Pan and into the French Fire?," in *Cambodia and the West, 1500–2000*, ed. T. O. Smith (London: Palgrave Macmillan, 2018), 37–63, at 49.

30. Hall, "Eleventh-Century Commercial Developments," 424.

31. Hall, "Eleventh-Century Commercial Developments," 424.

32. The reasons for the downfall of Angkor remain contested among historians, with myriad hypotheses forwarded to account both for the diminished importance of the once powerful kingdom and the rapidity of its decline. In all likelihood, the demise was gradual and related to numerous factors acting in concert. See, for example, Dan Penny,

"Social Upheaval in Ancient Angkor Resulting from Fluvial Response to Land Use and Climate Variability," *Past Global Changes* 22, no. 1 (2014): 32–33; Alison K. Carter, Miriam T. Stark, Seth Quintus, Yijie Zhuang, Hong Wang, Piphal Heng, and Rachna Chhay, "Temple Occupation and the Tempo of Collapse at Angkor Wat, Cambodia," *PNAS* 116, no. 25 (2019): 12226–12231; and Dan Penny, Tegan Hall, Damian Evans, and Martin Polkinghorne, "Geoarchaeological Evidence from Angkor, Cambodia, Reveals a Gradual Decline Rather than a Catastrophic 15th-Century Collapse," *PNAS* 116, no. 11 (2019): 4871–4876.

33. Geoff Wade, "An Early Age of Commerce in Southeast Asia, 900–1300 CE," *Journal of Southeast Asian Studies* 40, no. 2 (2009): 221–265, at 222. See also Kenneth R. Hall, "The Coming of the West: European Cambodian Marketplace Connectivity, 1500–1800," in *Cambodia and the West, 1500–2000*, ed. T. O. Smith (London: Palgrave Macmillan, 2018), 7–36.

34. Hall, "The Coming of the West," 11.

35. Hall, "The Coming of the West," 11.

36. Michael Vickery, *Cambodia, 1975–1982* (Chiang Mai, Thailand: Silkworm Books, 1984), 13.

37. Jean-Christophe Diepart and David Dupuis, "The Peasants in Turmoil: Khmer Rouge, State Formation and the Control of Land in Northwest Cambodia," *Journal of Peasant Studies* 41, no. 4 (2014): 445–468, at 450.

38. Chandler, *A History of Cambodia*, 107. See also Margaret Slocomb, "Cultures and Histories of Resistance in Cambodia," in *Conservation and Development in Cambodia: Exploring Frontiers of Change in Nature, State and Society*, ed. Sarah Milne and Sango Mahanty (New York: Routledge, 2015), 225–237; and Milton E. Osborne, *The French Presence in Cochinchina and Cambodia* (Chiang Mai, Thailand: White Lotus, 1997).

39. Chandler, *A History of Cambodia*, 108.

40. Diepart and Dupuis, "The Peasants in Turmoil," 450.

41. Diepart and Sem, *Cambodian Peasantry*, 12.

42. Chandler, *A History of Cambodia*, 100.

43. Diepart and Sem, *Cambodian Peasantry*, 12.

44. Chandler, *A History of Cambodia*, 102–103.

45. Kalyanee E. Mam, "An Oral History of Family Life under the Khmer Rouge," Yale Center for International and Area Studies Working Paper Series, GS10 (New Haven, Conn.: Yale Center for International and Area Studies, 1999), 3. See also May Ebihara, "Intervillage, Intertown, and Village-City Relations in Cambodia," *Annals of the New York Academy of Sciences* 220, no. 1 (1973): 358–375; May Ebihara, "Residence Patterns in a Khmer Peasant Village," *Annals of the New York Academy of Sciences* 293, no. 1 (1977): 51–68; and May Ebihara, *Svay: A Khmer Village in Cambodia* (Ithaca, N.Y.: Cornell University Press, 2018).

46. Susan H. Lee, *"Rice Plus": Widows and Economic Survival in Rural Cambodia* (New York: Routledge, 2006), 25–27.

47. Chandler, *A History of Cambodia*, 104.

48. Michael Vickery, *Kampuchea: Politics, Economics, and Society* (Boulder, Colo.: Lynn Rienner, 1986), 51.

49. David Chandler, William R. Roff, John R. W. Smail, David Joel Steinberg, Robert

H. Taylor, Alexander Woodside, and David K. Wyatt, *In Search of Southeast Asia: A Modern History*, rev. ed. (Honolulu: University of Hawaii Press, 1987), 186.

50. Chandler et al., *In Search of Southeast Asia*, 187.

51. Montserrat López Jerez, "Colonial and Indigenous Institutions in the Fiscal Development of French Indochina," in *Fiscal Capacity and the Colonial State in Asia and Africa, c. 1850–1960*, ed. Ewout Frankema and Anne Booth (Cambridge: Cambridge University Press, 2019), 110–136.

52. Jerez, "Colonial and Indigenous Institutions," 119.

53. Chandler, *A History of Cambodia*, 153.

54. Helmers, "Rice in the Cambodian Economy," 2.

55. Helmers, "Rice in the Cambodian Economy," 2; Rice, *Famine in the Remaking*, 142.

56. Helmers, "Rice in the Cambodian Economy," 2–3. Beyond these two systems, there were other productive arrangements, including larger holdings in the possession of ethnic Vietnamese and Chinese landowners.

57. Helmers, "Rice in the Cambodian Economy," 3.

58. Margaret Slocomb, *An Economic History of Cambodia in the Twentieth Century* (Singapore: National University of Singapore Press, 2010), 71.

59. Slocomb, *An Economic History of Cambodia*, 52.

60. Sokbunthoeun So, "The Politics and Practice of Land Registration at the Grassroots," in *Cambodia's Economic Transformation*, ed. Caroline Hughes and Kheang Un (Copenhagen: NIAS Press, 2011), 136–160, at 139.

61. Diepart and Dupuis, "The Peasants in Turmoil," 451; Tully, "Cambodia in the Nineteenth Century," 51. See also Ray Russell, "Land Law in the Kingdom of Cambodia," *Property Management* 15, no. 2 (1997): 101–110; Anne Y. Guillou, "The Question of Land in Cambodia: Perceptions, Access, and Use since De-Collectivization," *Moussons: Recherche en sciences humaines sur l'Asie du Sud-Est* 9–10 (2006): 299–324; Mathieu Guérin, "Khmer Peasants and Land Access in Kompong Thom Province in the 1930s," *Journal of Southeast Asian Studies* 43, no. 3 (2012): 441–462; and Alice Beban and Courtney Work, "The Spirits Are Crying: Dispossessing Land and Possessing Bodies in Rural Cambodia," *Antipode* 46, no. 3 (2014): 593–610.

62. Diepart and Dupuis, "The Peasants in Turmoil," 451.

63. Tully, "Cambodia in the Nineteenth Century," 51.

64. Diepart and Sem, *Cambodian Peasantry*, 13.

65. Diepart and Sem, *Cambodian Peasantry*, 13.

66. Diepart and Sem, *Cambodian Peasantry*, 13.

67. Diepart and Sem, *Cambodian Peasantry*, 13; Ben Kiernan, "Introduction," in *Peasants and Politics in Kampuchea, 1942–1981*, ed. Ben Kiernan and Chanthou Boua (New York: M. E. Sharpe, 1982), 6–7.

68. Margaret Slocomb, *Colons and Coolies: The Development of Cambodia's Rubber Plantations* (Chiang Mai, Thailand: White Lotus, 2007); Michitake Aso, "Rubber and Race in Rural Colonial Cambodia (1920s–1954)," *History Faculty Scholarship* 23, nos. 12–13 (2010): 127–138; Jean-Christophe Diepart and Laura Schoenberger, "Concessions in Cambodia: Governing Profits, Extending State Power and Enclosing Resources from the Colonial Era to the Present," in *The Handbook of Contemporary Cambodia*, ed. Simon Springer and Kathryne Brickell (London: Routledge, 2016), 157–168; and Michitake

Aso, "Rubbery Revolution: Plantations as Battlefields in the First Indochina War, 1945–1954," in *Water and Power: Environmental Governance and Strategies for Sustainability in the Lower Mekong Basin*, ed. Mart A. Stewart and Peter A. Coclanis (Cham, Switzerland: Springer International, 2019), 29–47.

69. According to Michitake Aso, the first plantation in Cambodia was established in Kampot in 1911. See Aso, "Rubber and Race," 128.

70. Slocomb, *An Economic History of Cambodia*, 57, 62.

71. Diepart and Schoenberg, "Concessions in Cambodia," 158–159.

72. Slocomb, *An Economic History of Cambodia*, 51, 72.

73. Vickery, *Kampuchea*, 52.

74. Kiernan, "Introduction," 1–28, at 4.

75. Vickery, *Kampuchea*, 52.

76. Diepart and Dupois, "The Peasants in Turmoil," 452.

77. Slocomb, *An Economic History of Cambodia*, 71.

78. Raoul M. Jennar, *The Cambodian Constitutions* (Bangkok, Thailand: White Lotus, 1995), 35.

79. Slocomb, *An Economic History of Cambodia*, 76.

80. David Chandler, *The Tragedy of Cambodian History: Politics, War, and Revolution since 1945* (New Haven, Conn.: Yale University Press, 1991), 108.

81. Chandler, *The Tragedy of Cambodian History*, 89.

82. Quoted in David Ayers, *Anatomy of a Crisis: Education, Development, and the State in Cambodia, 1953-1998* (Chiang Mai, Thailand: Silkworm, 2003), 32.

83. Ayers, *Anatomy of a Crisis*, 32.

84. Chandler, *The Tragedy of Cambodian History*, 88–89; Rice, *Famine in the Remaking*, 151.

85. In 1960, Sihanouk's father died and Sihanouk assumed the new position of head of state, which he held for the next ten years. A new king was not selected, but neither was the monarchy abolished. See Marlowe Hood and David A. Ablin, "The Path to Cambodia's Present," in *The Cambodian Agony*, ed. David A. Ablin and Marlowe Hood (Armonk, N.Y.: M. E. Sharpe, 1990), xxii.

86. Oliver Hensengerth, *Transitions of Cambodia: War and Peace, 1954 to the Present*, Project Working Paper No. 2 (Universität Duisburg Essen: Institute for Development and Peace, 2008), 9.

87. Chandler, *The Tragedy of Cambodian History*, 87.

88. Michael Vickery, "Looking Back at Cambodia, 1942–76," in *Peasants and Politics in Kampuchea, 1942–1981*, ed. Ben Kiernan and Chanthou Boua (Armonk, N.Y.: M. E. Sharpe, 1982), 89–126, at 101.

89. Chandler, *The Tragedy of Cambodian History*, 87.

90. Kenton Clymer, *Troubled Relations: The United States and Cambodia since 1870* (DeKalb: Northern Illinois University Press, 2007), 57.

91. Margaret Slocomb, "The Nature and Role of Ideology in the Modern Cambodian State," *Journal of Southeast Asian Studies* 37, no. 3 (2006): 375–395, at 379.

92. Chandler, *The Tragedy of Cambodian History*, 89; Slocomb, *An Economic History of Cambodia*, 77. See also Stuart Simmonds, "Laos and Cambodia: The Search for Unity and Independence," *International Affairs* 49, no. 4 (1973): 574–583, at 580.

93. Helmers, "Rice in the Cambodian Economy," 4.
94. Kenton J. Clymer, "The Perils of Neutrality: The Break in US-Cambodian Relations, 1965," *Diplomatic History* 23, no. 4 (1999): 613.
95. Rice, *Famine in the Remaking*, 152.
96. Helmers, "Rice in the Cambodian Economy," 5.
97. Rice, *Famine in the Remaking*, 152.
98. Rice, *Famine in the Remaking*, 152; Helmers, "Rice in the Cambodian Economy," 4.
99. Slocomb, "The Nature and Role of Ideology," 380.
100. Courtney Work and Alice Beban, "Mapping the 'Srok': The Mimeses of Land Titling in Cambodia," *Sojourn: Journal of Social Issues in Southeast Asia* 31, no. 1 (2016): 37–80, at 49.
101. Kiernan, "Introduction," 6–7; Diepart and Sem, *Cambodian Peasantry*, 15.
102. Slocomb, *An Economic History of Cambodia*, 120.
103. Ben Kiernan, *How Pol Pot Came to Power: A History of Communism in Kampuchea, 1930–1975* (New Haven, Conn.: Yale University Press, 1996), xv.
104. Donald M. Seekins, "Historical Setting," in *Cambodia: A Country Study*, ed. R. R. Ross (Washington, D.C.: U.S. Government Printing Office, 1990), 3–71, at 32–34.
105. Hood and Ablin, "The Path to Cambodia's Present," xxi.
106. Sihanouk was aware of covert operations engineered by the CIA to destabilize his government or actually remove him from power. See Clymer, "The Perils of Neutrality," 613–614.
107. Hood and Ablin, "The Path to Cambodia's Present," xxii.
108. Helmers, "Rice in the Cambodian Economy," 4.
109. Donald Kirk, "Cambodia's Economic Crisis," *Asian Survey* 11, no. 3 (1971): 238–255, at 240.
110. Hood and Ablin, "The Path to Cambodia's Present," xxii–xxiii.
111. Ben Kiernan, "The Samlaut Rebellion, 1967–1968," in *Peasants and Politics in Kampuchea, 1942–1981*, ed. Ben Kiernan and Chanthou Boua (New York: M. E. Sharpe, 1982), 168.
112. Helmers, "Rice in the Cambodian Economy," 5; Rice, *Famine in the Remaking*, 153.
113. Diepart and Sem, *Cambodian Peasantry*, 15. See also Sokbunthoeun So, "Political Economy of Land Registration in Cambodia" (PhD diss., Northern Illinois University, 2009).
114. Chandler, *The Tragedy of Cambodian History*, 163–166. See also Kiernan, "The Samlaut Rebellion, 1967–1968," 166–205.
115. Peter Manning, *Transitional Justice and Memory in Cambodia: Beyond the Extraordinary Chambers* (New York: Routledge, 2017), 43.
116. Kiernan, "The Samlaut Rebellion, 1967–1968," 166.
117. Donald Kirk, *Wider War* (New York: Praeger, 1971), 78.
118. Chandler, *The Tragedy of Cambodian History*, 179–180.
119. Chandler, *The Tragedy of Cambodian History*, 180.
120. Chandler, *The Tragedy of Cambodian History*, 180; Slocomb, *An Economic History of Cambodia*, 107.
121. Hood and Ablin, "The Path to Cambodia's Present," xxiii.
122. Ben Kiernan, "Conflict in the Kampuchean Communist Movement," *Journal of*

Contemporary Asia 10, nos. 1–2 (1980): 7–74; Ben Kiernan, "Origins of Khmer Communism," *Southeast Asian Affairs* (1981): 161–180; Matthew Edwards, "The Rise of the Khmer Rouge in Cambodia: Internal or External Origins?," *Asian Affairs* 35, no. 1 (2004): 56–67; and Steve Heder, *Cambodian Communism and the Vietnamese Model: Imitation and Independence, 1930–1975* (Bangkok: White Lotus, 2004).

123. Kiernan, "Origins of Khmer Communism," 162–163.

124. Hood and Ablin, "The Path to Cambodia's Present," xxxii.

125. Elizabeth Becker details that many of the Issaraks refused to work with the Communists and refused to join in a united front with them against the French. This would lead to a permanent split in Cambodia between Communist and non-Communist independence movements. See Elizabeth Becker, *When the War Was Over: The Voices of Cambodia's Revolution and Its People* (New York: Simon & Schuster, 1986), 70.

126. David Chandler, "From 'Cambodge' to 'Kampuchea': State and Revolution in Cambodia, 1863–1979," *Thesis Eleven* 50, no. 1 (1997): 39.

127. Manning, *Transitional Justice*, 42.

128. Becker, *When the War Was Over*, 71.

129. Chandler, "From 'Cambodge' to 'Kampuchea,'" 39.

130. Quoted in Becker, *When the War Was Over*, 71.

131. Chandler, *The Tragedy of Cambodian History*, 108.

132. Chandler, *A History of Cambodia*, 187.

133. Chandler, *The Tragedy of Cambodian History*, 71; Kiernan, "Origins of Khmer Communism," 173.

134. Scott Ross, "'The Masters of the Khmer Rouge': Cambodia between China and Vietnam, 1954–1975" (PhD diss., University of Missouri, 2008), 10. See also Gareth Porter, "Vietnamese Communist Policy toward Kampuchea, 1930–1970," in *Revolution and Its Aftermath in Kampuchea: Eight Essays*, ed. David Chandler and Ben Kiernan (New Haven: Yale University Southeast Asia Studies, 1983), 57–98, at 69–70.

135. Heder, *Cambodian Communism*, 17–18.

136. Porter, "Vietnamese Communist Policy," 73.

137. Heder, *Cambodian Communism*, 49.

138. Kiernan, "Origins of Khmer Communism," 174–175.

139. Stephen Heder, "Kampuchea's Armed Struggle: The Origins of an Independent Revolution," *Bulletin of Concerned Asian Scholars* 11, no. 1 (1979): 2–23; Ben Kiernan, "Pol Pot and the Kampuchean Communist Movement," in *Peasants and Politics in Kampuchea, 1942–1981*, ed. Ben Kiernan and Chanthou Boua (Armonk, N.Y.: M. E. Sharpe, 1982), 227–317.

140. May Ebihara, "Perspectives on Sociopolitical Transformations in Cambodia/Kampuchea—a Review Article," *Journal of Asian Studies* 41, no. 1 (1981): 63–71, at 66.

141. Becker, *When the War Was Over*, 56.

142. Ben Kiernan, *The Pol Pot Regime: Race, Power, and Genocide in Cambodia under the Khmer Rouge, 1975–79* (New Haven, Conn.: Yale University Press, 1996), 13.

143. Becker, *When the War Was Over*, 81.

144. Philip Short, *Pol Pot: Anatomy of a Nightmare* (New York: Macmillan, 2005), 137. See also Ross, "'The Masters of the Khmer Rouge,'" 46.

145. Ross, "'The Masters of the Khmer Rouge,'" 47–48.

146. Kiernan, "Pol Pot," 254.

147. Kiernan, "Pol Pot," 254.

148. Ross, "'The Masters of the Khmer Rouge,'" 49–50. See also Short, *Pol Pot*, 146–147.

149. Heder, *Cambodian Communism*, 93.

150. Margaret Slocomb, *The People's Republic of Kampuchea, 1979–1989: The Revolution after Pol Pot* (Chiang Mai, Thailand: Silkworm Books, 2003), 10.

151. Heder, *Cambodian Communism*, 11.

152. Ross, "'The Masters of the Khmer Rouge,'" 51.

153. Slocomb, *The People's Republic of Kampuchea*, 11.

154. Ross, "'The Masters of the Khmer Rouge,'" 57.

155. Quoted in Short, *Pol Pot*, 161. See also Ross, "'The Masters of the Khmer Rouge,'" 60.

156. Ross, "'The Masters of the Khmer Rouge,'" 60.

157. Heder, "Kampuchea's Armed Struggle," 9.

158. Kate G. Frieson, "Revolution and Rural Response in Cambodia: 1970–1975," in *Genocide and Democracy in Cambodia: The Khmer Rouge, the United Nations and the International Community*, ed. Ben Kiernan (New Haven, Conn.: Yale University Southeast Asia Studies, 1993), 33–63, at 34.

CHAPTER 2. WITH FATAL PROGNOSIS

The epigraphs are from "Transcript of Telephone Conversation between President Nixon and the President's Assistant for National Security Affairs (Kissinger)," Nixon Presidential Materials, Henry A. Kissinger Telephone Conversation Transcripts, Box 21, Chronological File, National Archives, available at https://history.state.gov/historicaldocuments/frus1969-76v10/d97 (accessed January 3, 2021); and "Minutes of Cabinet Meeting," National Security Adviser, Memoranda of Conversation, Box 11, 4/16/75, Ford Library, available at https://history.state.gov/historicaldocuments/frus1969-76v10/d234 (accessed January 23, 2021).

1. "Memorandum from the President's Assistant for National Security Affairs (Kissinger) to President Nixon," Nixon Presidential Materials, NSC Files, Box 506, Country Files, Far East, Cambodia, Vol. 2, September 1969–9 April 1970, National Archives, available at https://history.state.gov/historicaldocuments/frus1969-76v06/d202 (accessed January 3, 2021).

2. William Rosoff, "Dissension in the Kingdom," in *Cambodia: The Widening War*, ed. Jonathan S. Grant, Laurence A. G. Moss, and Jonathan Unger (New York: Washington Square, 1971), 81–94, at 89–90.

3. Sydney H. Schanberg, "A Cambodian Anniversary Marked Only by Misery," *New York Times*, March 19, 1975, available at https://www.nytimes.com/1974/03/19/archives/a-cambodian-anniversary-marked-only-by-misery-a-difference-in-sound.html (accessed January 21, 2021).

4. Schanberg, "A Cambodian Anniversary."

5. Stian Rice, *Famine in the Remaking: Food System Change and Mass Starvation in Hawaii, Madagascar, and Cambodia* (Morgantown: West Virginia University Press,

2020), 154. See also Margaret Slocomb, *An Economic History of Cambodia in the Twentieth Century* (Singapore: National University of Singapore Press, 2010).

6. Schanberg, "A Cambodian Anniversary."

7. "Memorandum of Conversation," National Security Advisor, Kissinger-Scowcroft West Wing Office Files, Box 34, Vietnamese War (2), Camp David File, March 24–December 11, 1975, Ford Library, available at https://history.state.gov/historicaldocuments/frus1969-76v10/d191 (accessed January 3, 2021).

8. George Hildebrand and Gareth Porter, *Cambodia: Starvation and Revolution* (New York: Monthly Review Press, 1976), 12.

9. Michael E. Latham, "Redirecting the Revolution? The USA and the Failure of Nation-Building in South Vietnam," *Third World Quarterly* 27, no. 1 (2006): 27–41; and James M. Carter, *Inventing Vietnam: The United States and State Building, 1954–1968* (Cambridge: Cambridge University Press, 2008).

10. Carter, *Inventing Vietnam*, 6.

11. Latham, "Redirecting the Revolution?," 29–30.

12. Carter, *Inventing Vietnam*, 9.

13. Thomas C. Thayer, *War without Fronts: The American Experience in Vietnam* (Boulder, Colo.: Westview, 1985); Scott Sigmund Gartner and Marissa Edson Myers, "Body Counts and 'Success' in the Vietnam and Korean Wars," *Journal of Interdisciplinary History* 25, no. 3 (1995): 377–395; Gregory A. Daddis, "The Problem of Metrics: Assessing Progress and Effectiveness in the Vietnam War," *War in History* 19, no. 1 (2012): 73–98; Martin G. Clemis, *The Control War: The Struggle for South Vietnam, 1968–1975* (Norman: University of Oklahoma Press, 2018); and Oliver Belcher, "Sensing, Territory, Population: Computation, Embodied Sensors, and Hamlet Control in the Vietnam War," *Security Dialogue* 50, no. 5 (2019): 416–436.

14. Daddis, "The Problem of Metrics," 74.

15. See James A. Tyner, *War, Violence, and Population: Making the Body Count* (New York: Guilford, 2009), 74–81.

16. In 1969 the Provisional Revolutionary Government of South Vietnam was formed to provide a formal governmental structure to the NLF.

17. Wesley Attewell, "The Lifelines of Empire: Logistics as Infrastructural Power in Occupied South Vietnam," *American Quarterly* 72, no. 4 (2020): 909–935; Wesley Attewell, "Just-in-Time Imperialism: The Logistics Revolution and the Vietnam War," *Annals of the American Association of Geographers* 111, no. 5 (2021): 1329–1345.

18. Central Intelligence Agency, "Recent Developments in the Use of Cambodian Territory by the VC/NVA," available at https://www.cia.gov/readingroom/docs/CIA-RDP78T02095R000900070056-2.pdf (accessed January 9, 2021); Central Intelligence Agency, "Cambodia's Role in the Movement of Arms and Ammunition to the Vietnamese Communists," July 1, 1968, available at https://www.cia.gov/readingroom/docs/CIA-RDP82S00205R000100140005-4.pdf (accessed January 9, 2021).

19. Charles Smith, "Pressures on Laos," *Asian Affairs* 1, no. 3 (1970): 285–292, at 285.

20. Michel Foucault, *"Society Must Be Defended": Lectures at the Collège de France, 1975–1976*, trans. David Macey (New York: Picador, 2003), 240.

21. Walt W. Rostow, *The Stages of Economic Growth: A Non-Communist Manifesto* (Cambridge: Cambridge University Press, 1962), 107.

22. George C. Herring, *America's Longest War: The United States and Vietnam, 1950–1975*, 3rd ed. (New York: McGraw-Hill, 1996), 161.

23. Ben Kiernan and Taylor Owen, "Roots of U.S. Troubles in Afghanistan: Civilian Bombing Casualties and the Cambodian Precedent," *Asia-Pacific Journal* 8, no. 26-4 (June 2010): 10.

24. Kenton Clymer, *Troubled Relations: The United States and Cambodia since 1870* (DeKalb: Northern Illinois University Press, 2007), 99–100, 137.

25. Clymer, *Troubled Relations*, 99. Sihanouk's role and responsibility remain a source of contention. Clymer maintains that Sihanouk did not give his approval for military encroachment into Cambodia; he did, however, tolerate *limited* engagement. For example, Sihanouk stomached certain demands of both the DRV and the United States to operate within Cambodia's borders. However, as Clymer explains, these were specific and limited arrangements, agreed to only in a desperate hope to keep the violence away from Cambodia and to retain his country's independence and neutrality.

26. Jeffrey Kimball, *Nixon's Vietnam War* (Lawrence: University Press of Kansas, 1998); David F. Schmitz, *Richard Nixon and the Vietnam War* (Lanham, Md.: Rowman & Littlefield, 2014).

27. Pierre Asselin, *A Bitter Peace: Washington, Hanoi, and the Making of the Paris Agreement* (Chapel Hill: University of North Carolina Press, 2002), 14.

28. Schmitz, *Richard Nixon and the Vietnam War*, 31–32.

29. Scott S. Gartner, "Differing Evaluations of Vietnamization," *Journal of Interdisciplinary History* 24, no. 2 (1998): 243–262; Karlyn K. Campbell, *The Great Silent Majority: Nixon's 1969 Speech on Vietnamization* (College Station: Texas A&M University Press, 2014); David L. Prentice, "Choosing 'the Long Road': Henry Kissinger, Melvin Laird, Vietnamization, and the War over Nixon's Vietnam Strategy," *Diplomatic History* 40, no. 3 (2016): 445–474.

30. Jeffrey Kimball, "The Nixon Doctrine: A Sage of Misunderstanding," *Presidential Studies Quarterly* 36, no. 1 (2006): 59–74, at 65.

31. Prentice, "Choosing 'the Long Road,'" 461.

32. Geoffrey Warner, "Leaving Vietnam: Nixon, Kissinger and Ford, 1969–1975. Part One: January 1969–January 1972," *International Affairs* 87, no. 6 (2011: 1485–1506, at 1489.

33. Operation Menu comprised six bombing campaigns, known as Breakfast, Lunch, Snack, Dinner, Supper, and Dessert. Each campaign targeted a specific base area located in Cambodia. See Ben Kiernan, "The American Bombardment of Kampuchea, 1969–1973," *Vietnam Generation* 1, no. 1 (1989): 4–14; William Shawcross, *Sideshow: Kissinger, Nixon, and the Destruction of Cambodia*, rev. ed. (New York: Cooper Square, 2002); Taylor Owen and Ben Kiernan, "Bombs over Cambodia," *Walrus Magazine*, October 2006, 62–69; and Ben Kiernan and Taylor Owen, "Making More Enemies Than We Kill? Calculating U.S. Bomb Tonnages Dropped on Laos and Cambodia, and Weighing Their Implications," *Asia-Pacific Journal* 13, no. 16 (2015): 1–9. In the end, Nixon's bombing campaign would prove mostly ineffectual in achieving the hoped-for objectives. As described in an assessment provided by the CIA, "The B-52 bombing effort has been the least valuable, for several reasons. In general, there is a dearth of suitable targets in Cambodia such as massed forces and concentrated storage areas. . . . Most important, however, we simply do not have enough high-quality targetting information to provide certain or even probable targets for many of the B-52 strikes now run against Cambodian territory." See Cen-

tral Intelligence Agency, "The Employment of U.S. Air Power over Cambodia between 1 July and 15 August 1973," available at https://www.cia.gov/readingroom/docs/CIA-RDP80T01719R0004000320002-4.pdf (accessed January 9, 2021).

34. Lon Nol had recently been appointed prime minister by Sihanouk.

35. Arnold Isaacs, *Without Honor: Defeat in Cambodia* (Baltimore: Johns Hopkins University Press, 1983), 200.

36. Isaacs, *Without Honor*, 200.

37. "Minutes of Washington Special Actions Group Meeting," March 19, 1970, Nixon Presidential Materials, NSC Files, NSC Institutional Files (H-Files), Box H-114, WSAG Minutes, Originals, 1969–1970, National Archives, available at https://history.state.gov/historicaldocuments/frus1969-76v06/d203 (accessed January 23, 2021).

38. Isaacs, *Without Honor*, 201.

39. Isaacs, *Without Honor*, 201.

40. Isaacs, *Without Honor*, 199.

41. Donald M. Seekins, "Historical Setting," in *Cambodia: A Country Study*, ed. R. R. Ross (Washington, D.C.: U.S. Government Printing Office, 1990), 3–71, at 43–44. Khmer Rouge members of GRUNK claimed that it was not a government-in-exile because Khieu Samphan and other officials remained in Cambodia. Pol Pot, Ieng Sary, and Nuon Chea were not publicly identified as top leaders—although political and military authority was firmly in their hands.

42. Schmitz, *Richard Nixon and the Vietnam War*, 45.

43. Schmitz, *Richard Nixon and the Vietnam War*, 75.

44. "Memorandum from President Nixon to his Assistant for National Security Affairs (Kissinger)," Nixon Presidential Materials, White House Special Files, President's Personal File, Box 2, Memorandum for the President, January–December 1970, April 1970, National Archives, available at https://history.state.gov/historicaldocuments/frus1969-76v06/d245 (accessed January 23, 2021).

45. U.S. General Accounting Office, *U.S. Assistance to the Khmer Republic (Cambodia)*, October 10, 1973, available at https://www.gao.gov/assets/210/200096.pdf (accessed January 27, 2021).

46. Quoted in Wilfred P. Deac, *Road to the Killing Fields: The Cambodian War of 1970–1975* (College Station: Texas A&M University Press, 1997), 77.

47. Richard M. Nixon, "Address to the Nation on the Situation in Southeast Asia," April 30, 1970, https://www.nixonfoundation.org/2017/09/address-nation-situation-southeast-asia-april-30-1970/ (accessed July 5, 2022).

48. Quoted in Shawcross, *Sideshow*, 145.

49. Isaacs, *Without Honor*, 204.

50. "Memorandum from President Nixon to the Chairman of the Washington Special Actions Group (Kissinger)," Nixon Presidential Materials, NSC Files, Box 510, Country Files, Far East, Cambodia, Vol. 8, 20 June 1970–20 July 1970, National Archives, available at https://history.state.gov/historicaldocuments/frus1969-76v06/d339 (accessed January 3, 2021).

51. Central Intelligence Agency, "Political Improvement in Cambodia, Obstacles and Possibilities," July 24, 1973, available at https://www.cia.gov/readingroom/docs/CIA-RDP80T01719R000400310003-4.pdf (accessed January 9, 2021).

52. "Memorandum from Richard Kennedy and William Stearman of the National Se-

curity Council Staff to the President's Assistant for National Security Affairs (Kissinger)," Nixon Presidential Materials, NSC Files, Box 1338, Unfiled Material, NSC Unfiled, 1973, National Archives, available at https://history.state.gov/historicaldocuments/frus1969-76v10/d104 (accessed January 3, 2021).

53. Central Intelligence Agency, "A Review of CIA Judgments on the Probable Situation in Cambodia after the U.S. Bombing Halt on 15 August 1973," September 14, 1973, available at https://www.cia.gov/readingroom/docs/CIA-RDP80B01495R000600160028-2.pdf (accessed January 9, 2021).

54. Central Intelligence Agency, "Taking Stock in Cambodia," February 18, 1972, available at https://www.cia.gov/readingroom/docs/CIA-RDP85T00875R002000110043-7.pdf (accessed January 9, 2021).

55. "Memorandum of Conversation, Washington, January 29, 1973, 1:15–2:30 p.m.," Nixon Presidential Materials, NSC Files, Box 1030, Presidential/HAK Memoranda of Conversations, National Archives, available at https://history.state.gov/historicaldocuments/frus1969-76ve08/d104 (accessed January 3, 2021).

56. "Memorandum for the President's File by the President's Assistant for National Security Affairs (Kissinger)," Nixon Presidential Materials, NSC Files, Kissinger Office Files, Box 94, Country Files, Far East, China Exchanges, May 16–June 13, 1973, National Archives, available at https://history.state.gov/historicaldocuments/frus1969-76v18/d34 (accessed January 3, 2021).

57. "Memorandum of Conversation," Nixon Presidential Materials, NSC Files, Kissinger Office Files, Box 105, Country Files, Far East, Vietnam, GVN Memcons, May–June 1973, National Archives, available at https://history.state.gov/historicaldocuments/frus1969-76v10/d85 (accessed January 3, 2021).

58. "Memorandum of Conversation, Washington, July 25, 1973, 5:04–5:28 p.m.," Nixon Presidential Materials, NSC Files, Box 504, Country Files, Far East, Australia, January 1972–December 31, 1973, National Archives, available at https://history.state.gov/historicaldocuments/frus1969-76v12/d35 (accessed January 3, 2021).

59. "Memorandum of Conversation," National Security Advisor, Kissinger Reports on USSR, China, and Middle East Discussions, Box 2, China Memcons and Reports, November 25–29, 1974, Ford Library, available at https://history.state.gov/historicaldocuments/frus1969-76v18/d93 (accessed January 3, 2021).

60. Asselin, *A Bitter Peace*, 183.

61. Quoted in Asselin, *A Bitter Peace*, 183.

62. Asselin, *A Bitter Peace*, 183–184. See also Jeffrey Kimball, "The Case of the 'Decent Interval': Do We Now Have a Smoking Gun?" *SHAFR Newsletter* 32, no. 3 (2001): 35–39; Frank Snepp, *Decent Interval: An Insider's Account of Saigon's Indecent End Told by the CIA's Chief Strategy Analyst in Vietnam* (Lawrence: University Press of Kansas, 2002); Jussi Hanhimaki, "Selling the 'Decent Interval': Kissinger, Triangular Diplomacy, and the End of the Vietnam War, 1971–73," *Diplomacy & Statecraft* 14, no. 1 (2003): 159–194; Ken Hughes, "Fatal Politics: Nixon's Political Time Table for Withdrawing from Vietnam," *Diplomatic History* 34, no. 3 (2010): 497–506. For a more critical take on the "decent interval" thesis, see Pierre Asselin, "Kimball's Vietnam War," *Diplomatic History* 30, no. 1 (2006): 163–167.

63. "Minutes of Washington Special Actions Group Meeting," July 10, 1973, Nixon

Presidential Materials, NSC Files, NSC Institutional Files (H-Files), Box H-117, WSAG Meeting Minutes, National Archives, available at https://history.state.gov/historical documents/frus1969-76v10/d92 (accessed January 3, 2021).

64. "Minutes of Washington Special Actions Group Meeting," February 7, 1973, National Archives, Nixon Presidential Materials, NSC Files, NSC Institutional Files (H-Files), Box H-116, WSAG Meeting Minutes, National Archives, available at https://history.state.gov/historicaldocuments/frus1969-76v10/d10 (accessed January 3, 2021).

65. "Minutes of Washington Special Actions Group Meeting," October 2, 1973, Nixon Presidential Materials, NSC Files, NSC Institutional Files (H-Files), Box H-117, WSAG Meeting Minutes, National Archives, available at https://history.state.gov/historical documents/frus1969-76v10/d109 (accessed January 3, 2021).

66. Central Intelligence Agency, "Military Assistance Alternatives for Cambodia," April 22, 1970, available at https://www.cia.gov/readingroom/docs/CIA-RDP80R01720R000200030003-0.pdf (accessed January 9, 2021).

67. "Minutes of the Washington Special Actions Group Meeting," March 28, 1973, Nixon Presidential Materials, NSC Files, NSC Institutional Files (H-Files), Box H-117, WSAG Meeting Minutes, National Archives, available at https://history.state.gov/historicaldocuments/frus1969-76v10/d36 (accessed January 3, 2021).

68. "Telephone Conversation between President Nixon and the White House Chief of Staff (Haig)," Nixon Presidential Materials, White House Tapes, Conversation No. 44–120, National Archives, available at https://history.state.gov/historicaldocuments/frus1969-76v10/d37 (accessed January 3, 2021).

69. Sydney H. Schanberg, "Lon Nol Says U.S. Vows Full Support, *New York Times*, January 8, 1973, available at https://www.nytimes.com/1973/01/08/archives/lon-nol-says-us-vows-full-suppport.html (accessed January 21, 2021).

70. Isaacs, *Without Honor*, 217.

71. Shawcross, *Sideshow*, 294–295.

72. "Memorandum of Conversation," National Security Advisor, Kissinger Reports on USSR, China, and Middle East Discussions, Box 2, China Memcons and Reports, November 25–29, 1974, Ford Library, available at https://history.state.gov/historical documents/frus1969-76v18/d97 (accessed January 3, 2021).

73. Donald Kirk, "Cambodia's Economic Crisis," *Asian Survey* 11, no. 3 (1971): 246.

74. Sydney H. Schanberg, "Cambodian Economy Is Badly Hurt by War," *New York Times*, July 5, 1970, available at https://www.newyorktimes.com/1970/07/05/archives/cambodian-economy-is-badly-hurt-by-war-cambodian-economy-damaged-by.html (accessed January 21, 2021).

75. Central Intelligence Agency, "Military Assistance Alternatives for Cambodia," April 22, 1970.

76. Central Intelligence Agency, "The Impact of the Fighting in Cambodia on the Economy," June 1, 1970, available at https://www.cia.gov/readingroom/docs/CIA-RDP85T00875R001600030085-5.pdf (accessed January 9, 2021).

77. Rice, of course, was not the only foodstuff in short supply. According to Hildebrand and Porter, prior to the economic collapse of Cambodia, the Khmer ate more fish and meat than the Vietnamese and Laotians. Along with abundant fruit, these foods provided the protein and vitamins necessary to supplement rice in the Khmer diet. How-

ever, as early as October 1971, meat, poultry, and fish had largely disappeared from the diet of the poor in Phnom Penh; and by the beginning of 1975, the poor had virtually nothing to supplement what little rice they could acquire. See Hildebrand and Porter, *Cambodia: Starvation and Revolution*, 24.

78. Slocomb, *An Economic History of Cambodia*, 147.

79. Quoted in Slocomb, *An Economic History of Cambodia*, 148.

80. Slocomb, *An Economic History of Cambodia*, 148.

81. Hildebrand and Porter, *Cambodia: Starvation and Revolution*, 20; Slocomb, *An Economic History of Cambodia*, 149.

82. Rice, *Famine in the Remaking*, 156; Hildebrand and Porter, Cambodia: Starvation and Revolution, 20.

83. Hildebrand and Porter, *Cambodia: Starvation and Revolution*, 20.

84. Slocomb, *An Economic History of Cambodia*, 144.

85. Bridget Conley and Alex de Waal, "The Purposes of Starvation: Historical and Contemporary Uses," *Journal of International Criminal Justice* 17 (2019): 699–722, at 721.

86. Hildebrand and Porter, *Cambodia: Starvation and Revolution*, 21.

87. Hildebrand and Porter, *Cambodia: Starvation and Revolution*, 21; Slocomb, *An Economic History of Cambodia*, 144; Office of the Inspector-General of Foreign Assistance, Inspection Report, "Cambodia: An Assessment of Humanitarian Needs and Relief Efforts," March 12, 1975, available at https://www.govinfo.gov/app/details/GPO-CRECB-1975-pt6/ (accessed January 30, 2021).

88. Sydney H. Schanberg, "Cambodian Fighting Is Creating New Refugees by the Thousands," *New York Times*, May 27, 1973, available at https://www.nytimes.com/1973/05/27/archives/cambodian-fighting-is-creating-new-refugees-by-the-thousands.html (accessed January 21, 2021).

89. Office of the Inspector-General of Foreign Assistance, Inspection Report, "Cambodia," March 12, 1975.

90. U.S. General Accounting Office, "Follow-Up Review of Problems of War Victims, Civilian Health, and War-Related Casualties in Cambodia," available at https://www.gao.gov/assets/120/112323.pdf (accessed January 27, 2021).

91. As of 1973 the Cambodian government no longer published any estimates, and the United States Embassy judged the number at two hundred thousand. See U.S. General Accounting Office, "Follow-Up Review of Problems."

92. U.S. General Accounting Office, *Problems in the Khmer Republic (Cambodia) Concerning War Victims, Civilian Health, and War-Related Casualties*, February 2, 1972, available at https://www.gao.gov/assets/210/204505.pdf (accessed January 28, 2021).

93. U.S. General Accounting Office, *Problems in the Khmer Republic (Cambodia)*.

94. Hildebrand and Porter, *Cambodia: Starvation and Revolution*, 27.

95. Office of the Inspector-General of Foreign Assistance, Inspection Report, "Cambodia: An Assessment of Humanitarian Needs and Relief Efforts," March 12, 1975, available at https://www.govinfo.gov/app/details/GPO-CRECB-1975-pt6/ (accessed January 30, 2021).

96. Hildebrand and Porter, *Cambodia: Starvation and Revolution*, 24.

97. Rice, *Famine in the Remaking*, 158.

98. Rice, *Famine in the Remaking*, 158.

99. U.S. General Accounting Office, *U.S. Assistance to the Khmer Republic*.
100. U.S. General Accounting Office, *U.S. Assistance to the Khmer Republic*.
101. Hildebrand and Porter, *Cambodia: Starvation and Revolution*, 33.
102. Hildebrand and Porter, *Cambodia: Starvation and Revolution*, 19–20.
103. U.S. General Accounting Office, "Follow-Up Review of Problems."
104. U.S. General Accounting Office, "Follow-Up Review of Problems." See also Hildebrand and Porter, *Cambodia: Starvation and Revolution*, 35.
105. Office of the Inspector-General of Foreign Assistance, Inspection Report, "Cambodia," March 12, 1975.
106. Hildebrand and Porter, *Cambodia: Starvation and Revolution*, 36.
107. Israel Yost, "The Food for Peace Arsenal," *NACLA Newsletter* 5, no. 3 (1971): 1–7, at 1–2.
108. Gareth Porter and George C. Hildebrand, *The Politics of Food: Starvation and Agricultural Revolution in Cambodia* (Washington, D.C.: Indochina Resource Center, 1975), 11. See also Yost, "The Food for Peace Arsenal," 3–4; and Rice, *Famine in the Remaking*, 158.
109. Yost, "The Food for Peace Arsenal," 3.
110. Hildebrand and Porter, *Cambodia: Starvation and Revolution*, 36.
111. Rice, *Famine in the Remaking*, 166, emphasis in original.
112. Hildebrand and Porter, *Cambodia: Starvation and Revolution*, 21.
113. Hildebrand and Porter, *Cambodia: Starvation and Revolution*, 30.
114. U.S. General Accounting Office, *Report on the Payment of Phantom Troops in the Cambodian Military Forces*, July 3, 1973, available at https://www.gao.gov/assets/120/113347.pdf (accessed January 27, 2021). See also Hildebrand and Porter, *Cambodia: Starvation and Revolution*, 30.
115. U.S. General Accounting Office, *U.S. Assistance to the Khmer Republic*; U.S. General Accounting Office, *Report on the Payment of Phantom Troops*, July 3, 1973.
116. Sydney H. Schanberg, "Cambodian War Enriches the Corrupt, Debases the Poor," *New York Times*, November 30, 1972, available at https://www.nytimes.com/1972/11/30/archives/cambodian-war-enriches-the-corrupt-debases-the-poor.html (accessed January 21, 2021).
117. Schanberg, "Cambodian War Enriches the Corrupt."
118. Rice, *Famine in the Remaking*, 159.
119. Hildebrand and Porter, *Cambodia: Starvation and Revolution*, 24.
120. U.S. General Accounting Office, *Problems in the Khmer Republic (Cambodia)*, February 2, 1972.
121. Office of the Inspector-General of Foreign Assistance, Inspection Report, "Cambodia: An Assessment of Humanitarian Needs and Relief Efforts," March 12, 1975, available at https://www.govinfo.gov/app/details/GPO-CRECB-1975-pt6/ (accessed January 30, 2021).
122. Office of the Inspector-General of Foreign Assistance, Inspection Report, "Cambodia," March 12, 1975.
123. Office of the Inspector-General of Foreign Assistance, Inspection Report, "Cambodia," March 12, 1975.
124. Sydney H. Schanberg, "Siege in Cambodian Town Traps 30,000 Refugees," *New

York Times, February 24, 1975, available at https://www.nytimes.com/1975/02/24/archives/seige-in-cambodia-town-traps-30000-refugees-siege-in-cambodia-town.html (accessed January 21, 2021).

125. Office of the Inspector-General of Foreign Assistance, Inspection Report, "Cambodia," March 12, 1975.

126. Jan Ovesen and Ing-Britt Trankell, *Cambodians and Their Doctors: A Medical Anthropology of Colonial and Post-Colonial Cambodia* (Copenhagen, Denmark: Nordic Institute of Asian Studies, 2010), 79.

127. U.S. General Accounting Office, *Problems in the Khmer Republic (Cambodia)*, February 2, 1972.

128. Office of the Inspector-General of Foreign Assistance, Inspection Report, "Cambodia," March 12, 1975.

129. U.S. General Accounting Office, *Problems in the Khmer Republic (Cambodia)*, February 2, 1972.

130. Office of the Inspector-General of Foreign Assistance, Inspection Report, "Cambodia," March 12, 1975.

131. Sydney H. Schanberg, "Reporter's Notebook: Suffering Seems Endless in Phnom Penh," *New York Times*, March 29, 1975, available at https://www.nytimes.com/1975/03/29/archives/reporters-notebook-suffering-seems-endless-in-phnom-penh.html (accessed January 21, 2021).

132. Office of the Inspector-General of Foreign Assistance, Inspection Report, "Cambodia," March 12, 1975.

133. Office of the Inspector-General of Foreign Assistance, Inspection Report, "Cambodia," March 12, 1975.

134. "Minutes of Washington Special Actions Group Meeting," November 2, 1973, Nixon Presidential Materials, NSC Files, NSC Institutional Files (H-Files), Box H-117, WSAG Meeting Minutes, National Archives, available at https://history.state.gov/historicaldocuments/frus1969-76v10/d113 (accessed January 3, 2021).

135. Hildebrand and Porter, *Cambodia: Starvation and Revolution*, 33.

136. "Minutes of Washington Special Actions Group Meeting," July 10, 1973, Nixon Presidential Materials, NSC Files, NSC Institutional Files (H-Files), Box H-117, WSAG Meeting Minutes, National Archives, available at https://history.state.gov/historicaldocuments/frus1969-76v10/d92 (accessed January 3, 2021).

137. "Minutes of Washington Special Actions Group Meeting," July 10, 1973, National Archives, Nixon Presidential Materials, NSC Files, NSC Institutional Files (H-Files), Box H-117, WSAG Meeting Minutes, available at https://history.state.gov/historicaldocuments/frus1969-76v10/d92 (accessed January 3, 2021).

138. Quoted in Hildebrand and Porter, *Cambodia: Starvation and Revolution*, 38.

139. Hildebrand and Porter, *Cambodia: Starvation and Revolution*, 38.

CHAPTER 3. WORK MORE, GAIN MORE, BUT SPEND LESS CAPITAL

The epigraphs are from Document No. D55874, "Democratic Kampuchea: A Workers' and Peasants' State in South-East Asia," archived at the Documentation Center of Cambodia, Phnom Penh; and Document E3/799, "Minutes of the Plenary Meeting of the

920th Division," archived by the Extraordinary Chambers in the Courts of Cambodia (ECCC) at https://www.eccc.gov.kh/en/document/court/note-committee-division-920-meeting-report-about-enemy-situation-and-our-situation.

1. May Ebihara, "Intervillage, Intertown, and Village-City Relations in Cambodia," *Annals of the New York Academy of Sciences* 220, no. 1 (1973): 358–375; May Ebihara, "Residence Patterns in a Khmer Peasant Village," *Annals of the New York Academy of Sciences* 293, no. 1 (1977): 51–68; Ben Kiernan, "Introduction," in *Peasants and Politics in Kampuchea, 1942–1981*, ed. Ben Kiernan and Chanthou Boua (London: Zed, 1982), 1–28; May Ebihara, "Revolution and Reformulation in Kampuchean Village Culture," in *The Cambodian Agony*, ed. David A. Ablin and Marlowe Hood (Armonk, N.Y.: M. E. Sharpe, 1990), 16–61; May Ebihara, "A Cambodian Village under the Khmer Rouge," in *Genocide and Democracy in Cambodia: The Khmer Rouge, the United Nations and the International Community*, ed. Ben Kiernan (New Haven, Conn.: Yale University Southeast Asia Studies, 1993), 51–63; Kalyanee E. Mam, "An Oral History of Family Life under the Khmer Rouge," Yale Center for International and Area Studies Working Paper Series, GS10 (New Haven, Conn.: Yale Center for International and Area Studies, 1999); Siv Leng Chhor, "Destruction of Family Foundation in Kampuchea," *Searching for the Truth* 11 (2000): 22–23; Ratana C. Huy, "Khmer Rouge Wedding," *Searching for the Truth* 25 (2002): 26–28; Judy Ledgerwood and John Vijghen, "Decision-Making in Rural Khmer Villages," in *Cambodia Emerges from the Past: Eight Essays*, ed. Judy Ledgerwood (DeKalb: Center for Southeast Asian Studies, Northern Illinois University, 2002), 109–150; Zal Karkaria, "Failure through Neglect: The Women's Policies of the Khmer Rouge" (master's thesis, Concordia University, 2003); Patrick Heuveline and Bunnak Poch, "Do Marriages Forget Their Past? Marital Stability in Post-Khmer Rouge Cambodia," *Demography* 43 (2006): 99–125; Susan H. Lee, *"Rice Plus": Widows and Economic Survival in Rural Cambodia* (New York: Routledge, 2006); Katherine Brickell, "Gender Relations in the Khmer 'Home': Post-Conflict Perspectives" (PhD diss., London School of Economics and Political Science, 2007); Annuska Derks, *Khmer Women on the Move: Exploring Work and Life in Urban Cambodia* (Honolulu: University of Hawai'i Press, 2008); Neha Jain, "Forced Marriage as a Crime against Humanity," *Journal of International Criminal Justice* 6 (2008): 1013–1032; Peg LeVine, *Love and Dread in Cambodia: Weddings, Births, and Ritual Harm under the Khmer Rouge* (Singapore: National University of Singapore Press, 2010); Mathieu Guérin, "Khmer Peasants and Land Access in Kompong Thom Province in the 1930s," *Journal of Southeast Asian Studies* 43, no. 3 (2012): 441–462; Chan Pranith Phuong, "Forced Marriage to Avoid the Death," *Searching for the Truth*, (Third Quarter 2013): 18–19; Heidi Hoefinger, *Sex, Love and Money in Cambodia: Professional Girlfriends and Transactional Relationships* (New York: Routledge, 2014); Jean-Christophe Diepart, *The Fragmentation of Land Tenure Systems in Cambodia: Peasants and the Formalization of Land Rights* (Paris: Technical Committee on "Land Tenure and Development," 2015); and May Ebihara, *Svay: A Khmer Village in Cambodia* (Ithaca, N.Y.: Cornell University Press, 2018).

2. Lee, *"Rice Plus,"* 25–27.

3. Ebihara, "Revolution and Reformulation," 18.

4. Ebihara, "Revolution and Reformulation," 21.

5. Ebihara, "Revolution and Reformulation," 21.

6. "MK 82 Aircraft Bomb," Geneva International Centre for Humanitarian Demining (GICHD), available at http://characterisationexplosiveweapons.org/studies/annex-e-mk82-aircraft-bombs/ (accessed February 12, 2021).

7. Sydney H. Schanberg, "A Cambodian Landscape: Bomb Pits, Rubble, Ashes," *New York Times*, May 24, 1973, available at https://www.nytimes.com/1973/05/24/archives/a-cambodian-landscape-bomb-pits-rubble-ashes-bombing-is-responsible.html (accessed January 21, 2021).

8. Quoted in Schanberg, "A Cambodian Landscape."

9. Eric Prokosch, "Technology and Its Control: Antipersonnel Weapons," *International Social Science Journal* 28 (1976): 341–358, at 349. See also James A. Tyner, *Military Legacies: A World Made by War* (New York: Routledge, 2010).

10. Ebihara, "Revolution and Reformulation," 21.

11. Ebihara, "Revolution and Reformulation," 22.

12. Ebihara, "Revolution and Reformulation," 23.

13. Document E3/760, "Revolutionary Flag, Issue 6 June 1976," archived by the Extraordinary Chambers in the Courts of Cambodia (ECCC) at https://www.eccc.gov.kh/sites/default/files/documents/courtdoc/00509604-00509635_E3_760_EN.TXT.pdf.

14. Document E3/760, "Revolutionary Flag, Issue 6 June 1976."

15. Document E3/760, "Revolutionary Flag, Issue 6 June 1976."

16. Document E3/760, "Revolutionary Flag, Issue 6 June 1976."

17. Michael J. Watts, *Silent Violence: Food, Famine, and Peasantry in Northern Nigeria* (1983; reprint, Athens: University of Georgia Press, 2013), 1.

18. Administratively, each political unit (i.e., zone, region, district, subdistrict, and cooperative) was governed by a three-person committee consisting of a secretary, deputy secretary, and member. The zone committee, consequently, was responsible for overseeing the implementation of party plans and policies throughout its respective zone, and for delegating plans and policies to all other levels (e.g., regions, districts) in its zone. Likewise, the committees at the region, district, subdistrict, and cooperative levels fulfilled similar functions of implementing tasks designated by the CPK upper echelon. See Office of the Co-Prosecutors, *Co-Prosecutors' Rule 66 Final Submission* (public redacted version), Case No.: 002/19/09/20007–ECCC/OCIJ, page 54.

19. Office of the Co-Prosecutors, *Co-Prosecutors' Rule 66 Final Submission* (public redacted version), Case No.: 002/19/09/20007–ECCC/OCIJ, page 53.

20. Communist Party of Kampuchea (CPK), "The Party's Four-Year Plan to Build Socialism in All Fields, 1977–1980," in *Pol Pot Plans the Future*, ed. David P. Chandler, Ben Kiernan, and Chanthou Boua (New Haven, Conn.: Yale Center for International and Area Studies, 1988), 44–119.

21. CPK, "The Party's Four-Year Plan," 51.

22. CPK, "The Party's Four-Year Plan," 51.

23. Stian Rice, *Famine in the Remaking: Food System Change and Mass Starvation in Hawaii, Madagascar, and Cambodia* (Morgantown: West Virginia University Press, 2020), 168.

24. Communist Party of Kampuchea (CPK), "Preliminary Explanation before Reading the Plan, by the Party Secretary," in *Pol Pot Plans the Future: Confidential Leadership*

Documents from Democratic Kampuchea, 1976–1977, eds. David P. Chandler, Ben Kiernan, and Chanthou Boua (New Haven, Conn.: Yale University Press, 1988), 120–63, at 127.

25. In the early years of the Cold War, representatives of former colonies sought to forge an independent path, free from the dictates of either the Western powers or the Soviet Union. Known as the Non-Aligned Movement (NAM), this organization became a powerful political force that proclaimed a commitment to nationalism, the preservation of national dignity, and the realization of national power. Moreover, the NAM connoted an alliance with the forces of regionalism and national independence, as well as with the struggle for a new economic order, social and economic progress, and self-reliance. See, for example, Brian R. Tomlinson, "What Was the Third World?," *Journal of Contemporary History* 38, no. 2 (2003): 307–321; Jürgen Dinkel, "'Third World Begins to Flex Its Muscles': The Non-Aligned Movement and the North-South Conflict during the 1970s," in *Neutrality and Neutralism in the Global Cold War*, ed. Sandra Bott, Jussi M. Hanhimaki, Janick Schaufelbuehl, and Marco Wyss (New York: Routledge, 2015), 108–123; Robert B. Rakove, "The Rise and Fall of Non-Aligned Mediation, 1961–6," *International History Review* 37, no. 5 (2015): 991–1013; and Lorenz M. Lüthi, "The Non-Aligned Movement and the Cold War, 1961–1973," *Journal of Cold War Studies* 18, no. 4 (2016): 98–147.

26. Institute of Foreign Affairs, *Summit Declarations of Non-Aligned Movement (1961–2009)* (Kathmandu, Nepal: Institute of Foreign Affairs, 2011), 84. Notably, sixteen months earlier a resurgent had Asia witnessed the victory of the Khmer Rouge. Remarkably, this event seemingly heralded a broader victory of Third Worldism over colonialism and neocolonialism. Effectively, member states of the Non-Aligned Movement understood the CPK's *national* struggle as part of an *international* struggle. As stated in the declaration, member states "welcomed the triumph of the struggle of the peoples of Democratic Kampuchea, Lao People's Democratic Republic and the Socialist Republic of Vietnam against United States' imperialist aggression." In addition, the conference "congratulated Democratic Kampuchea on having remained faithful to the principles of Non-Alignment and paid tribute to its constant determination to defend them." The struggles of Democratic Kampuchea, notably, stood alongside "the success of the liberation struggle of Guinea-Bissau, Cape Verde, Mozambique, Angola, and Sao Tome and Principe." See Institute of Foreign Affairs, *Summit Declarations*, 102.

27. Document No. D55874, "Democratic Kampuchea: A Workers' and Peasants' State in South-East Asia," archived at the Documentation Center of Cambodia, Phnom Penh.

28. Document No. D55874, "Democratic Kampuchea: A Workers' and Peasants' State in South-East Asia," archived at the Documentation Center of Cambodia, Phnom Penh.

29. See my argument in James A. Tyner, *Red Harvests: Agrarian Capitalism and Genocide in Democratic Kampuchea* (Morgantown: West Virginia University Press, 2021), 33–38.

30. Karl D. Jackson, "The Ideology of Total Revolution," in *Cambodia, 1975–1978: Rendezvous with Death*, ed. Karl D. Jackson (Princeton, N.J.: Princeton University Press, 1989), 37–78, at 45.

31. Charles H. Twining, "The Economy," in *Cambodia, 1975–1978: Rendezvous with Death*, ed. Karl D. Jackson (Princeton, N.J.: Princeton University), 109–150, at 110.

32. Friedrich W. Y. Wu, "From Self-Reliance to Interdependence? Development Strategy and Foreign Economic Policy in Post-Mao China," *Modern China* 7, no. 4 (1981): 445–482, at 452.

33. Kempe R. Hope, "Self-Reliance and Participation of the Poor in the Development Process in the Third World," *Futures* 15, no. 6 (1983): 455–462, at 455.

34. Document No. E3/1612, "Meeting of the Standing Committee 9 October 1975," archived by the Extraordinary Chambers in the Courts of Cambodia (ECCC) at https://www.eccc.gov.kh/sites/default/files/documents/courtdoc/00183393-00183408_E3_1612_EN.TXT.pdf.

35. Hope, "Self-Reliance," 456.

36. CPK, "Preliminary Explanation," 150–151.

37. Tony Smith, "The Underdevelopment of Development Literature: The Case of Dependency Theory," *World Politics* 31, no. 2 (1979): 247–288; Michael P. Todaro, *Economic Development in the Third World*, 4th ed. (New York: Longman, 1989); Henry J. Bruton, "A Reconsideration of Import Substitution," *Journal of Economic Literature* 36, no. 2 (1998): 903–936; and Robert P. Potter, Tony Binns, Jennifer A. Elliott, and David Smith, *Geographies of Development*, 2nd ed. (New York: Pearson, 2004).

38. Rice, *Famine in the Remaking*, 168–169.

39. Document No. D00698, "Cooperation with the Ministry of Commerce," archived at the Documentation Center of Cambodia, Phnom Penh.

40. CPK, "The Party's Four-Year Plan," 46.

41. Communist Party of Kampuchea [CPK], "Report of Activities of the Party Center According to the General Political Tasks of 1976," in *Pol Pot Plans the Future: Confidential Leadership Documents from Democratic Kampuchea, 1976–1977*, ed. David Chandler, Ben Kiernan, and Chanthou Boua (New Haven, Conn.: Yale University Southeast Asia Studies, 1988), 177–212, at 200.

42. CPK, "The Party's Four-Year Plan, 51.

43. CPK, "The Party's Four-Year Plan," 106.

44. CPK, "The Party's Four-Year Plan," 51; Kent Helmers, "Rice in the Cambodian Economy: Past and Present," in *Rice Production in Cambodia*, ed. Harry J. Nesbitt (Manila: International Rice Research Institute, 1997), 1–14, at 6; and Rice, *Famine in the Remaking*, 169–170.

45. The Khmer Rouge, relatedly, initiated a spatial practice to rearrange the distribution of rice paddies. Historically, rice fields in Cambodia were arranged haphazardly in parcels of varying shapes and sizes, the end result being a pastiche of land-use patterns. Under the Khmer Rouge these paddies were reorganized into regular quadrangular plots—ostensibly a more efficient spatial arrangement of farming practices. Ebihara, "Intervillage, Intertown, and Village-City Relations," 26.

46. CPK, "Preliminary Explanation," 132.

47. Document E3/781, "Examination of Control and Implementation of the Policy Line on Restoring the Economy and Preparations to Build the Country in Every Sector," archived by the Extraordinary Chambers in the Courts of Cambodia (ECCC) at https://www.eccc.gov.kh/sites/default/files/documents/courtdoc/00523569-00523592_E3_781_EN.TXT.pdf.

48. See, for example, Joel R. Charny, "Appropriate Development Aid for Kampuchea,"

in *The Cambodian Agony*, ed. David A. Ablin and Marlowe Hood (Armonk, N.Y.: M. E. Sharpe, 1990), 243–266, at 258.

49. Document No. E3/752, "Revolutionary Male and Female Youth Issue 3, March 1976," archived by the Extraordinary Chambers in the Courts of Cambodia (ECCC) at https://www.eccc.gov.kh/sites/default/files/documents/courtdoc/00593548-00593577_E3_752_EN.TXT.pdf.

50. Document No. E3/752, "Revolutionary Male and Female Youth Issue 3, March 1976."
51. Document E3/781, "Examination of Control and Implementation of the Policy Line."
52. CPK, "The Party's Four-Year Plan," 89.
53. CPK, "The Party's Four-Year Plan," 89.
54. Rice, *Famine in the Remaking*, 174.
55. James A. Tyner, Mandy Munro-Stasiuk, Corrine Coakley, Sokvisal Kimsroy, and Stian Rice, "Khmer Rouge Irrigation Schemes during the Cambodian Genocide," *Genocide Studies International* 12, no. 1 (2018): 103–119; Corrine Coakley, Mandy Munro-Stasiuk, James A. Tyner, Sokvisal Kimsroy, Chhunly Chhay, and Stian Rice, "Extracting Irrigation Structure Networks from Pre–Landsat 4 Satellite Imagery Using Vegetation Indices," *Remote Sensing* 11, no. 20 (2019): 2397.
56. See, for example, "Interview with Van Rith in Khpop Commune, S'ang District, Kandal Province," archived at the Documentation Center of Cambodia, Phnom Penh.
57. Document E3/781, "Examination of Control and Implementation of the Policy Line."
58. Document E3/781, "Examination of Control and Implementation of the Policy Line."
59. CPK, "THE Party's Four-Year Plan," 90.
60. Document E3/781, "Examination of Control and Implementation of the Policy Line."
61. Document E3/781, "Examination of Control and Implementation of the Policy Line."
62. Document E3/781, "Examination of Control and Implementation of the Policy Line."
63. Document E3/781, "Examination of Control and Implementation of the Policy Line."
64. Rice, *Famine in the Remaking*, 170.
65. Communist Party of Kampuchea CPK, "Excerpted Report on the Leading Views of the Comrade Representing the Party Organization at a Zone Assembly," in *Pol Pot Plans the Future: Confidential Leadership Documents from Democratic Kampuchea, 1976–1977*, ed. David Chandler, Ben Kiernan, and Chanthou Boua (New Haven, Conn.: Yale University Southeast Asia Studies, 1988), 27.
66. Document E3/752, "Revolutionary Male and Female Youth Issue 3, March 1976."
67. CPK, "THE Party's Four-Year Plan," 112.
68. CPK, "THE Party's Four-Year Plan," 112.
69. Document No. E3/752, "Revolutionary Male and Female Youth Issue 3, March 1976."
70. Document No. E3/752, "Revolutionary Male and Female Youth Issue 3, March 1976."
71. Mam, "An Oral History of Family Life," 8.
72. Mam, "An Oral History of Family Life," 8.
73. Ebihara, "A Cambodian Village under the Khmer Rouge," 51–63, at 55.
74. Document No. E3/50, "Third Year Anniversary of the Organization of Peasant Cooperatives," archived by the Extraordinary Chambers in the Courts of Cambodia (ECCC) AT Https://www.eccc.gov.kh/sites/default/files/documents/courtdoc/00636008-00636043_E3_50_EN.TXT.pdf.
75. Document No. E3/50, "Third Year Anniversary of the Organization."

76. Timothy Carney, "The Unexpected Victory," in *Cambodia, 1975–1978: Rendezvous with Death*, ed. Karl D. Jackson (Princeton, N.J.: Princeton University Press, 1989), 29.

77. Carney, "The Unexpected Victory," 30.

78. Document No. E3/50, "Third Year Anniversary of the Organization."

79. Document E3/216, "Record of the Standing Committee's Visit to the Northwest Zone, 20–24 August 1975," archived by the Extraordinary Chambers in the Courts of Cambodia (ECCC) AT Https://www.eccc.gov.kh/sites/default/files/documents/courtdoc/2013-09-16%2010%3A12/E3_216_EN.PDF.

80. Document E3/216, "Record of the Standing Committee's Visit to the Northwest Zone, 20–24 August 1975."

81. Ebihara, "Revolution and Reformulation," 25.

82. Twining, "The Economy," 125.

83. Carney, "The Unexpected Victory," 13–35, at 28.

84. Twining, "The Economy," 125–126.

85. Twining, "The Economy," 127.

86. Document No. E3/752, "Revolutionary Male and Female Youth Issue 3, March 1976."

87. Document No. E3/748, "Revolutionary Flag Special Issue, October–November 1975," archived by the Extraordinary Chambers in the Courts of Cambodia (ECCC) at https://www.eccc.gov.kh/sites/default/files/documents/courtdoc/00495800-00495828_E3_748_EN.TXT.pdf.

88. Document E3/216, "Record of the Standing Committee's Visit to the Northwest Zone, 20–24 August 1975."

89. Ebihara, "Revolution and Reformulation," 26.

90. Tyner, *Red Harvests*.

91. Document E3/166, "Revolutionary Flag Issue 2–3 February–March 1976," archived by the Extraordinary Chambers in the Courts of Cambodia (ECCC) AT Https://www.eccc.gov.kh/sites/default/files/documents/courtdoc/00517813-00517848_E3_166_EN.TXT.pdf.

92. Document E3/166, "Revolutionary Flag Issue 2–3 February–March 1976."

93. Gavin Rae, *Critiquing Sovereign Violence: Law, Biopolitics, Bio-Juridicalism* (Edinburgh: Edinburgh University Press, 2021), 139.

94. Ben Kiernan, *The Pol Pot Regime: Race, Power, and Genocide in Cambodia under the Khmer Rouge, 1975–79* (New Haven, Conn.: Yale University Press, 1996); Ben Kiernan, "Ben Kiernan Replies to Sorpong Peou," *Holocaust and Genocide Studies* 12, no. 1 (1998): 213–214. For a contrasting view, see Stephen Heder, "Racism, Marxism, Labeling and Genocide in Ben Kiernan's *The Pol Pot Regime*," *South East Asia Research* 5, no. 2 (1997): 101–153.

95. Kiernan does not provide a definition of "race" or racism; he does explain that he uses "the terms 'race' and 'ethnicity' interchangeably, because of the emerging scholarly consensus that racial boundaries have no biological basis." See Kiernan, *The Pol Pot Regime*, 26.

96. Michel Foucault, *"Society Must Be Defended": Lectures at the Collège de France, 1975–1976*, trans. David Macey (New York: Picador, 2003), 261.

97. Foucault, *"Society Must Be Defended,"* 81.

98. Document No. D00674, "Communist Party of Kampuchea: Statute," archived at the Documentation Center of Cambodia, Phnom Penh.

99. Quoted in Henri Locard, *Pol Pot's Little Red Book: The Sayings of Ankar* (Chiang Mai, Thailand: Silkworm Books, 2004), 187–188. See also James A. Tyner, "Dead Labor, Landscapes, and Mass Graves: Administrative Violence during the Cambodian Genocide," *Geoforum* 52 (2014): 7–77.

100. Mam, "An Oral History of Family Life," 9.

101. Kalyanee Mam, "The Endurance of the Cambodian Family under the Khmer Rouge Regime: An Oral History," in *Genocide in Cambodia and Rwanda: New Perspectives*, ed. Susan E. Cook (New Haven, Conn.: Yale Center for International and Area Studies, 2004), 127–171, at 134–135.

102. Document No. E3/752, "Revolutionary Male and Female Youth Issue 3, March 1976," archived by the Extraordinary Chambers in the Courts of Cambodia (ECCC) at https://www.eccc.gov.kh/sites/default/files/documents/courtdoc/00593548-00593577_E3_752_EN.TXT.pdf.

103. Document No. E3/752, "Revolutionary Male and Female Youth Issue 3, March 1976."

104. Document No. E3/752, "Revolutionary Male and Female Youth Issue 3, March 1976."

105. The cans used for measurement were most often Nestle's condensed milk cans; each can could contain approximately two hundred grams of rice.

106. In reality, most workers did not even receive this basic minimum, with the notable exception being high-ranking officials and, to a lesser extent, Khmer Rouge cadres and base people.

107. Interestingly, the only food ration that was projected to vary over time was dessert. In 1977, workers were to receive dessert once every three days; by 1978 this allotment was increased to once every two days; and by 1979 workers were to receive dessert daily. In reality, again, workers rarely received desserts at any point.

108. CPK, "The Party's Four-Year Plan," 51. This translates into approximately 0.85 kilogram per day.

109. CPK, "The Party's Four-Year Plan," 54.

110. CPK, "The Party's Four-Year Plan, 56–57. The plan is unclear as to the distribution of the remaining one million tons.

111. CPK, "Excerpted Report," 20.

112. Twining, "The Economy," 130.

113. Ebihara, "Revolution and Reformulation," 23.

114. Ebihara, "Revolution and Reformulation," 23.

115. Document No. D21934, archived at the Documentation Center of Cambodia, Phnom Penh.

116. See, for example, Document No. D00707 and Document No. D02166, archived at the Documentation Center of Cambodia, Phnom Penh.

117. See for example Craig Etcheson, *After the Killing Fields: Lessons from the Cambodian Genocide* (Lubbock: Texas Tech University Press, 2005), 107–128. See also Michael Vickery, *Cambodia, 1975–1982* (Chiang Mai, Thailand: Silkworm Books, 1984), 88–172.

118. Randle C. DeFalco, "Justice and Starvation in Cambodia: The Khmer Rouge Famine," *Cambodia Law and Policy Journal* 2 (2014): 69.

119. Document No. E3/750, "Revolutionary Male and Female Youths Number 11 November 1975," archived by the Extraordinary Chambers in the Courts of Cambodia (ECCC) at https://www.eccc.gov.kh/sites/default/files/documents/courtdoc/2013-09-16%2010%3A26/E3_750_EN.PDF.

120. Document No. E3/11, "Revolutionary Flag Special Issue September 1977," archived by the Extraordinary Chambers in the Courts of Cambodia (ECCC) at https://www.eccc.gov.kh/sites/default/files/documents/courtdoc/00486212-00486266_E3_11_EN.TXT.pdf.

121. Document No. E3/11, "Revolutionary Flag Special Issue September 1977."

122. Document No. E3/798, "Minutes of the Meeting of Secretaries and Deputy Secretaries of Divisions and Independent Regiments," archived by the Extraordinary Chambers in the Courts of Cambodia (ECCC) at https://www.eccc.gov.kh/sites/default/files/documents/courtdoc/00183966-00183969_E3_798_EN.TXT.pdf.

123. Document No. E3/822, "Minutes of the Meeting [of] Comrade Tal of Division 290 and Division 170," archived by the Extraordinary Chambers in the Courts of Cambodia (ECCC) at https://www.eccc.gov.kh/en/document/court/minute-meeting-tal-division-290-and-division170-16-september-1976-1615-pm-first-page.

124. Randle DeFalco, "Accounting for Famine at the Extraordinary Chambers in the Courts of Cambodia: The Crimes against Humanity of Extermination, Inhumane Acts and Persecution," *International Journal of Transitional Justice* 5, no. 1 (2011): 142–158, at 151–52.

125. Document No. D21934, archived at the Documentation Center of Cambodia, Phnom Penh.

126. Communist Party of Kampuchea CPK, "Summary of the Results of the 1976 Study Session," in *Pol Pot Plans the Future: Confidential Leadership Documents from Democratic Kampuchea, 1976–1977*, ed. David Chandler, Ben Kiernan, and Chanthou Boua (New Haven, Conn.: Yale University Southeast Asia Studies, 1988), 175.

127. CPK, "Preliminary Explanation," 156.

128. CPK, "Preliminary Explanation," 156.

CHAPTER 4. ANOTHER CAMBODIAN WAR

The chapter title is from "Intelligence Memorandum Prepared in the Central Intelligence Agency," December 15, 1978, Office of Support Services (DI), Job 80T00634a: Production Case Files, Box 5, Central Intelligence Agency, available at https://history.state.gov/historicaldocuments/frus1977-80v22/d34 (accessed February 4, 2021). The epigraph is from "Report Prepared in the Office of the First Lady," undated, National Security Affairs, Brzezinski Material, Country File, Box 42, Kampuchea, 11–12/79, Carter Library, available at https://history.state.gov/historicaldocuments/frus1977-80v22/d71 (accessed February 4, 2021).

1. For in-depth discussion on the overthrow of the Khmer Rouge and the establishment of the People's Republic of Kampuchea, see Stephen R. Heder, *Kampuchean Occupation and Resistance*, Asian Studies Monograph No. 027 (Bangkok, Thailand: Institute of Asian Studies, Chulalongkorn University, 1980); Ben Kiernan, "New Light on the Ori-

gins of the Vietnam-Kampuchea Conflict," *Bulletin of Concerned Asian Scholars* 12, no. 4 (1980): 61–65; Nayan Chanda, *Brother Enemy: The War after the War* (New York: Collier Books, 1986); Margaret Slocomb, *The People's Republic of Kampuchea, 1979–1989: The Revolution after Pol Pot* (Chiang Mai, Thailand: Silkworm Books, 2003); Evan Gottesman, *Cambodia after the Khmer Rouge: Inside the Politics of Nation Building* (New Haven, Conn.: Yale University Press, 2003); and Tom Fawthrop and Helen Jarvis, *Getting Away with Genocide? Elusive Justice and the Khmer Rouge Tribunal* (London: Pluto, 2004). For a critical take on Vietnam's military intervention, see Laura Summers, "In Matters of War and Socialism, Anthony Barnett Would Shame and Honor Kampuchea Too Much," *Bulletin of Concerned Asian Scholars* 11, no. 4 (1979): 10–18. For a discussion on the subsequent famine relief efforts, see John Murlis, "An Analysis of Food Aid Information in Kampuchea to March 1980," *Disasters* 4, no. 3 (1980): 263–270; Linda Mason and Roger Brown, *Rice, Rivalry, and Politics: Managing Cambodian Relief* (Notre Dame: University of Notre Dame Press, 1983); and Eva Mysliwiec, *Punishing the Poor: The International Isolation of Kampuchea* (Oxford, UK: Oxfam 1988); and Joel R. Charny, "Oxfam's Cambodia Response and Effective Approaches to Humanitarian Action," in *Change Not Charity: Essays on Oxfam America's First 40 Years*, ed. Laura Roper (Boston: Oxfam, 2010), 165–174.

2. Chanda, *Brother Enemy*, 340.

3. Sophie Quinn-Judge, "Victory on the Battlefield; Isolation in Asia: Vietnam's Cambodia Decade, 1979–1989," in *The Third Indochina War: Conflict between China, Vietnam and Cambodia, 1972–79*, ed. Odd Arne Westad and Sophie Quinn-Judge (New York: Routledge, 2006), 207–230, at 211.

4. For an understanding of Vietnam's overthrow of the Khmer Rouge, see Chanda, *Brother Enemy* and Stephen J. Morris, *Why Vietnam Invaded Cambodia: Political Culture and the Causes of War* (Stanford, Calif.: Stanford University Press).

5. Heng Samrin had been a ranking member of the CPK for its Eastern Zone and political commissar and commander of its Fourth Division. Michael Leifer, "Kampuchea, 1979: From Dry Season to Dry Season," *Asian Survey* 20, no. 1 (1980): 33–41, at 34.

6. Ben Kiernan, "Kampuchea, 1979–81," *Southeast Asian Affairs* 8 (1982): 169.

7. Quoted in Morris, *Why Vietnam Invaded Cambodia*, 111.

8. Michael Hass, *Cambodia, Pol Pot, and the United States: The Faustian Pact* (New York: ABC-CLIO, 1991); Sheldon Neuringer, *The Carter Administration, Human Rights, and the Agony of Cambodia* (Lewistown, N.Y.: Edwin Mellon, 1993); Christopher Brady, *United States Foreign Policy towards Cambodia, 1977–1992: A Question of Realities* (New York: Springer, 1999); and Kenton Clymer, "Jimmy Carter, Human Rights, and Cambodia," *Diplomatic History* 27, no. 2 (2003): 245–278.

9. Chanda, *Brother Enemy*, 371; Memorandum of Conversation, "Secretary's Meeting with Foreign Minister Chatchai of Thailand," November 26, 1975, available at http://nsarchive.gwu/NSAEBB/NSAEBB198 (accessed February 15, 2016).

10. In 1982 the Coalition Government of Democratic Kampuchea was created, with the support of both China and the United States. Composed of various anti-PRK and anti-Vietnamese factions but dominated especially by former Khmer Rouge officials, the CGDK was recognized by the UN as the legitimate, sovereign power of Cambodia until elections were held in the early 1990s. See Ramses Amer, "The United Nations and Kam-

puchea: The Issue of Representation and Its Implications," *Bulletin of Concerned Asian Scholars* 22, no. 3 (1990): 52–60.

11. Chanda, *Brother Enemy*, 371.

12. Jenny Leigh Smith, "Hunger and Governance: The Food Supply in Cambodia, 1979–1980 and Beyond," in *Water and Power: Environmental Governance and Strategies for Sustainability in the Lower Mekong Basin*, ed. Mart A. Stewart and Peter A. Coclanis (Cham, Switzerland: Spring International, 2019), 17–27, at 21.

13. Heder, *Kampuchean Occupation and Resistance*, 27.

14. Heder, *Kampuchean Occupation and Resistance*, 27–28.

15. Fawthrop and Jarvis, *Getting Away with Genocide?*, 54.

16. Mason and Brown, *Rice, Rivalry, and Politics*, 18–19.

17. Heder, *Kampuchean Occupation and Resistance*, 29.

18. Meng Try Ea, "War and Famine: The Example of Kampuchea," in *Famine as a Geographical Phenomenon*, ed. Bruce Currey and Graeme Hugo (Hingham, Mass.: Kluwer Academic, 1984), 44.

19. Heder, *Kampuchean Occupation and Resistance*, 8.

20. Mysliwiec, *Punishing the Poor*, 11; Joel R. Charny, "Appropriate Development Aid for Kampuchea," in *The Cambodian Agony*, ed. David A. Ablin and Marlowe Hood (Armonk, N.Y.: M. E. Sharpe, 1990), 243–266, at 244; Chanthou Boua, "Development Aid and Democracy in Cambodia," in *Genocide and Democracy in Cambodia: The Khmer Rouge, the United Nations and the International Community*, ed. Ben Kiernan (New Haven, Conn.: Yale University Southeast Asia Studies, 1993), 273–283, at 274.

21. Heder, *Kampuchean Occupation and Resistance*, 40.

22. Heder, *Kampuchean Occupation and Resistance*, 30.

23. Quinn-Judge, "Victory on the Battlefield," 215.

24. Ian Harris, *Buddhism in a Dark Age: Cambodian Monks under Pol Pot* (Honolulu: University of Hawaii Press, 2013), 137; SungYong Lee, "Local Resilience and the Reconstruction of Social Institutions: Recovery, Maintenance and Transformation of Buddhist Sangha in Post–Khmer Rouge Cambodia," *Journal of Intervention and Statebuilding* 14, no. 3 (2020): 349–367, at 352.

25. Quoted in Elizabeth Becker, "The Politics of Famine in Cambodia," *Washington Post*, November 18, 1979, available at https://www.washingtonpost.com/archive/opinions/1979/11/18/the-politics-of-famine-in-cambodia/81f0849e-9d1a-493c-b92a-aa00a9d3b1db/ (accessed March 18, 2021).

26. Charny, "Appropriate Development Aid," 245; Mysliwiec, *Punishing the Poor*, 35.

27. Becker, "The Politics of Famine in Cambodia."

28. Leifer, "Kampuchea, 1979," 34–38.

29. Charny, "Oxfam's Cambodia Response," 165; Leifer, "Kampuchea, 1979," 39.

30. Becker, "The Politics of Famine in Cambodia."

31. "Letter from President Carter to Australian Prime Minister Fraser," February 14, 1979, National Security Affairs, Staff Material, Far East, Platt Chron Files, Box 66, 2/1–13/79, Carter Library, available at https://history.state.gov/historicaldocuments/frus1977-80v22/d263 (accessed February 4, 2021).

32. Fawthrop and Jarvis, *Getting Away with Genocide?*, 53.

33. "Memorandum of Conversation," January 30, 1979, National Security Affairs, State

Material, Office, Outside the System File, Box 47, China: President's Meeting with Vice Premier Deng: 1–2/79, Carter Library, available at https://history.state.gov/historical documents/frus1977-80v13/d207 (accessed February 4, 2021).

34. "Memorandum from Fritz Ermarth of the National Security Council Staff to the President's Assistant for National Security Affairs (Brzezinski)," January 17, 1979, National Security Affairs, State Material, Office, Presidential Advisory Board, Box 74, Far East: Box 2, Carter Library, available at https://history.state.gov/historicaldocuments/frus1977-80v13/d193 (accessed February 4, 2021).

35. Fawthrop and Jarvis, *Getting Away with Genocide?*, 58–59.

36. "Telegram from the Department of State to Certain Diplomatic Posts," January 8, 1979, RG 59, Central Foreign Policy File, D790009–1052, National Archives, available at https://history.state.gov/historicaldocuments/frus1977-80v22/d38 (accessed February 4, 2021).

37. "Telegram from the Embassy in Thailand to the Department of State," January 8, 1979, National Security Affairs, Brzezinski Material, Brzezinski Office File, Country Chron File, Box 56, Vietnam, 1978–1979, Carter Library, available at https://history.state.gov/historicaldocuments/frus1977-80v22/d170 (accessed February 4, 2021).

38. "Briefing Memorandum from the Acting Director of the Bureau of Intelligence and Research (Mark) to Secretary of State Vance," January 8, 1979, National Security Affairs, Brzezinski Material, Country File, Box 86, Vietnam, 1/79–1/81, Carter Library, available at https://history.state.gov/historicaldocuments/frus1977-80v22/d39 (accessed February 4, 2021).

39. Quoted in Pamela Sodhy, "A Survey of U.S. Post-Vietnam Policy and the Kampuchean Dilemma, 1975–89: A Southeast Asian View," *Contemporary Southeast Asia* 11, no. 3 (1989): 283–312, at 288.

40. Clymer, "Jimmy Carter, Human Rights, and Cambodia," 256.

41. Michael Vickery, "Democratic Kampuchea—CIA to the Rescue," *Bulletin of Concerned Asian Scholars* 14, no. 4 (1982): 45–54, at 45.

42. Clymer, "Jimmy Carter, Human Rights, and Cambodia," 258.

43. "Memorandum from the President's Assistant for National Security Affairs (Brzezinski) to President Carter," January 26, 1979, National Security Affairs, Brzezinski Material, Brzezinski Office File, Country Chron File, Box 3, Asia, 1979, Carter Library, available at https://history.state.gov/historicaldocuments/frus1977-80v22/d41 (accessed February 4, 2021).

44. Fawthrop and Jarvis, *Getting Away with Genocide?*, 61.

45. Mason and Brown, *Rice, Rivalry, and Politics*, 11.

46. Mason and Brown, *Rice, Rivalry, and Politics*, 15.

47. Evan Gottesman, *Cambodia after the Khmer Rouge: Inside the Politics of Nation Building* (New Haven, Conn.: Yale University Press, 2003), 80.

48. Mason and Brown, *Rice, Rivalry, and Politics*, 14.

49. Mason and Brown, *Rice, Rivalry, and Politics*, 13.

50. Mason and Brown, *Rice, Rivalry, and Politics*, 13.

51. Mason and Brown, *Rice, Rivalry, and Politics*, 15.

52. Quoted in Mason and Brown, *Rice, Rivalry, and Politics*, 16.

53. Mason and Brown, *Rice, Rivalry, and Politics*, 16.

54. Mason and Brown, *Rice, Rivalry, and Politics*, 17.
55. Charny, "Oxfam's Cambodia Response," 166.
56. Charny, "Oxfam's Cambodia Response," 166; Mason and Brown, *Rice, Rivalry, and Politics*, 29.
57. Charny, "Oxfam's Cambodia Response," 168.
58. Charny, "Oxfam's Cambodia Response," 167.
59. Mason and Brown, *Rice, Rivalry, and Politics*, 29.
60. Heder, *Kampuchean Occupation and Resistance*, 37.
61. Murlis, "An Analysis of Food Aid," 264.
62. Mason and Brown, *Rice, Rivalry, and Politics*, 28.
63. "Telegram from the Embassy in Thailand to the Department of State," October 23, 1979, National Security Affairs, Brzezinski Material, Cables File, Far East, Box 13, 9–11/79, Carter Library, available at https://history.state.gov/historicaldocuments/frus1977-80v22/d140 (accessed February 4, 2021).
64. "Telegram from the Embassy in Thailand to the Department of State," November 6, 1979, National Security Affairs, Brzezinski Material, Cables File, Far East, Box 13, 9–11/79, Carter Library, available at https://history.state.gov/historicaldocuments/frus1977-80v22/d70 (accessed February 4, 2021).
65. "Memorandum from the President's Assistant for National Security Affairs (Brzezinski) and the Special Representative for Economic Summits (Owen) to President Carter," October 12, 1979, National Security Affairs, Brzezinski Material, Brzezinski Office File, Country Chron File, Box 6, Cambodia, 1979, Carter Library, available at https://history.state.gov/historicaldocuments/frus1977-80v22/d62 (accessed February 4, 2021).
66. Clymer, "Jimmy Carter, Human Rights, and Cambodia," 262.
67. Clymer, "Jimmy Carter, Human Rights, and Cambodia," 263.
68. "Memorandum from Secretary of Defense Brown to President Carter," September 4, 1979, National Security Affairs, Brzezinski Material, Brzezinski Office File, Country Chron File, Box 50, Thailand 1979, Carter Library, available at https://history.state.gov/historicaldocuments/frus1977-80v22/d57 (accessed February 4, 2021).
69. Vickery, "Democratic Kampuchea—CIA to the Rescue," 45, 54.
70. Mason and Brown, *Rice, Rivalry, and Politics*, 30, 34.
71. Mason and Brown, *Rice, Rivalry, and Politics*, 35.
72. Mason and Brown, *Rice, Rivalry, and Politics*, 35.
73. "Report Prepared in the Office of the First Lady," undated, National Security Affairs, Brzezinski Material, Country File, Box 42, Kampuchea, 11–12/79, Carter Library, available at https://history.state.gov/historicaldocuments/frus1977-80v22/d71 (accessed February 4, 2021).
74. Clymer, "Jimmy Carter, Human Rights, and Cambodia," 262.
75. "Summary of Conclusions of a Special Coordination Committee Meeting," December 10, 1979, National Security Council, Institutional Files, 1977–1980, Box 106, SCC 233, Thailand-Cambodia, 12/10/79, Carter Library, available at https://history.state.gov/historicaldocuments/frus1977-80v22/d75 (accessed February 4, 2021).
76. Quoted in Clymer, "Jimmy Carter, Human Rights, and Cambodia," 264.
77. Quoted in Clymer, "Jimmy Carter, Human Rights, and Cambodia," 264–265.
78. "Memorandum from Director of Central Intelligence Turner to the President's As-

sistant for National Security Affairs (Brzezinski)," December 11, 1979, Central Intelligence Agency, CADRE C01434041, available at https://history.state.gov/historicaldocuments/frus1977-80v22/d76 (accessed February 4, 2021).

79. Ea, "War and Famine," 44.
80. Gottesman, *Cambodia after the Khmer Rouge*, 89.
81. Ea, "War and Famine," 44.
82. Jean-Christophe Diepart and Thol Sem, *Cambodian Peasantry and Formalization of Land Right: Historical Perspectives and Current Issues* (Paris: French Technical Committee on Land Tenure and Development, 2018), 22.
83. Fawthrop and Jarvis, *Getting Away with Genocide?*, 13.
84. Fawthrop and Jarvis, *Getting Away with Genocide?*, 15.
85. Orlin J. Scoville, "Relief and Rehabilitation in Kampuchea," Journal of Developing Areas 20, no. 1 (1985): 26.
86. Quinn-Judge, "Victory on the Battlefield," 215.
87. Mysliwiec, *Punishing the Poor*, 25.
88. Mysliwiec, *Punishing the Poor*, 26.
89. Diepart and Sem, *Cambodian Peasantry*, 22. See also Viviane Frings, *The Failure of Agricultural Collectivization in the People's Republic of Kampuchea, (1979–1989)*, Working Paper 80, The Center of Southeast Asian Studies (Clayton, Australia: Monash University, 1993) and Oliver Hensengerth, *Transitions of Cambodia: War and Peace, 1954 to the Present*, Project Working Paper No. 2 (Universität Duisburg Essen: Institute for Development and Peace, 2008).
90. Kiernan, "Kampuchea, 1979–81," 176.
91. Mysliwiec, *Punishing the Poor*, 28.
92. Mysliwiec, *Punishing the Poor*, 29.
93. Diepart and Sem, *Cambodian Peasantry*, 23.
94. Scoville, "Relief and Rehabilitation in Kampuchea," 27.
95. Kiernan, "Kampuchea, 1979–81," 176; Diepart and Sem, *Cambodian Peasantry*, 24.
96. Diepart and Sem, *Cambodian Peasantry*, 23.
97. Mysliwiec, *Punishing the Poor*, 28.
98. Mysliwiec, *Punishing the Poor*, 26.
99. Diepart and Sem, *Cambodian Peasantry*, 24.
100. Charny, "Appropriate Development Aid," 248.
101. Heder, *Kampuchean Occupation and Resistance*, 37.
102. Scoville, "Relief and Rehabilitation in Kampuchea," 27.
103. Diepart and Sem, *Cambodian Peasantry*, 24–25.
104. Diepart and Sem, *Cambodian Peasantry*, 26.
105. Mysliwiec, *Punishing the Poor*, 16.
106. Ea, "War and Famine," 45.
107. Smith, "Hunger and Governance," 26.
108. Quinn-Judge, "Victory on the Battlefield," 215.
109. Quinn-Judge, "Victory on the Battlefield," 215.
110. Mysliwiec, *Punishing the Poor*, 23.
111. Boua, "Development Aid," 274.
112. Quinn-Judge, "Victory on the Battlefield," 220.

113. Quinn-Judge, "Victory on the Battlefield," 216.

114. Jack Colhoun, "On the Side of Pol Pot: U.S. Supports Khmer Rouge," *Covert Action Quarterly* 34 (1990): 37–40, at 37.

115. John Pilger, "How Thatcher Gave Pol Pot a Hand," *New Statesman*, April 17, 2000, available at https://www.newstatesman.com/politics/politics/2014/04/how-thatcher-gave-pol-pot-hand (accessed March 25, 2021).

116. Fawthrop and Jordan, *Getting Away with Genocide?*, 62.

117. Mason and Brown, *Rice, Rivalry, and Politics*, 135–136.

118. Pilger, "How Thatcher Gave Pol Pot a Hand."

119. John Pilger, "The Long Secret Alliance: Uncle Sam and Pol Pot," *Covert Action Quarterly* 62 (1997): 5–9, at 6.

EPILOGUE

The first epigraph is quoted in Shashank Bengali, "How Dams and Climate Change Are Choking Asia's Great Lake," January 22, 2020, available at https://phys.org/news/2020-01-climate-asia-great-lake.html (accessed April 6, 2021). Phat Phalla is an environmental activist with the Fisheries Action Coalition Team, an alliance of Cambodian nongovernmental agencies. The second epigraph is quoted in Sun Narin, "Gripped by Drought, Cambodian Farmers Struggle against Changing Climate," Voice of America Cambodia, March 2, 2019, available at https://www.voacambodia.com/a/gripped-by-drought-cambodian-farmers-struggle-against-changing-climate/4809586.html (accessed November 27, 2019). Laing Thom is a farmer from Banteay Meanchey Province.

1. Jenny Leigh Smith, "Food Security and Food Sovereignty in Cambodia, 1979–1989," Conference Paper No. 61, presented at the 5th International Conference of the BRICS Initiative for Critical Agrarian Studies, October 13–16, 2017, Moscow, Russia, available at https://www.iss.nl/sites/corporate/files/2017-11/BICAS%20CP%205-61%20Smith.pdf (accessed May 24, 2021).

2. Viviane Frings, *The Failure of Agricultural Collectivization in the People's Republic of Kampuchea, (1979–1989)*, Working Paper 80, The Center of Southeast Asian Studies (Clayton, Australia: Monash University, 1993), at 41. See also Anne Y. Guillou, "The Question of Land in Cambodia: Perceptions, Access, and Use since Decollectivization," *Moussons: Recherche en sciences humaines sur l'Asie du Sud-Est*, 9–10(2006): 299–324; Oliver Hensengerth, *Transitions of Cambodia: War and Peace, 1954 to the Present*, Project Working Paper No. 2 (Universität Duisburg Essen: Institute for Development and Peace, 2008); and Jean-Christophe Diepart and Thol Sem, *Cambodian Peasantry and Formalization of Land Right: Historical Perspectives and Current Issues* (Paris: French Technical Committee on Land Tenure and Development, 2018).

3. Julio A. Jeldres, "The UN and the Cambodian Transition," *Journal of Democracy* 4, no. 4 (1993): 104–116, at 105.

4. Jeldres, "The UN and the Cambodian Transition," 106–107; Aurel Croissant and Philip Lorenz, *Comparative Politics of Southeast Asia: An Introduction into Government and Politics* (Cham, Switzerland: Springer International 2018), 39.

5. Simon Springer, "The Neoliberalization of Security and Violence in Cambodia's Transition," In *Human Security in East Asia: Challenges for Collaborative Action*, ed. Sor-

pong Peou (New York: Routledge, 2008), 137–153; Simon Springer, "Violence, Democracy, and the Neoliberal 'Order': The Contestation of Public Space in Posttransitional Cambodia," *Annals of the Association of American Geographers* 99, no. 1 (2009): 138–162; Thomas Kolnberger, "'Voices' from the UNTAC Files: Policy and Politics of Accommodation in Phnom Penh after the Khmer Rouge," *South East Asia Research* 23, no. 3 (2015): 377–404; and Simon Springer, *Violent Neoliberalism: Development, Discourse, and Dispossession in Cambodia* (New York: Palgrave Macmillan, 2015).

6. Springer, "Violence, Democracy, and the Neoliberal 'Order,'" 143. See also Khatharya Um, "Cambodia in 1989: Still Talking but no Settlement," *Asian Survey* 30, no. 1 (1990): 96–104.

7. Springer, "Violence, Democracy, and the Neoliberal 'Order,'" 143.

8. Springer, *Violent Neoliberalism*, 27.

9. Jeldres, "The UN and the Cambodian Transition," 111.

10. Springer, "The Neoliberalization of Security," 134.

11. Springer, "The Neoliberalization of Security," 134.

12. Springer, "The Neoliberalization of Security," 135; Springer, *Violent Neoliberalism*, 28.

13. Springer, "The Neoliberalization of Security," 136.

14. Croissant and Lorenz, *Comparative Politics of Southeast Asia*, 40; Simon Springer, "Articulated Neoliberalism: The Specificity of Patronage, Kleptocracy, and Violence in Cambodia's Neoliberalization," *Environment and Planning A* 43, no. 11 (2011): 2554–2570, at 2566.

15. Alice Beban, Laura Schoenberger, and Vanessa Lamb, "Pockets of Liberal Media in Authoritarian Regimes: What the Crackdown on Emancipatory Spaces Means for Rural Social Movements in Cambodia," *Journal of Peasant Studies* 47, no. 1 (2020): 95–115, at 99. See also Ian Scoones, Marc Edelman, Saturnino M. Borras Jr., Ruth Hall, Wendy Wolford, and Ben White, "Emancipatory Rural Politics: Confronting Authoritarian Populism," *Journal of Peasant Studies* 45, no. 1 (2018): 1–20.

16. Caroline Hughes, "Transnational Networks, International Organizations and Political Participation in Cambodia: Human Rights, Labor Rights and Common Rights," *Democratization* 14, no. 5 (2007): 834–852, at 836; Springer, "Articulated Neoliberalism," 2557.

17. Croissant and Lorenz, *Comparative Politics of Southeast Asia*, 41; Springer, *Violent Neoliberalism*, 140; Springer, "Articulated Neoliberalism," 2560. See also Laura Schoenberger and Alice Beban, "'They Turn Us into Criminals': Embodiments of Fear in Cambodian Land Grabbing," *Annals of the American Association of Geographers* 108, no. 5 (2018): 1338–1353; Anne Hennings, "The Dark Underbelly of Land Struggles: The Instrumentalization of Female Activism and Emotional Resistance in Cambodia," *Critical Asian Studies* 51, no. 1 (2019): 103–119; Kheang Un, *Cambodia: Return to Authoritarianism* (Cambridge: Cambridge University Press, 2019).

18. Croissant and Lorenz, *Comparative Politics of Southeast Asia*, 41.

19. Kheang Un and Sokbunthoeun So, "Land Rights in Cambodia: How Neopatrimonial Politics Restricts Land Policy Reform," *Pacific Affairs* 84, no. 2 (2011): 289–308, at 294.

20. Kheang Un, "State, Society and Democratic Consolidation: The Case of Cambodia," *Pacific Affairs* 79, no. 2 (2006): 225–245, at 230, 244.

21. Springer, "Violence, Democracy, and the Neoliberal 'Order,'" 146; Springer, "The Neoliberalization of Security," 139.

22. Rhoda E. Howard-Hassmann, "Faminogenesis: State Policies That Undermine the Right to Food," *Netherlands Quarterly of Human Rights* 29, no. 4 (2011): 560–590, at 561.

23. Ian G. Baird, "The Global Land Grab Meta-Narrative, Asian Money Laundering and Elite Capture: Reconsidering the Cambodian Context," *Geopolitics* 19, no. 2 (2014): 431–453, at 438. See also Saturnino M. Borras Jr. and Jennifer C. Franco, "Global Land Grabbing and Trajectories of Agrarian Change: A Preliminary Analysis," *Journal of Agrarian Change* 12, no. 1 (2012): 34–59, at 34.

24. Derek Hall, "Primitive Accumulation, Accumulation by Dispossession and the Global Land Grab," *Third World Quarterly* 34, no. 9 (2013): 1582–1604, at 1583. See also Jim Glassman, "Primitive Accumulation, Accumulation by Dispossession, Accumulation by 'Extra-Economic' Means," *Progress in Human Geography* 30, no. 5 (2006): 608–625.

25. Wendy Wolford, Saturnino M. Borras Jr., Ruth Hall, Ian Scoones, and Ben White, "Governing Global Land Deals: The Role of the State in the Rush for Land," *Development and Change* 44, no. 2 (2013): 189–210, at 197.

26. Fred Magdoff, "Twenty-First-Century Land Grabs: Accumulation by Agricultural Dispossession," *Monthly Review* 65, no. 1 (2013): 1–18, at 1.

27. Philip Hirsch, *Land Dispossession / Land Grabbing* (Vientiane, Lao PDR: Mekong Land Research Forum, 2018), 1.

28. Wolford et al., "Governing Global Land Deals," 192; Hall, "Primitive Accumulation," 1583.

29. Hirsch, *Land Dispossession / Land Grabbing*, 3–4.

30. Wolford et al., "Governing Global Land Deals," 192.

31. Wolford et al., "Governing Global Land Deals," 192.

32. Saturnino M. Borras Jr. and Jennifer C. Franco, "Global Land Grabbing and Political Reactions 'from Below,'" *Third World Quarterly* 34, no. 9 (2013): 1723–1747, at 1729.

33. Wolford et al., "Governing Global Land Deals," 193.

34. Wolford et al., "Governing Global Land Deals," 193.

35. Lorenzo Cotula, "The International Political Economy of the Global Land Rush: A Critical Appraisal of Trends, Scale, Geography and Drivers," *Journal of Peasant Studies* 39, nos. 3–4 (2012): 649–680; Ben White, Saturnino M. Borras Jr., Ruth Hall, Ian Scoones, and Wendy Wolford, "The New Enclosures: Critical Perspectives on Corporate Land Deals," *Journal of Peasant Studies* 39, nos. 3–4 (2012): 619–647; Matias E. Margulis, Nora McKeon, and Saturnino M. Borras Jr., "Land Grabbing and Global Governance: Critical Perspectives," *Globalizations* 10, no. 1 (2013): 1–23; and Tania Murray Li, "What Is Land? Assembling a Resource for Global Investment," *Transactions of the Institute of British Geographers* 39, no. 4 (2014): 589–602.

36. Xi Jiao, Carsten Smith-Hall, and Ida Theilade, "Rural Household Incomes and Land Grabbing in Cambodia," *Land Use Policy* 48 (2015): 317–328, at 317.

37. White et al., "The New Enclosures," 627.

38. Alice Beban and Courtney Work, "The Spirits Are Crying: Dispossessing Land and Possessing Bodies in Rural Cambodia," *Antipode* 46, no. 3 (2014): 593–610, at 599.

39. Simon Springer, "Violent Accumulation: A Postanarchist Critique of Property, Dispossession, and the State of Exception in Neoliberalizing Cambodia," *Annals of the*

Association of American Geographers 103, no. 3 (2013): 608–626; Arnim Scheidel, Katharine N. Farrell, Jesús Ramos-Martin, Mario Giampietro, and Kozo Mayumi, "Land Poverty and Emerging Ruralities in Cambodia: Insights from Kampot Province," *Environment, Development and Sustainability* 16, no. 4 (2014): 823–840; Natalia Scurrah and Philip Hirsch, *The Political Economy of Land Governance in Cambodia* (Vientiane, Lao PDR: 2015); and Arnim Scheidel, "Tactics of Land Capture through Claims of Poverty Reduction in Cambodia," *Geoforum* 75 (2016): 110–114.

40. Scurrah and Hirsch, *The Political Economy of Land Governance*, 6.

41. Diepart and Sem, *Cambodian Peasantry*, 27; Frank Van Acker, *Hitting a Stone with an Egg? Cambodia's Rural Economy and Land Tenure in Transition*, CAS Discussion Paper (Antwerpen, Belgium: Center for ASEAN Studies and Center for International Management and Development, 1999).

42. Scurrah and Hirsch, *The Political Economy of Land Governance*, 6.

43. Diepart and Sem, *Cambodian Peasantry*, 32; Jiao, Smith-Hall, and Theilade, "Rural Household Incomes," 318; Philippe Le Billon, "The Political Ecology of Transition in Cambodia, 1989–1999: War, Peace and Forest Exploitation," *Development and Change* 31, no. 4 (2000): 785–805, at 787. See also Philippe Le Billon, "Logging in Muddy Waters: The Politics of Forest Exploitation in Cambodia," *Critical Asian Studies* 34, no. 4 (2002): 563–586.

44. Scurrah and Hirsch, *The Political Economy of Land Governance*, 6.

45. Diepart and Sem, *Cambodian Peasantry*, 37; Van Acker, *Hitting a Stone with an Egg?*.

46. Diepart and Sem, *Cambodian Peasantry*, 43–44; Alice Beban, Sokbunthoeun So, and Kheang Un, "From Force to Legitimation: Rethinking Land Grabs in Cambodia," *Development and Change* 48, no. 3 (2017): 596.

47. Jiao, Smith-Hall, and Theilade, "Rural Household Incomes," 318.

48. Mark Grimsditch and Laura Schoenberger, *New Actions and Existing Policies: The Implementation and Impacts of Order 01* (Phnom Penh: The NGO Forum on Cambodia Land and Livelihoods Program, 2015), 60.

49. Springer, "Violent Accumulation," 608.

50. Pou Sovachana and Paul Chambers, "Human Insecurity Scourge: The Land Grabbing Crisis in Cambodia," in *Human Security and Cross-Border Cooperation in East Asia*, ed. Carolina G. Hernandez, Eun Mee Kim, Yōichi Mine, and Xiao Ren (Cham, Switzerland: Palgrave Macmillan, 2019), 181–203, at 184.

51. Scurrah and Hirsch, *The Political Economy of Land Governance*, 6–7.

52. Philippe Le Billon, *Wars of Plunder: Conflicts, Profits and the Politics of Resources* (London: Hurst, 2012).

53. Grimsditch and Schoenberger, *New Actions and Existing Policies*, 65–66.

54. Scurrah and Hirsch, *The Political Economy of Land Governance*, 16.

55. Jean-Christophe Diepart, *They Will Need Land! The Current Land Tenure Situation and Future Land Allocation Needs of Smallholder Farmers in Cambodia* (Vientiane, Lao PDR: Mekong Region Land Governance, 2016), 2–3.

56. Sovachana and Chambers, "Human Insecurity Scourge," 181.

57. LICADHO, *Land Grabbing and Poverty in Cambodia: The Myth of Development* (Phnom Penh, Cambodia: LICADHO, 2009), 1, 7. See also LICADHO, *On Stony Ground:*

A Look into Social Land Concessions (Phnom Penh, Cambodia: LICADHO, 2015) and Neil Loughlin and Sarah Milne, "After the Grab? Land Control and Regime Survival in Cambodia since 2012," *Journal of Contemporary Asia* 51, no. 3 (2021): 375–397.

58. Beban, So, and Un, "From Force to Legitimation," 596.

59. Vanessa Lamb, Laura Schoenberger, Carl Middleton, and Borin Un, "Gendered Eviction, Protest and Recovery: A Feminist Political Ecology Engagement with Land Grabbing in Rural Cambodia," *Journal of Peasant Studies* 44, no. 6 (2017): 1215–1234; Willemijn Verkoren and Chanrith Ngin, "Organizing against Land Grabbing in Cambodia: Exploring Missing Links," *Development and Change* 48, no. 6 (2017): 1336–1361; and Clara Mi Young Park, "'Our Lands Are Our Lives': Gendered Experiences of Resistance to Land Grabbing in Rural Cambodia," *Feminist Economics* 25, no. 4 (2019): 21–44.

60. Jiao, Smith-Hall, and Theilade, "Rural Household Incomes," 325.

61. Scheidel et al., "Land Poverty and Emerging Ruralities," 837.

62. Andrew R. Cock, "External Actors and the Relative Autonomy of the Ruling Elite in Post-UNTAC Cambodia," *Journal of Southeast Asian Studies* 41, no. 2 (2010): 241–265, at 263.

63. Bryan Tilt, *Dams and Development in China: The Moral Economy of Water and Power* (New York: Columbia University Press, 2015), 56.

64. Mekong River Commission, *Overview of the Hydrology of the Mekong Basin* (Vientiane, Laos: Mekong River Commission, 2005), 1, 8.

65. Mekong River Commission, *Overview of the Hydrology*, 1.

66. Mekong River Commission, *Overview of the Hydrology*, 9.

67. Mekong River Commission, *Overview of the Hydrology*, 9.

68. Mekong River Commission, *Overview of the Hydrology*, 2, 9.

69. Mekong River Commission, *Situation Report: Hydrological Conditions in the Lower Mekong River Basin in January–July 2020*, August 2020, available at https://www.mrcmekong.org/assets/Publications/Situation-report-Jan-Jul-2020.pdf (accessed April 6, 2021).

70. Mekong River Commission, *Overview of the Hydrology*, 9–10.

71. The importance of the Mekong River–Tonle Sap system extends into southern Vietnam. The seasonal storage of water in the Great Lake acts as a huge natural regulator for water flows downstream and thus affects the seasonal distribution of flows in the Vietnamese delta. As stored water flows out of the Great Lake into the Mekong during the dry season, the low flows of the mainstream are increased, providing water for irrigation. Furthermore, the continual flow of water into the delta, especially during the dry season, mitigates the amount of saltwater intrusion into the delta. Indeed, the annual flood pulse of the Tonle Sap is crucial for the sustainability of the Mekong Delta. Given its long history of modification, the delta is composed of myriad levees that direct the flow of water. Historically, these are regularly overtopped, and lower areas far from the main river systems are submerged. These "ponded water" zones are biologically rich and play a key role both in maintaining ecological diversity and by functioning as floodwater retention areas and as natural water purification systems. See Mekong River Commission, *Overview of the Hydrology*, 10, 49, 53.

72. Kenneth R. Olson and Lois Wright Morton, "Tonle Sap Lake and River and Confluence with the Mekong River in Cambodia," *Journal of Soil and Water Conservation* 73,

no. 3 (2018): 60A–66A, at 60A. See also Lois Wright Morton and Kenneth R. Olson, "The Pulses of the Mekong River Basin: Rivers and the Livelihoods of Farmers and Fishers," *Journal of Environmental Protection* 9 (2018): 431–459.

73. Nithya Natarajan, Katherine Brickell, and Laurie Parsons, "Climate Change Adaptation and Precarity across the Rural-Urban Divide in Cambodia: Towards a 'Climate Precarity' Approach," *ENE: Nature and Space* 2, no. 4 (2019): 899–921, at 907. See also Paula Nuorteva, Marko Keskinen, and Olli Varis, "Water, Livelihoods and Climate Change Adaptation in the Tonle Sap Lake Area, Cambodia: Learning from the Past to Understand the Future," *Journal of Water and Climate Change* 1, no. 1 (2010): 87–101; Heng Chan Thoeun, "Observed and Projected Changes in Temperature and Rainfall in Cambodia," *Weather and Climate Extremes* 7 (2015): 61–71; and Laurie Parsons and Sopheak Chann, "Mobilising Hydrosocial Power: Climate Perception, Migration and the Small Scale Geography of Water in Cambodia," *Political Geography* 75 (2019): https://doi.org/10.1016/j.polgeo.2019.102055.

74. Natarajan, "Climate Change Adaptation and Precarity," 907.

75. Olson and Morton, "Tonle Sap Lake and River," 66A.

76. Philip Hirsch, "The Changing Political Dynamics of Dam Building on the Mekong," *Water Alternatives* 3, no. 2 (2010): 312–323, at 313. See also Jeffrey W. Jacobs, "The United States and the Mekong Project," *Water Policy* 1, no. 6 (2000): 587–603; Chris Sneddon and Coleen Fox, "Rethinking Transboundary Waters: A Critical Hydropolitics of the Mekong Basin," *Political Geography* 25 (2006): 181–202; Christopher Sneddon, "The 'Sinew of Development': Cold War Geopolitics, Technical Expertise, and Water Resource Development in Southeast Asia, 1954–1975," *Social Studies of Science* 42, no. 4 (2012): 564–590; Christopher Sneddon, *Concrete Revolution: Large Dams, Cold War Geopolitics, and the U.S. Bureau of Reclamation* (Chicago: University of Chicago Press, 2015); and Philip Hirsch, "The Shifting Regional Geopolitics of Mekong Dams," *Political Geography* 51 (2016): 63–74.

77. Hirsch, "The Changing Political Dynamics," 313.

78. Akarath Soukhaphon, Ian G. Baird, and Zeb S. Hogan, "The Impacts of Hydropower Dams in the Mekong River Basin: A Review," *Water* 13, no. 3 (2021): 265, https://doi:10.3390/w13030265.

79. David Murray, "'From Battlefield to Market Place'—Regional Economic Cooperation in the Mekong Zone," *Geography* 79, no. 4 (1994): 350–353, at 350; Karen Bakker, "The Politics of Hydropower: Developing the Mekong," *Political Geography* 18 (1999): 209–232, at 213.

80. Soukhaphon, Baird, and Hogan, "The Impacts of Hydropower Dams"; Chris Sneddon, "Reconfiguring Scale and Power: The Khong-Chi-Mun Project in Northeast Thailand," *Environment and Planning A* 35, no. 12 (2003): 2229–2250, at 2236.

81. Carl Middleton and Jeremy Allouche, "Watershed or Powershed? Critical Hydropolitics, China and the 'Lancang-Mekong Cooperation Framework,'" *International Spectator* 51, no. 3 (2016): 100–117, at 100.

82. Soukhaphon, Baird, and Hogan, "The Impacts of Hydropower Dams."

83. Middleton and Allouche, "Watershed or Powershed?," 113.

84. Abby Seiff, "Did Cambodia's Most Famous River Stop Changing Course?" Vice World News, October 16, 2020, available at https://www.vice.com/en/article/dy8gv7/did

-cambodias-most-famous-river-stop-changing-course (accessed January 16, 2021); Brian Eyler, "2020 Status of Lower Mekong Mainstream and Tributary Dams," Stimson, January 10, 2020, available at https://www.stimson.org/2020/2020-status-of-lower-mekong-mainstream-and-tributary-dams/ (accessed April 6, 2021).

85. Bakker, "The Politics of Hydropower," 211.

86. Pichamon Yeophantong, "China's Dam Diplomacy in the Mekong Region: Three Game Changers," in *Water Governance Dynamics in the Mekong Region*, ed. David J. H. Blake and Lisa Robins (Petaling Jaya, Malaysia: Strategic Information and Research Development Center, 2016), 123–148.

87. Philip Hirsch, "China and the Cascading Geopolitics of Lower Mekong Dams," *Asia-Pacific Journal* 9, no. 20 (2011): 1–5, at 2.

88. Hirsch, "China and the Cascading Geopolitics," 3.

89. Stefan Lovgren, "Mekong River at Its Lowest in 100 Years, Threatening Food Supply," *National Geographic*, July 31, 2019, available at https://www.nationalgeographic.com/environment/2019/07/mekong-river-lowest-levels-100-years-food-shortages/#close (accessed January 16, 2021).

90. David J. H. Blake, "Recalling Hydraulic Despotism: Hun Sen's Cambodia and the Return of Strict Authoritarianism," *Austrian Journal of South-East Asian Studies* 12, no. 1 (2019): 69–89, at 76.

91. Blake, "Recalling Hydraulic Despotism," 76.

92. Blake, "Recalling Hydraulic Despotism," 76. See also Jean-Philippe Venot and Jean-Philippe Fontenelle, *Irrigation Policy in Cambodia: History, Achievements and Challenges of AFD's Interventions* (Montpellier, France: COSTEA, 2018).

93. Blake, "Recalling Hydraulic Despotism," 77–79.

94. Sreang Chheat, "Contesting China-Funded Projects in Cambodia: The Case of Stung Chhay Areng Hydropower," *Asian Studies Review* 46, no. 1 (2022): 19–35, https://doi:10.1080/10357823.2021.1919598.

95. On China's hydro-diplomacy, see Carla P. Freeman, "Dam Diplomacy? China's New Neighborhood Policy and Chinese Dam-Building Companies," *Water International* 42, no. 2 (2017): 187–206; Sebastian Biba, "China's 'Old' and 'New' Mekong River Politics: The Lancang-Mekong Cooperation from a Comparative Benefit-Sharing Perspective," *Water International* 43, no. 5 (2018): 622–641.

96. Blake, "Recalling Hydraulic Despotism," 80.

97. Philip Hirsch and Andrew Wyatt, "Negotiating Local Livelihoods: Scales of Conflict in the Se San River Basin," *Asia Pacific Viewpoint* 45, no. 1 (2004): 51–68; Marko Keskinen, Mira Käkönen, Prom Tola, and Olli Varis, "The Tonle Sap Lake, Cambodia: Water-Related Conflicts with Abundance of Water," *Economics of Peace and Security Journal* 2, no. 2 (2007): 49–59; Mauricio E. Arias, Thomas A. Cochrane, Matti Kummu, Hannu Lauri, Gordon W. Holtgrieve, Jorma Koponen, and Thanapon Piman, "Impacts of Hydropower and Climate Change on Drivers of Ecological Productivity of Southeast Asia's Most Important Wetland," *Ecological Modelling* 272 (2014): 252–263; Marko Keskinen, Paradis Someth, Aura Salmivaara, and Matti Kummu, "Water-Energy-Food Nexus in a Transboundary River Basin: The Case of Tonle Sap Lake, Mekong River Basin," *Water* 7 (2015): 5416–5436; and Aura Salmivaara, Matti Kummu, Olli Varis, and Marko Kes-

kinen, "Socio-Economic Changes in Cambodia's Unique Tonle Sap Lake Area: A Spatial Approach," *Applied Spatial Analysis and Policy* 9, no. 3 (2016): 413–432.

98. Mekong River Commission, *Situation Report*; see also Seiff, "Did Cambodia's Most Famous River Stop?"

99. Keskinen et al., "Water-Energy-Food Nexus," 5427.

100. Chris Sneddon, "Nature's Materiality and the Circuitous Paths of Accumulation: Dispossession of Freshwater Fisheries in Cambodia," *Antipode* 39, no. 1 (2007): 167–193, at 175.

101. Sneddon, "Nature's Materiality," 175.

102. Sneddon, "Nature's Materiality," 177.

103. Quoted in Seiff, "Did Cambodia's Most Famous River Stop?"

104. Seiff, "Did Cambodia's Most Famous River Stop?"

105. Natarajan, Brickell, and Parsons, "Climate Change Adaptation and Precarity," 907.

106. Quoted in Sun Narin, "Pursat Farmers Struggle to Keep Rice Fields Irrigated, Worries Increase over Migration and Debt," Voice of America Cambodia, December 24, 2019, available at https://www.voacambodia.com/a/pursat-farmers-struggle-to-keep-rice-fields-irrigated-worries-increase-over-migration-and-debt/5217932.html (accessed December 26, 2019).

107. Nuorteva, Keskinen, and Varis, "Water, Livelihoods and Climate Change," 96, 98.

INDEX

Abramowitz, Morton, 109, 114
accumulation by dispossession, 137
Agamben, Giorgio, 10–11
Angkor, 21–23, 34, 83
Association of Southeast Asian Nations (ASEAN), 107, 109, 130
autarky, 81, 132

Bakker, Karen, 147
bare life, 11–12, 14, 66, 71, 73
base people, 92, 103, 104, 111
Battambang (city), 24, 27, 62
Battambang (province), 27, 33–34, 37, 44, 62, 65
Beban, Alice, 34, 139, 142
Becker, Elizabeth, 42
biopolitics: Cambodian People's Party and, 135; Communist Party of Kampuchea and, 78; concept of, 4, 8; famine and, 13; food provision system and, 78; United States and, 117
biopower, 8
black market, 36, 46, 64, 69
Blake, David, 149, 150
bombing, 13, 45, 54–55, 61–62, 65, 76–77, 128, 168–69n33
Brzezinski, Zbigniew, 110, 114, 116–117, 124

Cambodian People's Party (CPP), 131–135, 139–141, 143, 149–150
Carter, Jimmy, 115–117, 124
Carter, Rosalynn, 115–116
Chanda, Nayan, 100
Chandler, David, 23, 24, 32, 39
Chinese Communist Party (CCP), 44

climate change, 138, 145–146, 149, 151–153
Clymer, Kenton, 32, 110, 115
Coalition Government of Democratic Kampuchea (CGDK), 130, 131, 183–84n10
Cock, Andrew, 143
collectives, 1, 88, 90
commission, crimes of, 7, 9, 87, 98, 129
commons, 21, 30, 31, 122, 140
communes, 2, 77, 87–88
communism, 32, 39, 42, 56, 73, 110, 146
Communist Party of Kampuchea (CPK): agriculture and, 2, 20, 77, 80, 82–83, 86, 89–90, 128; famine and, 1, 14, 87–96, 96–98, 128; foreign exchange and, 78, 81; Four-Year Plan and, 79, 82–87, 94; industry and, 82, 84; infrastructure and, 2, 77, 83, 85–86; irrigation and, 20, 84; Non-Aligned Movement and, 80–81; origins of, 38–44; People's Republic of Kampuchea and, 107, 112, 119–120, 139; planning and, 1, 79, 82, 139. *See also* Democratic Kampuchea
Conley, Bridget, 63
cooperatives, 35, 78, 88–90, 102, 104, 120

dams: Cambodian People's Party and, 143–152; China and, 146–152; Communist Party of Kampuchea and, 84; People's Republic of Kampuchea and, 122
DeFalco, Randle, 97
Democratic Kampuchea: administrative organization and, 78–79; agriculture and, 79–83, 85–87, 87–96; currency and, 91; social relations in, 88–89; technology and, 83–84; water-management and, 84;

Democratic Republic of Vietnam (DRV; North Vietnam), 13, 39, 41, 43–44, 47, 49, 51–52, 55–57, 60–61, 73
Deng Xiaoping, 44, 59
Devereux, Stephen, 5–6
de Waal, Alex, 4, 6, 10, 63
Diepart, Jean-Christophe, 24, 29, 121–123
displacement, 27, 30, 64–65, 67, 77, 88, 98, 128, 135–136, 138–139, 142, 151
dispossession, 29, 31, 98, 135–137, 139, 142

Ea, Meng-Try, 14
Ebihara, May, 42, 75, 77, 88, 90, 95
Economic Land Concessions (ELCs), 134, 140–141
Edkins, Jenny, 6, 10, 11
enclosures, 29, 30, 140
Essex, Jamey, 12
evictions, 136

famine: Cambodian Civil War and, 61–72; Democratic Kampuchea and, 87–96, 96–98; People's Republic of Kampuchea, 106–118; sovereign violence and, 7–12
famine crimes, 4–9, 128–129, 136
famine relief: aid organizations and, 125; Communist Party of Kampuchea and, 77, 89; Necro-geopolitics and, 106–118; People's Republic of Kampuchea and, 15, 106–118; United States and, 66, 125, 129
faminogenesis, 6, 12
First Indochina War, 31–38
food insecurity, 15, 87, 127, 130, 146, 151
food provisioning system, 1, 5, 12–13, 15, 78, 98, 111, 122, 128, 136, 140
food rations, 1, 78, 87, 94–95, 99, 129
food security, 142–143, 149, 151
forests and forestry, 25, 29, 94, 121, 139, 145
Foucault, Michel, 8–11, 82, 92
French protectorate, 25–31
Frieson, Kate, 45
Frings, Viviane, 130
FUNCINPEC, 130, 132, 133, 134

gender relations, 25, 75–76, 87–88, 93
Geneva Accords, 39, 41, 48
geopolitics: Cambodian People's Party and, 132; China and, 147; Communist Party of Kampuchea and, 14, 44, 128; famine relief and, 106–118; food security and, 149

Gottesman, Evan, 118

Hall, Derek, 137
Heder, Steve, 44, 104, 122
Heng Samrin, 101, 107–108, 110–115, 117, 119–122, 124, 139
Hildebrand, George, 62, 63, 66, 68, 69, 70, 73, 74
Hirsch, Philip, 137, 146
Ho Chi Minh, 31, 38, 48
Ho Chi Minh Trail, 44, 51–52, 54
Holodomor, 6
homo sacer, 11, 66
households, 21, 25, 34, 64, 75, 121–122, 141–143, 149–152
Howard, Jim, 112–113
Hughes, Carolina, 134
humanitarian: aid, 67, 104, 114–115, 124; crises, 3, 66–67, 72–73, 106–107, 114, 116, 124; intervention, 103, 115; law, 110; needs, 66, 68, 112; relief, 2, 72, 113, 119, 125
Hunger Plan, Nazi, 6
Hun Sen, 132–135, 139, 150
hydrology: Angkor and, 22, China and, 136, 143–144, 147, 150; colonialism and, 26–27, 33; Khmer Rouge and, 75, 84, 86, 93, 95, 102, 120–121, 123; precolonial Cambodia and, 18, 25
hydro-necropolitics, 143–152
hydropower, 136, 146–147, 149–152

Ieng Sary, 41, 75, 101
import-substitution industrialization, 82
international aid, 108, 110, 112–113, 120, 123–124, 150
International Committee of the Red Cross (ICRC), 107, 110–116, 119
international donors, 110, 118, 120, 134–136, 140, 149
irrigation: Angkor and, 22; Cambodian People's Party and, 147, 149–151; French colonialism and, 26–27; Khmer Rouge, 85, 86, 93, 95, 102, 127; Norodom Sihanouk and, 34; rice production and, 18, 20, 22, 25, 95; United States and, 33, 62

Jarvis, Helen, 110, 119

Keen, David, 6
Khieu Samphan, 41, 97

Index   199

Khmer Issarak, 31, 38, 165n125
Khmer People's Revolutionary Party (KPRP), 31, 39, 41–42
Khmer Rouge. *See* Communist Party of Kampuchea (CPK)
Kiernan, Ben, 36, 43, 91–92
Kingdom of Cambodia (modern): contemporary politics in, 129–136; Economic Land Concessions (ELCs) and, 134, 140–141; hydropower and, 143–152; land grabs and, 137–143; Land Law of 2001, 140–141
Kingdom of Cambodia (under Norodom Sihanouk), 31–38
Kissinger, Henry, 46, 48, 55–61, 66, 73–74, 102
Kompong Som (Sihanoukville), 33, 62, 63, 64
Kratie, 101, 144
Krom Samaki, 120–123, 130

Lancang Jiang, 144, 147, 149
land grabs, 136, 137–143, 149–150
landownership, 16, 28, 36, 89–90, 120–121, 130, 139
letting die, 8, 9, 12
livelihoods, 21, 82, 91, 140, 142, 143, 147, 149, 153
logging, 29, 134, 138, 147
Lon Nol: famine and, 61–72; regime of, 47–48, 55–61

Magdoff, Fred, 137
Malthus, Thomas, 4–5
Mam, Kalyanee, 88
Marcus, David, 6
Mbembe, Achille, 1, 10, 12
Mekong Basin, 143–144, 149–150, 152
Mekong Delta, 26
Mekong River, 17–18, 23–24, 33, 60, 63, 85–86, 101, 133, 143–152

Nally, David, 13
necro-geopolitics, 106–118, 149
necropolitics: Cambodian People's Party and, 137–143; Communist Party of Kampuchea and, 14–15, 77–78, 87, 98; concept of, 3–4, 10–12; famine and, 10; state-induced famine and, 10, 129; United States and, 49, 110
neoliberalism, 132, 146
new people, 89, 92, 104
Nixon, Richard M., 46, 49, 54–61, 66, 73, 76
Non-Aligned Movement, 80–82

North Vietnam. *See* Democratic Republic of Vietnam (DRV)

omission, crimes of, 7, 9, 98, 129
Operation Menu, 55, 168–69n33
Oxfam, 112–113

Paris Peace Accords (1973), 59
Paris Peace Accords (1991), 91, 131, 132, 147
People's Republic of Kampuchea (PRK): aid organizations and, 107, 110–118; biopolitics and, 104–105; famine relief and, 15, 106–118; geopolitics and, 102, 106; rural economy and, 119–123
Phnom Penh: civil war and, 46–47, 58–59, 62–63, 73; colonial era and, 22; Communist Party of Kampuchea and, 42, 78, 86; famine and, 60, 62, 64, 69–71, 73–74, 76, 105, 111, 118–119; People's Republic of Kampuchea and, 101; precolonial era and, 23–25; refugees and, 64–65, 70–72
Pol Pot: agriculture and, 90, 120; Democratic Republic of Vietnam, 100–101, 108; famine and, 97, 99; geopolitics and, 43–44, 107; ideology and, 41–44; planning and, 80, 82–83; United States and, 109–111, 114–115, 124–125
Porter, Gareth, 62, 63, 66, 68, 69, 70, 73, 74
primitive accumulation, 28, 137
Public Law 480 (PL-480), 67–68

Quinn-Judge, Sophie, 119

Rae, Gavin, 9, 11
Red Cross. *See* International Committee of the Red Cross
refugees: Cambodian Civil War and, 63–72; People's Republic of Kampuchea and, 102–106
Republic of Vietnam (South Vietnam), 13, 35, 39, 41, 43, 48–61, 66, 69, 73, 146
responsibility to protect, 7
Rice, Stian, 34, 82
rice cultivation in Cambodia, 18–21
rights, negative, 7, 136
rights, positive, 7, 136

Samlaut Rebellion, 37
Schanberg, Sydney, 47, 64, 69, 70, 71, 72, 76
Scheidel, Arnim, 143

Index

Schmitt, Carl, 11
Scoville, Orlin, 119
Second Indochina War, 48–61, 146
self-determination, 81
self-reliance, 43, 78–87
Sen, Amartya, 5
Sihanouk, Norodom: China, 35, 56, 58; Communist Party of Kampuchea and, 37, 39, 41–45, 52, 58, 86, 91; Democratic Republic of Vietnam and, 44; regime of, 31–38; rice production and, 36; rural poverty and, 35, 46, 71; United States and, 35, 43, 46–47, 54–55, 58–59
Sihanouk Trail, 52, 54
Sihanoukville. *See* Kompong Som
Sirik Matak, 46, 47, 55
Slocomb, Margaret, 27, 28, 30, 31, 33, 34, 37
Smith, Jenny, 123, 130
socialism: Buddhist, 32–33; building, 41, 92, 94–95; Democratic Republic of Vietnam and, 41; Khmer, 32–33, 94
Socialist Republic of Vietnam (SRV), 100
social justice, 142
South Vietnam. *See* Republic of Vietnam
sovereign violence, 4, 7–12, 66, 99
Springer, Simon, 132, 133, 134, 135
state duties, 7
state-induced famine, 4–15, 17, 73, 125, 128–129, 136–138, 142–143, 151, 153

state racism, 9, 11, 91–92
sustainability, 150–151

Thailand, 3, 35, 47, 64, 103, 105, 108–109, 113–117, 124–125, 131, 143–144, 146–147
Third Indochina War, 100–102
Tonle Sap: flood-pulse system and, 145, 146, 151; Mekong River and, 17–18, 21–24, 85, 120, 144–146, 150–152

United Nations (UN), 7, 102, 107, 112, 116, 124, 129, 130, 146
United Nations High Commission on Refugees (UNHCR), 115
United Nations International Children's Emergency Fund (UNICEF), 107, 111–116
United Nations Transitional Authority in Cambodia (UNTAC), 131, 132, 133, 134

Vickery, Michael, 30, 32, 110, 115
"Vietnamese Starvation Policy," 117–118
Vietnam War: First Indochina War, 31–38; Second Indochina War, 48–61, 146; Third Indochina War, 100–102

Watts, Michael, 6, 12, 16, 17, 78
Wolford, Wendy, 137
Work, Courtney, 139

GEOGRAPHIES OF JUSTICE AND SOCIAL TRANSFORMATION

1. *Social Justice and the City*, rev. ed.
   BY DAVID HARVEY
2. *Begging as a Path to Progress: Indigenous Women and Children and the Struggle for Ecuador's Urban Spaces*
   BY KATE SWANSON
3. *Making the San Fernando Valley: Rural Landscapes, Urban Development, and White Privilege*
   BY LAURA R. BARRACLOUGH
4. *Company Towns in the Americas: Landscape, Power, and Working-Class Communities*
   EDITED BY OLIVER J. DINIUS AND ANGELA VERGARA
5. *Tremé: Race and Place in a New Orleans Neighborhood*
   BY MICHAEL E. CRUTCHER JR.
6. *Bloomberg's New York: Class and Governance in the Luxury City*
   BY JULIAN BRASH
7. *Roppongi Crossing: The Demise of a Tokyo Nightclub District and the Reshaping of a Global City*
   BY ROMAN ADRIAN CYBRIWSKY
8. *Fitzgerald: Geography of a Revolution*
   BY WILLIAM BUNGE
9. *Accumulating Insecurity: Violence and Dispossession in the Making of Everyday Life*
   EDITED BY SHELLEY FELDMAN, CHARLES GEISLER, AND GAYATRI A. MENON
10. *They Saved the Crops: Labor, Landscape, and the Struggle over Industrial Farming in Bracero-Era California*
    BY DON MITCHELL
11. *Faith Based: Religious Neoliberalism and the Politics of Welfare in the United States*
    BY JASON HACKWORTH
12. *Fields and Streams: Stream Restoration, Neoliberalism, and the Future of Environmental Science*
    BY REBECCA LAVE
13. *Black, White, and Green: Farmers Markets, Race, and the Green Economy*
    BY ALISON HOPE ALKON
14. *Beyond Walls and Cages: Prisons, Borders, and Global Crisis*
    EDITED BY JENNA M. LOYD, MATT MITCHELSON, AND ANDREW BURRIDGE
15. *Silent Violence: Food, Famine, and Peasantry in Northern Nigeria*
    BY MICHAEL J. WATTS
16. *Development, Security, and Aid: Geopolitics and Geoeconomics at the U.S. Agency for International Development*
    BY JAMEY ESSEX
17. *Properties of Violence: Law and Land-Grant Struggle in Northern New Mexico*
    BY DAVID CORREIA
18. *Geographical Diversions: Tibetan Trade, Global Transactions*
    BY TINA HARRIS
19. *The Politics of the Encounter: Urban Theory and Protest under Planetary Urbanization*
    BY ANDY MERRIFIELD
20. *Rethinking the South African Crisis: Nationalism, Populism, Hegemony*
    BY GILLIAN HART
21. *The Empires' Edge: Militarization, Resistance, and Transcending Hegemony in the Pacific*
    BY SASHA DAVIS
22. *Pain, Pride, and Politics: Social Movement Activism and the Sri Lankan Tamil Diaspora in Canada*
    BY AMARNATH AMARASINGAM
23. *Selling the Serengeti: The Cultural Politics of Safari Tourism*
    BY BENJAMIN GARDNER
24. *Territories of Poverty: Rethinking North and South*
    EDITED BY ANANYA ROY AND EMMA SHAW CRANE
25. *Precarious Worlds: Contested Geographies of Social Reproduction*
    EDITED BY KATIE MEEHAN AND KENDRA STRAUSS
26. *Spaces of Danger: Culture and Power in the Everyday*
    EDITED BY HEATHER MERRILL AND LISA M. HOFFMAN

27. *Shadows of a Sunbelt City: The Environment, Racism, and the Knowledge Economy in Austin*
BY ELIOT M. TRETTER

28. *Beyond the Kale: Urban Agriculture and Social Justice Activism in New York City*
BY KRISTIN REYNOLDS AND NEVIN COHEN

29. *Calculating Property Relations: Chicago's Wartime Industrial Mobilization, 1940–1950*
BY ROBERT LEWIS

30. *In the Public's Interest: Evictions, Citizenship, and Inequality in Contemporary Delhi*
BY GAUTAM BHAN

31. *The Carpetbaggers of Kabul and Other American-Afghan Entanglements: Intimate Development, Geopolitics, and the Currency of Gender and Grief*
BY JENNIFER L. FLURI AND RACHEL LEHR

32. *Masculinities and Markets: Raced and Gendered Urban Politics in Milwaukee*
BY BRENDA PARKER

33. *We Want Land to Live: Making Political Space for Food Sovereignty*
BY AMY TRAUGER

34. *The Long War: CENTCOM, Grand Strategy, and Global Security*
BY JOHN MORRISSEY

35. *Development Drowned and Reborn: The Blues and Bourbon Restorations in Post-Katrina New Orleans*
BY CLYDE WOODS
EDITED BY JORDAN T. CAMP AND LAURA PULIDO

36. *The Priority of Injustice: Locating Democracy in Critical Theory*
BY CLIVE BARNETT

37. *Spaces of Capital / Spaces of Resistance: Mexico and the Global Political Economy*
BY CHRIS HESKETH

38. *Revolting New York: How 400 Years of Riot, Rebellion, Uprising, and Revolution Shaped a City*
GENERAL EDITORS: NEIL SMITH AND DON MITCHELL
EDITORS: ERIN SIODMAK, JENJOY ROYBAL, MARNIE BRADY, AND BRENDAN O'MALLEY

39. *Relational Poverty Politics: Forms, Struggles, and Possibilities*
EDITED BY VICTORIA LAWSON AND SARAH ELWOOD

40. *Rights in Transit: Public Transportation and the Right to the City in California's East Bay*
BY KAFUI ABLODE ATTOH

41. *Open Borders: In Defense of Free Movement*
EDITED BY REECE JONES

42. *Subaltern Geographies*
EDITED BY TARIQ JAZEEL AND STEPHEN LEGG

43. *Detain and Deport: The Chaotic U.S. Immigration Enforcement Regime*
BY NANCY HIEMSTRA

44. *Global City Futures: Desire and Development in Singapore*
BY NATALIE OSWIN

45. *Public Los Angeles: A Private City's Activist Futures*
BY DON PARSON
EDITED BY ROGER KEIL AND JUDY BRANFMAN

46. *America's Johannesburg: Industrialization and Racial Transformation in Birmingham*
BY BOBBY M. WILSON

47. *Mean Streets: Homelessness, Public Space, and the Limits of Capital*
BY DON MITCHELL

48. *Islands and Oceans: Reimagining Sovereignty and Social Change*
BY SASHA DAVIS

49. *Social Reproduction and the City: Welfare Reform, Child Care, and Resistance in Neoliberal New York*
BY SIMON BLACK

50. *Freedom Is a Place: The Struggle for Sovereignty in Palestine*
BY RON J. SMITH

51. *Loisaida as Urban Laboratory: Puerto Rico Community Activism in New York*
BY TIMO SCHRADER

52. *Transecting Securityscapes: Dispatches from Cambodia, Iraq, and Mozambique*
BY TILL F. PAASCHE AND JAMES D. SIDAWAY

53. *Non-Performing Loans, Non-Performing People: Life and Struggle with Mortgage Debt in Spain*
BY MELISSA GARCÍA-LAMARCA

54. *Disturbing Development in the Jim Crow South*
BY MONA DOMOSH

55. *Famine in Cambodia: Geopolitics, Biopolitics, Necropolitics*
BY JAMES A. TYNER

56. *Well-Intentioned Whiteness: Green Urban Development and Black Resistance in Kansas City*
BY CHHAYA KOLAVALLI

57. *Urban Climate Justice: Theory, Praxis, Resistance*
EDITED BY JENNIFER L. RICE, JOSHUA LONG, AND ANTHONY LEVENDA

58. *Abolishing Poverty: Toward Pluriverse Futures and Politics*
BY VICTORIA LAWSON, SARAH ELWOOD, MICHELLE DAIGLE, YOLANDA GONZÁLEZ MENDOZA, ANA GUTIÉRREZ GARZA, JUAN HERRERA, ELLEN KOHL, JOVAN LEWIS, AARON MALLORY, PRISCILLA MCCUTCHEON, MARGARET MARIETTA RAMÍREZ, AND CHANDAN REDDY

Printed in the USA
CPSIA information can be obtained
at www.ICGtesting.com
CBHW010004090724
11322CB00008B/435